Marriage, Family and Relationships

Marriage, Family and Relationships

Biblical, doctrinal and
contemporary perspectives

Edited by
Thomas A. Noble, Sarah K. Whittle and Philip S. Johnston

APOLLOS

APOLLOS (an imprint of Inter-Varsity Press)
36 Causton Street, London SW1P 4ST, England
Website: www.ivpbooks.com
Email: ivp@ivpbooks.com

First published 2017

British Library Cataloguing in Publication Data
A catalogue record for this book is available from the British Library.

ISBN: 978-1-78359-539-6 paperback
     978-1-78359-540-2 ebook

Set in Monotype Garamond 11/13pt
Typeset in Great Britain by CRB Associates, Potterhanworth, Lincolnshire
Printed and bound in Great Britain by Ashford Colour Press Ltd, Gosport, Hampshire

Inter-Varsity Press publishes Christian books that are true to the Bible and that communicate the gospel, develop discipleship and strengthen the church for its mission in the world.

IVP originated within the Inter-Varsity Fellowship, now the Universities and Colleges Christian Fellowship, a student movement connecting Christian Unions in universities and colleges throughout Great Britain, and a member movement of the International Fellowship of Evangelical Students. Website: www. uccf.org.uk. That historic association is maintained, and all senior IVP staff and committee members subscribe to the UCCF Basis of Faith.

CONTENTS

CONTRIBUTORS

Andy Angel, Vicar, St Andrew's Church, Burgess Hill, West Sussex

Daniel I. Block, Gunther H. Knoedler Professor Emeritus of Old Testament, Wheaton College, Wheaton, Illinois

Rosalind Clarke, Online Pastor, Lichfield Diocese

Barry Danylak, Pastor of Single Adult Ministries, Centre Street Church, Calgary

Andrew Goddard, Senior Research Fellow, Kirby Laing Institute for Christian Ethics, Cambridge

Stephen R. Holmes, Senior Lecturer in Systematic Theology, University of St Andrews

David Instone-Brewer, Tyndale House, Cambridge

Philip Johnston, Affiliated Lecturer and Senior Tutor, Hughes Hall, Cambridge

A. T. B. McGowan, Professor of Theology, University of The Highlands and Islands

Nicholas J. Moore, Assistant Curate, All Saints' Church, Stranton, Hartlepool

Onesimus Ngundu, Research Assistant, Cambridge University Library

Thomas A. Noble, Research Professor in Theology, Nazarene Theological Seminary, Kansas City; Senior Research Fellow in Theology, Nazarene Theological College, Manchester

Oliver O'Donovan, Emeritus Professor of Christian Ethics, University of Edinburgh; Honorary Professor of Divinity, University of St Andrews

Ian Paul, Associate Minister, St Nicholas' Church, Nottingham; Managing Editor, Grove Books; Adjunct Professor in New Testament, Fuller Theological Seminary

Andrew Sloane, Senior Lecturer in Old Testament and Christian Thought, Morling College, Sydney

Katherine Smith, Lecturer in Old Testament, Bible College SA, Adelaide

Elaine Storkey, Lecturer in Developing a Christian Mind, University of Oxford; High Table member, Newnham College, Cambridge

Sarah Whittle, Research Fellow in Biblical Studies, Nazarene Theological College, Manchester; Postgraduate Student Adviser, University of St Andrews

ABBREVIATIONS

General

Gk	Greek
Heb.	Hebrew
NT	New Testament
OT	Old Testament
par(s)	parallel(s)
tr.	translated

Bible versions

AV	Authorized (King James) Version
ESV	English Standard Version
LXX	Septuagint
MT	Masoretic Text
NASB	New American Standard Bible
NIV	New International Version
NRSV	New Revised Standard Version
RSV	Revised Standard Version

Apocrypha and pseudepigrapha

Jdt.	Judith
Macc.	Maccabees

Pss. Sol.	*Psalms of Solomon*
Sir.	Sirach
Tob.	Tobit
Wis.	Wisdom of Solomon

Other ancient texts

TB	Babylonian Talmud

Modern works

AB	Anchor Bible
AJS	Association for Jewish Studies
AThR	*Anglican Theological Review*
BECNT	Baker Exegetical Commentary on the New Testament
BET	Beiträge zur evangelischen Theologie
BibInt	*Biblical Interpretation*
BSL	Biblical Studies Library
BST	Bible Speaks Today
BZAW	Beihefte zur Zeitschrift für die alttestamentliche Wissenschaft
CBQ	*Catholic Biblical Quarterly*
HCOT	Historical Commentary on the Old Testament
HThKNT	Herders theologischer Kommentar zum Neuen Testament
HTR	*Harvard Theological Review*
ICC	International Critical Commentary
JBL	*Journal of Biblical Literature*
JETS	*Journal of the Evangelical Theological Society*
JSNT	*Journal for the Study of the New Testament*
JSOTSup	Journal for the Study of the Old Testament, Supplement Series
LNTS	Library of New Testament Studies
NICGT	New International Commentary on the Greek Text
NICOT	New International Commentary on the Old Testament
NovT	*Novum Testamentum*
NovTSup	Novum Testamentum Supplement Series
NTS	*New Testament Studies*
OBT	Overtures to Biblical Theology
OTC	Old Testament Commentary
OTL	Old Testament Library

RevExp	*Review & Expositor*
SBL	Society of Biblical Literature
SBLDS	Society of Biblical Literature Dissertation Series
SC	*Sources Chrétiennes*
SJT	*Scottish Journal of Theology*
SNTSMS	Society for New Testament Studies Monograph Series
SP	Sacra Pagina
TDNT	*Theological Dictionary of the New Testament*
TynB	*Tyndale Bulletin*
VT	*Vetus Testamentum*
WBC	Word Biblical Commentary
WTJ	*Westminster Theological Journal*
WUNT	Wissenschaftliche Untersuchungen zum Neuen Testament

INTRODUCTION

Thomas A. Noble, Sarah K. Whittle and Philip S. Johnston

Family life has undergone revolutionary changes in Western society in the last sixty years. Within living memory, the pattern had remained almost the same as it had been for centuries, seemingly since time immemorial. Yes, the nuclear family had gradually become more isolated, but marriage was still the norm and divorce was rare. Fathers were the main breadwinners and mothers were house-wives or worked to supplement income. Cohabitation was socially unacceptable, and only a small minority of children were illegitimate. In the United Kingdom, men in same-sex relationships were still subject to prosecution and imprison-ment for 'gross indecency'. But in the later twentieth century, new cultural trends appeared. Promotion of the permissive society ended censorship in the theatre, a new fashion emerged for satire, deference to the establishment ended and authority figures became suspect. Along with these changes in culture came reaction against so-called Victorian morality. The lowering of the age of majority ended the regulation of relations between the sexes in student halls of residence. Laws against Sunday trading and gambling were increasingly relaxed, divorce became easier, and homosexual relations between consenting adults in private were decriminalized. Gradually, divorce rates rose, cohabitation became normal, illegitimacy was no longer a stigma, and same-sex relationships became socially acceptable and indeed celebrated. Unknown to the public until recently, the permissive society also had a hidden underside in the exploitation and abuse of the young by some leading entertainers, in some children's homes and, we now learn, by some football coaches. But while the more recent revelation of paedophilia has horrified public opinion, it has not led to any significant questioning of the general trend towards a more permissive approach to sexual ethics.

Social and cultural change

The changes affecting marriage, family and relationships over this period since the end of the Second World War have been part of wider social and cultural change. The same period has seen the decline of church membership in the UK from its peak in the 1950s, and 'the death of Christian Britain' has been documented by Callum Brown and others.[1] However, despite criticism of permissive trends, Christians have generally welcomed many of the cultural and social changes. Legalism and class distinctions, along with snobbery, racism and hypocrisy, are now seen as vices attached to the old social attitudes. The principle of equality has become a given in public ethics, so equal treatment for people of different classes and races is fundamental. When this principle is applied to marriage and family and to relationships between the sexes, then family life comes under scrutiny. Few Christians (if any) have therefore been opposed to the equal treatment of husbands and wives before the law, and it appears that only a minority of Christians were publicly opposed to the legislation establishing civil partnerships in the United Kingdom in 2004. Certainly, clear arguments were presented that same-sex relations were contrary to historic and biblical Christian ethics. The biblical basis for this was defended by several scholars, including for example Richard Hays,[2] and most exhaustively by Robert Gagnon.[3] Even when some Christians argued that same-sex relations should be accepted, they acknowledged that this would be contrary to the biblical position and would have to be based on scientific grounds.[4] But while the new law was generally agreed to be contrary to the biblical view of same-sex relationships, given that the country was *de facto* secular (whatever was legally true

---

1. Callum G. Brown, *The Death of Christian Britain* (London: Routledge, 2001).

2. Richard Hays, *The Moral Vision of the New Testament* (San Francisco: Harper, 1996), pp. 379–406.

3. Robert A. J. Gagnon, *The Bible and Homosexual Practice* (Nashville: Abingdon, 2001).

4. See, for example, William Loader, *The New Testament on Sexuality* (Grand Rapids: Eerdmans, 2012) and the brief summary of his position in Preston Sprinkle (ed.), *Two Views on Homosexuality, the Bible, and the Church* (Grand Rapids: Zondervan, 2016), pp. 17–48.

of the state), it seemed difficult to object to the change in the law. Christians might take a different view, but had to accept many features of a tolerant, multicultural society with which they did not necessarily agree.

But when, in 2013, the Marriage (Same Sex Couples) Act was passed by Parliament, a line was crossed. A number of other Western nations have also crossed this line, putting them at odds with most of the world. Given the churches' historic role in marriage law and customs, and given the church's historic teaching on marriage, the conflict between the historic Christian conscience and the law in these Western nations is now evident. The churches were taken by surprise at the speed of this development, which came about for political reasons rather than from widespread public demand. Several denominations are now seriously split on their view of same-sex relations since many Christians, including some who identify as evangelicals, are prepared to accept and support the changes. But the reason why this change in the law is different is that it seems to be totally contrary to what till then had been the agreed and long-established Christian doctrine of marriage. Despite differences between Roman Catholics and Protestants as to whether marriage is a sacrament, it had been seen by all Christians as ordained by God. According to the Book of Common Prayer, it is the 'joining together of a man and woman' in an 'honourable estate, instituted of God in the time of man's innocency'. The related view of marriage as indissoluble had already shifted, at least among Protestants, in the acceptance of divorce, but the notion that a marriage may take place between two people of the same sex is completely unprecedented. Until recent times it has been completely unthinkable, not only among Christians, but also in the Abrahamic religious traditions of Judaism and Islam.

This is the context in which the Tyndale Fellowship for Biblical and Theological Research convened a conference in July 2016 on 'Marriage, Family and Relationships'. This was not a conference of bishops or denominational leaders charged with making any decisions or enacting legislation or canon law. It was a conference of theologians and scholars engaged in research, and therefore perhaps enjoying a greater freedom to debate and disagree. But it was not intended to be a forum for debating the polarizing views now represented in the churches. It was rather intended to be a place where evangelical scholars, committed to the historic Christian view of marriage and the historic Christian understanding of the Scriptures, could interact and discuss their research together. It was important to set the particular debate over same-sex relations within the wider context of the Christian doctrine of marriage and the biblical understanding of the family. Far from being stuck in merely conventional and unthinking conservatism, participants exhibited a freedom to examine how far Western culture had shaped the cultural assumptions of Christendom in the past, and to explore the implications of biblical faith for fresh thinking on the Christian view of marriage, family and relationships.

Altogether some fifty papers were presented, including the seven Tyndale Lectures given annually in the overlapping fields of Old Testament, New Testament, Biblical Archaeology, Biblical Theology, Christian Doctrine, Philosophy of Religion, and Ethics and Social Theology. Many of these papers will no doubt be published elsewhere, but sixteen have been brought together in this volume as a coherent collection.

Biblical studies

In the Old Testament section, Daniel Block focuses on the key book of Deuteronomy. Rather than patriarchy, he sees there a 'patricentric' view of the family. This highlights not the authority of the father in the family, but the responsibility of the father for the family. Katy Smith examines Leviticus, arguing that the two verses outlawing sexual relations between men have to be placed in the context of positive teaching on the relational order of creation and society. Rosalind Clarke examines the multiple levels of interpretation of the Song of Songs. Even at the so-called literal level the Song is about many things: sexuality and redemption, wisdom and women, marriage and kingship. But read as a canonical text of Holy Scripture, the exemplary role of King Solomon and his bride not only honours love and marriage but also speaks of the relationship between God and Israel. Given Jesus' own references to himself as the bridegroom, New Testament writers then apply this to Christ and his church.

In the New Testament studies, our understanding of marriage is placed in eschatological context. Andy Angel addresses the sensitive topic of the sexuality of God incarnate. Past reluctance even to think about this has to give way to clear thinking, for two reasons: first, our more explicit discussion today of sexuality, and second, the continued commitment of Christian orthodoxy to the full humanity of Christ. Two chapters follow which examine exegetical issues in 1 Corinthians 7, a key chapter for Paul's view of marriage. Barry Danylak considers the debate whether Paul's statement in verse 1, 'It is well for a man not to touch a woman', is a quotation from an ascetic Corinthian group or a statement of his own view. Despite the apparent conflict with Genesis 2:18, 'It is not good that the man should be alone', for Danylak, Paul's argument is that while physical progeny was a mark of God's blessing under the old covenant, in the light of the resurrection of Christ there is a new role for single people within the new family which is the church. Paul himself is an example as a spiritual father. Sarah Whittle wrestles with Paul's instruction in 1 Corinthians

7:29, 'Let even those who have wives be as though they had none', arguing that it has to be understood in the context of Paul's apocalyptic framework. Marriage belongs to 'this present age' which is passing away. Ian Paul takes this theme further, engaging with the declaration by Jesus that in the resurrection there will be no marriage, and considering whether this implies the end of the differentiation between the sexes.

If these chapters encourage us to think again about the positive role of the celibate within the church, Nicholas Moore's examination of Hebrews 12:5–13 takes us to the role of the Christian family, and in particular, to parental discipline. Family discipline is God-ordained and, while potentially flawed, provides a minor but important argument that those in the household of God should submit to his fatherly discipline. David Instone-Brewer considers Jesus' teaching on sexual ethics in Matthew. Before replying to a question on divorce, Jesus criticized polygamy, rejected the teaching that divorce was required in cases of adultery, and seemed to allow for celibacy, contrary to the command to 'be fruitful and multiply'. But where he did not pronounce on an issue, Instone-Brewer argues that he was probably in line with the received rabbinic interpretation of Torah. Turning to rabbinic and other Jewish sources, he concludes that, while they condemned homosexual acts, they recognized that some men had homosexual tendencies and took steps to avoid temptation.

The doctrine of marriage

Onesimus Ngundu introduces the doctrinal studies with a valuable survey of the history of Christian marriage law and customs. Developments in Europe and the West have added customs and expectations which are not strictly biblical, and from an African perspective, can present problems. Andrew McGowan addresses the task of Christian dogmatics, taking his starting point from the late John Webster's examination of the roles of reason, revelation and Scripture. The theologian must take seriously the dogmatic tradition of the church and, in examining the debate over same-sex relations, has to take seriously the doctrine of original sin as understood by Augustine, Luther and Calvin. This means that we must understand human beings to be damaged in every part of their being, and in particular that all are 'enemies in their minds' (Col. 1:21). Given that 'the god of this age has blinded the minds of unbelievers' (2 Cor. 4:4), we have to take into account the *noetic* effects of sin. No one can claim, therefore, 'This is the way God made me'. We are all damaged in different ways by sin, and this leads some to reject the biblical truth about sexuality.

Oliver O'Donovan identifies the doctrine of marriage as arising out of the doctrine of creation and therefore the doctrine of human nature. Marriage has long been understood in the West as furthering three 'good effects', respectively physical, moral and spiritual: *proles*, the good of children; *fides*, the good of life-long faithfulness and companionship; and *sacramentum*, that it points to the union of Christ and his church. And while synods and councils today may alter *theologoumena* (teaching on specific matters of conduct, for example), they are not free to alter *dogmata*, established Christian doctrine. Pastoral accommodation is one thing, for example accommodating polygamous marriages in societies where this has been the accepted custom; but it is quite another to change doctrine, for example by overturning the universal doctrine of the church that marriage is between a man and a woman. The theological case for such a change in church doctrine has not been made.

Contemporary perspectives

Andrew Goddard's paper addresses the proposals of Robert Song, perhaps the best attempt at a Christian doctrine of marriage respectful of Scripture and tradition but accommodating same-sex unions. Song develops a wider proposal for non-procreative covenant partnerships within which same-sex unions may take their place. But Goddard takes his argument apart, rejecting the notion that the advent of Christ changes marriage in such a way that the fundamental distinction should not be between homosexual and heterosexual unions but between procreative and non-procreative covenants.

Andrew Sloane addresses theological questions raised by developments in biology, psychology and sociology, particularly the recognition of various forms of intersex, gender dysphoria and the cultural construction of gender roles. He attempts to reflect the complexity of affirming the goodness and diversity of our created, bodily, sexed and gendered existence, and at the same time the brokenness of the world and human experience. He suggests that we need to recognize our diversity and the centrality of relationships, and discusses what role medical intervention should play in dealing with gender dysphoria and intersex.

Elaine Storkey's chapter follows the horrifying evidence for the abuse of women across the world presented in her recent book, *Scars Across Humanity*.[5]

---

5. Elaine Storkey, *Scars Across Humanity: Understanding and Overcoming Violence against Women* (London: SPCK, 2015).

Here she focuses on two particular evils, the deliberate killing of girls before and after birth, and intimate-partner abuse and rape. She examines sociological and biological explanations for these widespread behaviour patterns and finds them inadequate. We cannot do without the ethical and theological perspective which grounds human personhood in the goodness of God and so gives us the concept of structural sin.

Finally, Stephen Holmes tries to understand the recent radical changes in cultural assumptions which have quite suddenly made the church's historic doctrine of marriage seem obscurantist and obsolescent to so many. Whereas in the early Christian centuries there was a new embracing of celibacy in the light of the resurrection of Christ, in the post-Freudian era sexual activity is seen as essential to human well-being. It makes the requirement for those attracted to the same sex to be celibate appear cruel. The focus on 'companionate marriage' and the demoting of the role of procreation mean that opposition to gay marriage seems an outdated prejudice. And if sexual norms are socially constructed, then no argument remains against same-sex marriage. Holmes advocates that if we are to argue from Scripture and Christian tradition for the historical Christian doctrine of marriage, we have to address the ways in which we in the modern West had already allowed pagan, romantic notions of love and marriage into the church. If we are to be heard, we need a more biblical and modest understanding of marriage as an ascetic practice, a new understanding of the centrality of procreation to marriage, and a new understanding of the role of celibacy in the church.

Altogether, these chapters are essential reading for all who are concerned with the church's teaching on marriage and the family. They balance a clear loyalty to the church's historic and biblical teaching with a recognition that all doctrine is contextualized. In the context of today, despite the growth of other religions in the West, educated and informed opinion is predominantly secular, and legislation no longer reflects the historic place of the Christian faith in society. The church therefore has to accept that a gap has opened up between what wider society thinks is true and right, and the convictions of Christian ethics. Christians have to learn to be counter-cultural. But the church's presentation of its ethical teaching also has to be self-critical, differentiating between what is true to biblical revelation and what has been shaped by later cultural developments, and fully aware of how unchanging Christian convictions need to be presented to constantly changing culture and society.

PART 1:

BIBLICAL PERSPECTIVES

1. THE PATRICENTRIC VISION OF FAMILY ORDER IN DEUTERONOMY

Daniel I. Block

Introduction

It is more than a quarter of a century since David Clines declared Genesis 1 – 3 'irredeemably androcentric' and in so doing rejected the authority of the Bible for modern readers.[1] Troubled by the tone of Clines' expression and especially by his rejection of the Bible's authority, fifteen years ago I made my first focused foray into biblical perspectives related to family roles and ethics.[2] At that time I suggested that if we would understand the normative view of the family in both the First and the New Testaments, we need to replace the words 'patri-archy' and 'patriarchal' with 'patricentricity' and 'patricentric'. While this

---

1. David J. A. Clines, 'What Does Eve Do to Help? And Other Irredeemably Androcentric Orientations in Genesis 1–3', ch. 1, in idem, *What Does Eve Do to Help? And Other Readerly Questions to the Old Testament*, JSOTSup 94 (Sheffield: Sheffield Academic Press, 1990), pp. 25–48.

2. See Daniel I. Block, 'Marriage and Family in Ancient Israel', in K. Campbell (ed.), *Marriage and Family in the Biblical World* (Downers Grove: IVP, 2003), pp. 33–102. See also Block, '"You shall not covet your neighbor's wife": A Study in Deuteronomic Domestic Ideology', *JETS* 53 (2010), pp. 449–74; republished in idem, *The Gospel According to Moses: Theological and Ethical Reflections on the Book of Deuteronomy* (Eugene: Cascade, 2012), pp. 137–73.

proposal has received encouraging support from some,[3] others continue to argue for retaining the word *patriarchy* in evangelical discourse on the family.[4] However, given the detrimental effects rigid patriarchalism has had on our families on the one hand, and the ideal domestic portrait painted by the First Testament on the other, the issue certainly deserves another look.

Here I shall explore further the patricentric ideals of family relationships, especially the roles fathers were to play within the household in the everyday life of Israelites once they had crossed into the Promised Land, as portrayed in Moses' speeches in Deuteronomy. Deuteronomy is clear that Israel's mission before a watching world was to demonstrate the transformative effects of divine grace in shaping the culture. Once in Canaan, the Israelites were to function as a restored humanity in microcosm. At the end of his third address, Moses declared YHWH's determination to set this nation 'high above all the nations that he has made for [his] fame and renown and glory', and that they would be 'a holy people to YHWH your God as he promised' (Deut. 26:19).[5] If and when they would fulfil their commission as 'lights of the world' (Matt. 5:14–16), then the peoples around would recognize Israel's unique privileges in having a God who was near and who heard them when they cried out to him, and who had graciously revealed his will to them (Deut. 4:6–8).

Definitions

Before we explore the Deuteronomic vision of patricentrism, we need to define our terms. Sociologists and anthropologists identify several different paradigms of domestic and communal administration.

Patriarchy: 'the system of male dominance by which men as a group acquire and maintain power over women as a group'.[6] Some Christians object that we

---

3. See Andreas J. Köstenberger, with David W. Jones, *God, Marriage and Family: Rebuilding the Biblical Foundation* (Wheaton: Crossway, 2004), pp. 93–107, passim; Andreas J. Köstenberger and Margaret E. Köstenberger, *God's Design for Man and Woman: A Biblical-Theological Survey* (Wheaton: Crossway, 2014), pp. 60–1, passim.

4. Russell D. Moore, 'After Patriarchy, What? Why Egalitarians Are Winning the Gender Debate', *JETS* 49 (2006), pp. 569–76.

5. Unless otherwise indicated all biblical translations in this chapter are the author's.

6. As defined by Kathy E. Ferguson, 'Patriarchy', in Helen Tierney (ed.), *Views from the Sciences*, vol. 1 of *Women's Studies Encyclopedia* (New York: Greenwood, 1989), p. 265.

cannot let secular writers define 'the grammar of our faith',[7] but the fact remains that their definitions determine how many people think. This is true both in the broader culture and among those who are theologically and biblically illiterate. Within evangelical contexts we may insist on our idealized and nuanced definitions, but then we lose all prospects of addressing the world out there.

Matriarchy: If *patriarchy* involves 'a system in which men rule', then we would expect *matriarchy* to involve 'a system in which women rule'.[8] However, some feminists do not view matriarchy as the female variety of patriarchy, but idealize it as either an egalitarian world in harmony with nature or a world in which maternal values (nurture and care-giving) apply to everyone, male and female.[9] It seems these are the only terms under which it is possible to identify any matriarchal culture at all.[10]

Diarchy: a system in which rule is shared by two persons, usually with clearly delineated areas of responsibility. In domestic contexts this would involve roles divided by gender, for example the husband/father leading in the procurement of food and heavy work (hunting, tilling) and the wife/mother leading in the processing and preparing of food (tending garden plants, cooking).

See further Pavla Miller, 'Patriarchy', in Bonnie G. Smith (ed.), *The Oxford Encyclopedia of Women in World History* (Philadelphia: Oxford University Press, 2010), 3:419–24.

7. Moore, 'After Patriarchy, What?', p. 574.

8. Thus most standard dictionaries.

9. For a summary statement, see Heide Goettner-Abendroth, 'Matriarchy', <http://www.hagia.de/en/matriarchy.html>. For fuller discussion, see idem, *Societies of Peace: Matriarchies Past, Present, and Future* (Toronto: Inanna Publications, 2009); *Matriarchal Societies: Studies on Indigenous Cultures across the Globe* (New York: Peter Lang, 2012).

10. Using very specific criteria, anthropologists have identified several societies as led by females: the Mosuo in China, the Minangkabau in Indonesia (the largest known matrilineal society), the Akan of Ghana, the Bribri in Costa Rica, the Tibeto-Burman Garos and the Nagovisi in New Guinea. However, while some of these societies are matrilineal, they are not actually matriarchal in administration and government. For further discussion of matriarchy, see Peggy Reeves Sanday, *Women at the Center: Life in a Modern Matriarchy* (Ithaca: Cornell University Press, 2002); idem, 'Matriarchy', in Smith (ed.), *Oxford Encyclopedia of Women*, 3:192–5.

Egalitarian government: a system in which all members of a household are equal
and have equal access to positions of authority and rule. In a truly egalitarian
household roles are not defined either by gender or age.

Anarchy: a system that is uncontrolled by convention or regulation, and in which
no member of the household has authority to exert power over anyone else,
or to try to ensure order. Usually this results in a chaotic and turbulent
environment.

Having identified the possibilities, we shall now explore which of them fits
the ideal biblical pattern. Of course, at the outset we must distinguish between the
realities in ancient Israel as reflected in the narrative texts, and the ideals as prom-
ulgated in the constitutional documents. As is well known, the narratives often
paint troubling pictures of male abuse in household situations. I have addressed
elsewhere the problem in the book of Judges,[11] but such abuse was not limited to
this troubled period in Israel's history. From the patriarchal narratives we note the
abuses by Abraham and Isaac, both of whom in flagrant self-interest were willing
to sacrifice their wives to save their own skins (Gen. 12:10–20; 20:1–18; 26:7–11).
David's offences involving women are also well documented: his polygyny
(involving his wives Ahinoam, Abigail, Maacah, Haggith, Abital, Eglah, Bathsheba
and concubines; 2 Sam. 3:2–5; 1 Chr. 3:1–9) and his adultery with Bathsheba (2 Sam. 11 – 12). But these images contrast sharply with the portrayal of
righteous ideals in Deuteronomy (cf. Deut. 16:20), to which we now turn.

The androcentricity of Deuteronomy

Given the pervasively androcentric character of both the Hebrew Bible and
the New Testament,[12] we should not be surprised by the androcentricity of

---

11. Daniel I. Block, 'Unspeakable Crimes: The Abuse of Women in the Book of
    Judges', *The Southern Baptist Theological Journal* 2 (1998), pp. 46–55.

12. Carol L. Meyers notes that, of the 1,426 personal names in the Hebrew Bible, 1,315
    (89%) identify men and only 111 (9%) identify women. See 'Every Day Life: Women
    in the Period of the Hebrew Bible', in Carol A. Newsome and Sharon H. Ringe
    (eds.), *The Women's Bible Commentary* (Louisville: Westminster/John Knox, 1992),
    p. 245. For alternative but similar statistics, see Karla G. Bohmbach, 'Names and
    Naming in the Biblical World', in Carol Meyers (ed.), *Women in Scripture: A Dictionary
    of Named and Unnamed Women in the Hebrew Bible, the Apocryphal/Deuterocanonical
    Books, and the New Testament* (Boston: Houghton Mifflin, 2000), pp. 33–9.

Deuteronomy. Cast as a collection of Moses' final pastoral addresses to his congregation, a major concern of this book is to govern the behaviour of men. The tone is established by the recitation of the Decalogue at the beginning of the second address (5:6–21). The second person of direct address in the book ('you') is always masculine. While the masculine in Hebrew is often used generically for everyone without specific reference to gender, never are women addressed directly as women. Indeed, when women's well-being and women's conduct are at issue, the style adopted is telling. These regulations are concerned primarily with men's treatment of women, rather than the conduct of the women themselves. The second person is reiterated in the motive clause following the prescribed response to an offence, 'Thus *you* shall purge the evil from your midst' (21:21; 22:21, 22, 24).

The captive bride (21:10–14). This text is expressly addressed to males, and deals with the woman in the third person ('she').

The second-ranked wife (21:15–17). This text is cast in the third person ('If a man . . .') and focuses on the man's responsibility to the second-ranked wife, rather than on her rights or her behaviour.

The mother of a rebellious son (21:18–21). After opening in the third person masculine like the previous text ('If a man . . .'), the text quickly expands the focus to the son's 'father and mother' and thereafter uses third person plural terms, which are masculine by default.

The wife falsely accused of lying about her virginity (22:13–21). This ordinance also begins in the third person ('If a man . . .'). While ostensibly dealing with a woman whom the husband accuses of deceit at their wedding, the focus is actually on a man whose accusations are proved false. As a brief addendum it prescribes how the wife is to be treated should the accusations be true, with instructions for the (male) elders of the town (vv. 20–21).

Accomplices in adultery and victims of rape (22:22–29). This ordinance is complex, involving at least four different scenarios. The series begins with a hypothetical case involving a man's action, 'If a man is found . . .' (v. 22), and the focus continues to be on the male (vv. 23–27). None of these cases is addressed to the female involved.

The divorced woman (24:1–4). This case also begins with a hypothetical situation involving a man ('If a man . . .'). Although the man finds something problematic in his wife, the emphasis throughout is on his conduct.

Levirate marriage (25:5–10). The ordinance opens with a note on a domestic scene from the male perspective, 'When brothers live together and one of them dies . . .'. Its concern is the maintenance of the dead man's name and estate, but the focus then shifts to his widow's response in the face of her brother-in-law's refusal to marry her.

The disrespectful woman (25:11–12). This is the most enigmatic text of the series. Here the issue is a woman's attempt to rescue her husband from an attacker, specifically her inappropriate grabbing of his genitals. Unlike the preceding ordinances, this one actually concerns primarily the actions of a woman. It could have been cast as a second person feminine command: 'If your husband is fighting . . . you (fem.) may not . . .'. In the end, though, the ordinance is addressed to those responsible for maintaining order: 'Then *you* (masc.) shall cut off her hand' (v. 12).

These cases reinforce the androcentric character of the book of Deuteronomy. But does an androcentric culture require domestic patriarchalism? If we accept the definition of patriarchy given above, the answer is not necessarily 'yes'. Just because texts – even constitutional texts that present social ideals – are androcentric, this does not mean the social structures will be patriarchal. Indeed, Deuteronomy especially raises the question whether or not patriarchy characterizes the ideals presented in the Mosaic Torah, especially as the term is generally understood and as defined above. As I argued previously, if we would accurately represent the ideals of the Torah, we need to replace the word *patriarchy* with *patricentrism*, for several reasons.

First, the domestic counterpart to androcentrism (as envisioned by Moses in Deuteronomy) is not patriarchy but patricentrism. Androcentrism need not by definition be preoccupied with structures of power and control; rather it may be concerned primarily with loci of responsibility and care. The patricentric Israelite disposition concerning the household is reflected transparently in the designation of a family unit (whether nuclear or extended) as a 'father's house' (*bêt 'āb*). As in most ancient Near Eastern cultures, Israelite families were patrilineal (descent traced through the father's line),[13] patrilocal (married women joined their husband's household), and patriarchal in some sense (the father governed the household).[14] However, the term 'patricentric' says more about the genealogical relationships than about power. A household could be nuclear

---

13. See the genealogies in Genesis 5, 10, 36, etc.

14. For discussion see R. Patai, *Family, Love and the Bible* (London: MacGibbon & Kee, 1960), pp. 17–18.

(father, mother, children), but it could also extend to three or four generations (cf. Deut. 5:9) and include elderly parents and even grandparents,[15] and it often contained other members (male and female servants). However, the core involved the blood relatives, the descendants of the household head, along with the wives of male members. This accounts for the book's oft-expressed concern for 'the alien, the fatherless, and the widow', who were economically vulnerable because they lacked an adult male (usually the father, but possibly an older brother) who would take care of them.[16]

Second, the term *patriarchy*, literally 'the rule of the father', places inordinate emphasis on the power a father exercised over his household.[17] In recent years feminist interpreters have helpfully pointed out the dark side of patriarchy reflected in many biblical narratives.[18] However, such approaches tend to interpret abusive male behaviour as natural expressions of patriarchy, despite the fact that the authors often deliberately cite such conduct to demonstrate the degeneracy of the times and the persons involved.[19] By definition, heads of households exercised authority over their families. But with the Canaanization

---

15. Cf. Karel van der Toorn, *Family Religion in Babylonia, Syria and Israel: Continuity and Change in the Forms of Religious Life* (Leiden: Brill, 1996), pp. 194–205; J. David Schloen, *The House of the Father as Fact and Symbol: Patrimonialism in Ugarit and the Ancient Near East* (Winona Lake: Eisenbrauns, 2001), pp. 147–50. Schloen argues that in Iron Age Israel only one third of the households would have consisted of joint families with more than one conjugal couple and their immature children.

16. Deut. 10:18; 14:29; 16:11, 14; 24:19–21; 26:12–13; 27:19.

17. See, for example, Patai's discussion of 'The Powers of the Patriarch', *Family, Love and the Bible*, pp. 114–24.

18. These interpreters are correct in characterizing as abusive: Abraham's passing off his wife Sarah as his sister (Gen. 12:10–20), Lot's offer of his two daughters to the thugs of Sodom (Gen. 19:8), Jephthah's sacrifice of his daughter (Judg. 11:34–40), the Israelite men's authorization of Benjaminite warriors to kidnap girls for wives (Judg. 21:19–24), David's adultery with Bathsheba and murder of her husband (2 Sam. 11:1–27), Amnon's rape of his half-sister Tamar (2 Sam. 13:1–19), to name just a few horrendous episodes. For a keen analysis of some of these troubling texts, see Phyllis Trible, *Texts of Terror: Literary Feminist Readings of Biblical Narratives*, OBT (Philadelphia: Fortress, 1984).

19. Nowhere is this more evident than in the book of Judges, the central thrust of which is to expose the Canaanization of Israelite society. The horrendous abuse of women in the book represents but one of the symptoms of a culture gone horribly wrong. See Block, 'Unspeakable Crimes', pp. 46–55.

of the Israelites, their normatively compassionate patriarchy rapidly degenerated to a cancerous, corrupt, irresponsible, self-centred and exploitative exercise of power. The energies of the household were invested in maintaining the status and power of its head rather than the well-being of its members (see the figure below). But this was a far cry from the normative ideal of patriarchy.[20] Because many associate this term *a priori* with this kind of abuse, the expression is best avoided.[21]

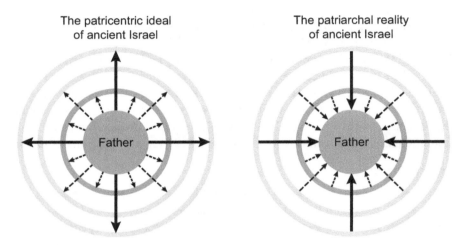

Third, *patricentrism* reflects the normative biblical disposition toward the role of the head of a household in Israel more accurately than *patriarchy*. It is clear that, just as the father's house was the nucleus of the clan, so the father was the nucleus of the father's house. And just as in a physical sense the house inhabited by the head of the extended family represented the nucleus of the compound, so the head of the family functioned as its centre. Like the spokes of a wheel, family life ideally radiated outward from him. In fact, as Johannes Pedersen

---

20. Remarkably, the verb *māšal*, 'to rule, govern', characterizes the relationship of the father (*'āb*) to his household only once in the Hebrew Bible, viz. Gen. 3:16, where it expresses a symptom of the world gone wrong after the entrance of sin.

21. So also Carol Meyers, who prefers to characterize Israelite society in general as *androcentric* rather than *patriarchal*; see 'The Family in Early Israel', in L. G. Perdue, J. Blenkinsopp, J. J. Collins and C. Meyers (eds.), *Families in Ancient Israel* (Louisville: Westminster John Knox, 1997), pp. 34–5. But as the phrase 'father's house' suggests, families in particular were *patricentric*.

noted long ago, 'wherever a man goes he takes "his house" with him'.[22] Biblical genealogies trace descent through the male line;[23] a married couple resided within the household of the groom; in references to a man and his wife or a man and his children the man is generally named first (Gen. 7:7); children were born to the father (Gen. 21:1–7); fathers negotiated family disputes (Gen. 13:1–13; 31:1–55); God generally addressed heads of the household (Gen. 3:9; 12:1; 35:1);[24] when families worshipped, the head of the household took the initiative (Gen. 9:13–22; 12:7–8; 35:2–15; cf. Job 1:4–5); when a man died without descendants his 'name' died (Deut. 25:5–6; Ruth 4:5, 10; 1 Sam. 24:18–22). In short, the ideal domestic community was built around the father; if in every respect it bore his stamp, it also looked to him as the one primarily responsible for its well-being.[25]

Patricentrism in the book of Deuteronomy

But how does this picture play out in the ideal Israelite world that Moses laid out in the book of Deuteronomy? Despite Deuteronomy's pervasive concern for the well-being of the family, especially in chapters 12 – 26, remarkably the expression 'father's house' occurs only twice, and that in one sentence in 22:21. Regarding a woman who proved not to have been a virgin at marriage, Moses prescribed: 'Then the men of her town shall bring the young woman out to the door of her father's house, and they shall kill her by stoning, because she has committed this outrage in Israel by prostituting her father's house.'

---

22. Johannes Pedersen, *Israel: Its Life and Culture* (Atlanta: Scholars Press, 1991; reprint of the 1926 edition), 1:51. See, for example, the deliverance of Noah and his house, which included his wife and his sons' wives (Gen. 7:1, 13).

23. The exceptional inclusion of four women in the genealogy of Jesus in Matthew 1 is driven by the rhetorical aims of the evangelist.

24. This normal pattern throws into even sharper relief the exceptional character of Judges 13:1–23, where the divine envoy prefers to address an otherwise unnamed woman concerning the birth of a child to her husband, Manoah, who is named.

25. For full discussion, see Rebekah Lee Josberger, 'Between Rule and Responsibility: The Role of the 'AB as Agent of Righteousness in Deuteronomy's Domestic Ideology', Ph.D. dissertation, The Southern Baptist Theological Seminary, Louisville, 2007; Block, 'Marriage and Family in Ancient Israel', pp. 33–102.

Patricentrism in the Decalogue (5:6–22)

Although most evangelical readers today assume the Decalogue is authoritative for all Christians, few are aware that strictly speaking this foundational document of YHWH's covenant with Israel is addressed primarily to the male head of an Israelite household.[26] The 'you' (masculine singular throughout) is an adult male, who is responsible for the practice of religion in the 'household' (5:8–10) and thereby the welfare of the family; who in a particular sense bears the name of YHWH (v. 11); who is in charge of the work of the household (vv. 13–14); whose 'household' includes sons and daughters, male and female servants, resident aliens, draught animals and other livestock (v. 14); and who is tempted to take his neighbour's wife, as well as his home and fields, servants, animals and any other property (v. 21).[27] We must note, however, that this identification of the male head of the household as the primary addressee does not absolve others of the Decalogue's authority over them. But they represent secondary audiences. In keeping with a fundamental tenet of biblical leadership, the primary function of leaders is not defined in terms of the tasks they are expected to perform but

---

26. My arguments for this interpretation are developed more fully in Daniel I. Block, 'The Decalogue in the Hebrew Scriptures', in Jeffrey Greenman and Timothy Larsen (eds.), *Reading the Decalogue through the Centuries* (Louisville: Westminster John Knox, 2012), pp. 9–11; 'Reading the Decalogue Right to Left: The Ten Principles of Covenant Relationship in the Hebrew Bible', in *How I Love Your Torah O LORD! Studies in the Book of Deuteronomy* (Eugene: Cascade, 2011), pp. 30–4.

27. If the significance of the 'you' is to be extended, it might include the father's wife, whose honorific status within the household the fourth command explicitly guards. Although the male head's adultery with the neighbour's wife would inevitably have implications for his own marriage, remarkably the document says nothing about his treatment of his own wife. Undoubtedly the mother was to promote and be as exercised about the well-being of the entire household as the father. On her status within the household, see further below. Based on the discourse grammar of the Decalogue, with Roman Catholics and Lutherans (as opposed to Reformed Protestants), I identify the command to honour father and mother as the fourth (rather than fifth) command. For brief discussion, see Block, 'Excursus A: How Shall We Number the Ten Commands?' following 'Reading the Decalogue Right to Left', pp. 56–60. For more detailed defence of this interpretation, see Jason S. DeRouchie, 'Counting the Ten: An Investigation into the Numbering of the Decalogue', in Jason S. DeRouchie, Jason Gile and Kenneth J. Turner (eds.), *For Our Good Always: Studies in the Message and Influence of Deuteronomy in Honor of Daniel I. Block* (Winona Lake: Eisenbrauns, 2013), pp. 93–126.

in terms of the kinds of persons they are to be. If the primary function of the head of the nation was to embody the ethical and spiritual values of the community (Deut. 17:14–20), the same was true for heads of households. The household's members should be able to observe the head and know what kinds of persons they were to be. Therefore, if idolatry or adultery were wrong for the household heads, they were also wrong for the rest of the family.

Contrary to the views of many, the Decalogue is not a gentlemen's agreement protecting the status of men or guaranteeing them a certain economic standard or enabling them to live in peace, while the rest of the household are over-looked.[28] Rather, this document recognizes and reins in the temptation of heads of households to act like little Pharaohs (cf. the reference to Egypt, v. 6), exploiting those in their charge and running roughshod over them in the way that the Egyptians had treated their forebears (v. 15). Indeed the document itself may be viewed as a bill of rights, protecting the well-being of the household *against* the abuse of fathers who are concerned only about themselves and care little for those who live under their roof, as illustrated in Table 1.1 overleaf.[29]

Recognizing that the male head wields the power in the household, the Decalogue seeks to limit the wrongful exercise of that power. Like other leadership institutions, it assumes that people in leadership occupy these positions for the sake of those whom they lead, in contrast to prevailing perspectives and the constant temptation to view others as props for the leader's status and well-being.[30] However, the modifications in Deuteronomy to the Exodus version of the commands regarding coveting (Deut. 5:21a; cf. Exod. 20:17a) caution against treating women as mere chattels. The inclusion of 'your mother' in the charge to honour parents (Deut. 5:16) suggests the Israelite ideal moves in the direction of complementarianism (parents may play different roles,

---

28. See most recently the blog post by Cheryl B. Anderson, 'Audience of the Ten Commandments', at <http://www.bibleodyssey.org/tools/video-gallery/a/audience-of-the-ten-commandments-anderson.aspx>. Accessed 2 July 2016.

29. This approach differs fundamentally from that of David Clines, who argues that the document was drafted to secure the interests of elites and those who wield power. See D. J. A. Clines, 'The Ten Commandments, Reading from Left to Right', in J. Davies, G. Harvey and W. G. E. Watson (eds.), *Words Remembered, Texts Renewed: Essays in Honour of John F. A. Sawyer*, JSOTSup 195 (Sheffield: Sheffield Academic Press, 1995), pp. 97–112.

30. For further discussion, see Daniel I. Block, 'Leader, Leadership, Old Testament', in Katherine Doob Sakenfeld (ed.), *New Interpreter's Dictionary of the Bible* (Nashville: Abingdon, 2008), 3:620–6.

Table 1.1

The Decalogue as the world's oldest Bill of Rights		
Command		**Rights involved**
	I am YHWH your God, who brought you out of the land of Egypt, out of the house of slavery.	The basis of the Bill of Rights in redemption (cf. Deut. 6:20–25)
1	You shall have no other gods before me; you shall not make for yourself a carved image . . . to bow down to them or serve them.	YHWH has the right to his people's exclusive allegiance.
2	You shall not bear the name of YHWH your God in vain.	YHWH has the right to proper representation and loyal service.
3	Remember the Sabbath day, to keep it holy.	A man's household has the right to days of rest (i.e. humane treatment).
4	Honour your father and your mother.	A man's parents have the right to his respect and care.
5	You shall not murder.	Others have the right to life.
6	You shall not commit adultery.	Others have the right to sexual purity and secure marriages.
7	You shall not steal.	Others have the right to property.
8	You shall not bear false witness against your neighbour.	A man's neighbour has the right to an honest representation and reputation, especially in court.
9	You shall not covet your neighbour's wife.	A man's neighbour has the right to freedom from fear that he desires his wife.
10	You shall not covet your neighbour's house, field, human resources, animal resources, or anything else.	A man's neighbours have the right to freedom from fear that he desires their household resources.

but they were worthy of equal honour).[31] That Leviticus 19:3 (Heb. 19:2) places 'mother' before 'father' in its call for respect from children, and that a home could also be identified as a 'mother's house', especially in accounts involving

---

31. This image pervades the book of Proverbs, which not only portrays a noble woman as creatively and energetically engaged in economic activity for her household (31:10–31), but also twice characterizes her instruction as teaching (*tôrāh*), and frequently identifies her as worthy of honour equal to that of a child's father (10:1; 15:20; 19:26; 20:20; 23:22, 25; 28:24; 29:15).

daughters (Gen. 24:28; Ruth 1:8; Song 3:4; 8:2), may not reflect an egalitarian diarchy, but certainly assume a complementarian relationship and equal onto-logical status.[32]

Patricentrism in the specific instructions in Deuteronomy 12 – 26

When we read Deuteronomy as a whole we notice its pervasively patricentric – as opposed to patriarchal – perspective. It is all about the heads of households seeking the well-being of those in their charge, rather than protecting their status and power. In particular, it pays special attention to women's rights, as long recognized by scholars.[33]

1. *The concern for widows* (10:17–18, passim). We begin with Deuteronomy's remarkable concern for the members of the community marginalized and economically vulnerable because they lack the security provided by a male figure, either a father or husband. Beginning in 10:18 and on nine further occasions, the book declares the responsibility of Israelites, particularly of household heads, for the well-being of the widow, the fatherless and the alien.[34]

2. *Invitations to participate in worship* (12:12, passim). Like the 'Book of the Covenant' in Exodus 21 – 23, the Deuteronomic Torah requires all males to gather at the central sanctuary three times a year for the Festivals of Passover and Unleavened Bread, Weeks, and Booths (16:16; cf. Exod. 23:14–17; 34:23). However, in contrast to the segregation that would characterize worship centuries later in Herodian times, Deuteronomy invites women, both free and slave, to worship freely in the presence of YHWH at the central sanctuary (12:12, 18; 16:11, 14; 31:12).

3. *The manumission of female slaves* (15:12). Whereas the regulations concerning the manumission of indentured slaves in the Book of the Covenant had spoken only of male slaves (Exod. 21:2–11), the corresponding instructions in Deuter-onomy 15 expressly stipulate that the law applies to both male and female slaves (v. 12).

4. *Military exemption for new husbands* (20:7). Like the instructions involving a newly constructed house (v. 5) and a newly planted vineyard (v. 6), the one-year

---

32. Hence the command to honour father and mother (5:16; cf. Lev. 19:3), and the involvement of mothers in cases involving children (Deut. 21:18–21).

33. Thus Moshe Weinfeld, *Deuteronomy 1–11: A New Translation with Introduction and Commentary*, AB 5 (New York: Doubleday, 1991), p. 318; idem, *Deuteronomy and the Deuteronomic School* (Winona Lake: Eisenbrauns, 2014; reprint of 1972 Oxford edition), pp. 282–92.

34. See footnote 16 above.

exemption of a newly betrothed man from military service appears to be interested primarily in his enjoyment of his new commitment. However, this ordinance also has the interests of his bride in mind. She would hope to have conceived a child before he leaves for his tour of duty 'lest he die and another man take her'. Further, 24:5 speaks expressly of the man tending to his new wife's happiness for the year.

5. *The captive bride* (21:10–14). For women, few circumstances are more fearful than conquest by a foreign army. It is clear from the concluding motive clause, 'because you have degraded her' (21:14),[35] that the goal here is to prevent male abuse of women in warfare. This paragraph assumes a soldier's right to marry a woman in circumstances where contractual arrangements with the bride's family are impossible,[36] and then to divorce her. But it appeals to Israelite men to be both humane and charitable in their treatment of foreign women who are forced to become a part of the Israelite community through no decision or fault of their own.

6. *The second-ranked wife* (21:15–17). Bigamous and polygamous marriages provide fertile soil for the mistreatment of women. This text assumes that one of the wives will be favoured by the man, which could lead to favoured treatment of her son when his property is divided. The present provision secures the status and well-being of the son of a rejected wife who happened to be the first-born. Since children were responsible for the care of their parents in old age, it also protects the interests and rights of the second-ranked wife.

7. *The mother of a rebellious son* (21:18–21). While the opening clause, 'If a man . . .', reflects the patricentrism of ancient Israel, the instructions on dealing with the 'stubborn and rebellious son' modify this by explicitly including the child's mother *with* his father as the aggrieved party, and by involving her in every phase of the legal process: *they* chastise him; *they* seize

---

35. Contrary to common understanding (e.g. Richard D. Nelson, *Deuteronomy: A Commentary*, OTL (Louisville: Westminster John Knox, 2002), p. 254; J. G. McConville, *Deuteronomy*, Apollos OTC 5 (Leicester: Apollos, 2002), p. 330) the verb here ('*innâ*, piel) does not refer to 'rape' or 'sexual abuse'. Ellen van Wolde has demonstrated that in juridical contexts the word serves an evaluative function, expressing downward social movement, and should be translated 'debased': 'Does '*innâ* Denote Rape? A Semantic Analysis of a Controversial Word', *VT* 52 (2002), pp. 528–44.

36. *Contra* Carolyn Pressler, *The View of Women Found in the Deuteronomic Family Laws*, BZAW 216 (Berlin/New York: de Gruyter, 1993), p. 11.

him; *they* bring him out; *they* tell the elders of the child's insubordination to *them*. These instructions prevent the male head of the household from operating only in self-interest, and force him also to protect his wife from abuse by a son.

8. *The wife falsely accused of lying about her virginity* (22:13–21). This paragraph divides into two parts, a primary case involving a false accusation (vv. 13–19) and a counter-case in which the charges prove to be true (vv. 20–21). Whereas the latter makes no attempt to defend a woman who is actually guilty of lying, the former goes to great lengths to protect a woman from false accusations by her husband. The text (a) invites the woman's parents (both father and mother) to come to her defence – a remarkable provision in a patrilocal society; (b) calls for a public hearing of the case before the elders – commensurate with the public nature of the slander; (c) invites the presentation of objective evidence to counter the false accusations; (d) provides for the turning of the tables between the accused and the plaintiff; (e) calls for the public disciplining of the man; (f) secures the honour of the woman's parents by forcing the man to pay compensation for his charge of 'damaged goods'; and (g) prohibits the man from divorcing the woman, thus ensuring her economic well-being for life.

Many modern readers will find the last prescription unpalatable. Surely divorce is better than living with a man who has publicly defamed his wife. However, ancient texts should be read in the light of their own intention rather than modern conventions. From the perspective of the husband, this order assumes that punishment will have a rehabilitative effect; having been publicly shamed he will return to his wife and assume his responsible role in caring for her. From the perspective of the woman, this order guarantees her security; she will be cared for all her days. From the perspective of her parents, they may keep the bride price (plus the fine); but more importantly, they can relax because their daughter is restored to a socially protective environment.[37] From the perspective of the community, the elders who witnessed the proceedings become guarantors of the man's good behaviour.

9. *The victims of rape* (22:23–29). Here Moses provides instructions for two scenarios involving rape of a virgin, distinguished by whether or not the victim is engaged. The first case is interesting for the distinction it draws between rape

---

37. This is difficult for modern Westerners to understand, given the high value we place on individual physical, psychological and emotional well-being, as opposed to the well-being of the community.

in a town (vv. 23–24) and out in the country (vv. 25–27).[38] It assumes that if the act occurs in town an innocent woman will cry for help and either her fiancé or her townspeople will rescue her. However, since there is no one in the countryside to hear her protests, it gives her the benefit of the doubt and assumes her innocence. Meanwhile the man must be executed.[39]

The second case involves a virgin who is not engaged. Whereas Exodus 22:16 (Heb. 22:17) considers the man's actions to be seductive, here Moses speaks of the man seizing the woman and 'lying' with her. The prescribed response focuses entirely on the man. Because he has deflowered and degraded the woman, he must pay her father fifty shekels. This payment is not a fine (as in v. 19) but the bride price, since she then becomes a wife whom he can never divorce. On the surface it looks like Deuteronomy has tightened the law recorded in Exodus and eliminated all other options for the poor woman but to become the wife of her violator.[40] However, the issue is probably not that simple. The point here is that, if the man pays the bride price and the father agrees to accept him as a son-in-law, the man must fulfil all the marital duties that come with sexual intercourse, and in so doing guarantee the woman's social security.

10. *The divorced woman* (24:1–4). This text has been the subject of more attention than most of the above. Interpretations vary, but the key is found in properly identifying where the unit shifts from 'if' (the protasis) to 'then' (the

---

38. This compares with ancient Hittite laws that distinguish rape cases occurring in the mountains and those in a woman's house, the latter being deemed a capital offence. See HL ¶¶197–198, in Martha T. Roth, *Law Collections from Mesopotamia and Asia Minor*, SBL Writings from the Ancient World Series 6, 2nd ed. (Atlanta: Scholars Press, 1997), p. 237.

39. Texts like this answer accusations of double standards, as in the unsigned article on 'Adultery' in Tierney (ed.), *Women's Studies Encyclopedia*: 'The double standard, that only the woman's infidelity deserves serious punishment, has permeated thinking in all patriarchal societies. It rests in large part on the idea of a woman as property' (p. 14). According to Gerda Lerner, 'Hebrew men enjoyed complete sexual freedom within and outside marriage'; Gerda Lerner, *The Creation of Patriarchy* (New York: Oxford University Press, 1986), p. 170. Comments like this are wrong, not only because they disregard the evidence of this text in Deuteronomy, but also because they ignore the fact that the Decalogue is addressed to men and does not even consider female adultery.

40. According to Gerda Lerner, 'Implicitly, this forces a woman into an indissoluble marriage with her rapist (Deut. 22:28–29)'; *Creation of Patriarchy*, p. 170.

apodosis). The syntax is admittedly ambiguous, but the following table represents the most likely flow and structure of the text:

The problem	When a man takes a woman and marries her, if she finds no favour in his eyes because he has found some defect in her,
The prevailing practice	and he writes her a certificate of divorce, and he puts it in her hand, and sends her out of his house,
The complication	if she departs from his house, and goes and becomes another man's wife, and if the latter man hates her, and he writes her a certificate of divorce, and puts it in her hand, and he sends her out of his house, if the latter man dies, who took her to be his wife,
The proscription	then her former husband, who sent her away, may not take her again to be his wife, after she has been declared defiled,
The rationale	for that is an abomination before YHWH, and you shall not bring sin upon the land that YHWH your God is giving you as a grant.

Contrary to common opinion, this text does not authorize or even regulate divorce *per se* – the practice is assumed – but seeks to prevent further abuse by a husband after he has divorced his wife (cf. 21:10–14). Technically the primary issue is not divorce but palingamy, i.e. remarriage to a former spouse.[41] Moses protects the woman from abuse by her first husband, by reiterating the existent procedures for releasing wives from marriage. Further, he insists that when a husband divorces his wife he relinquishes his authority over her. Having humiliated her by insisting she declare herself unclean, he may not reclaim her if she has remarried and then loses her later husband through divorce or death. The legislation protects the woman by requiring the husband to produce a severance document as legal proof for the dissolution of the marriage. Without this document the husband could demand to have her back at any time; and if she were to remarry, he could accuse her of adultery.[42]

---

41. Cf. Raymond Westbrook, 'Prohibition on Restoration of Marriage in Deuteronomy 24:1–4', in S. Japhet (ed.), *Studies in Bible 1986*, Scripta Hierosolymitana 31 (Jerusalem: Magnes, 1986), p. 388; Pressler, *View of Women*, pp. 46–7. For the traditional interpretation, see Gordon Hugenberger, *Marriage as a Covenant: Biblical Law and Ethics as Developed from Malachi*, BSL (Winona Lake: Eisenbrauns, 1998), pp. 76–81.

42. So also Christopher J. H. Wright, *God's People in God's Land* (Grand Rapids: Eerdmans, 1990), p. 217.

11. *Levirate marriage* (25:5–10). The primary purpose of this institution was to secure the integrity of families and inherited estates, which were threatened when a married man died without having fathered an heir. This could be achieved by the widow marrying the deceased's brother, i.e. his nearest unmarried male relative. The first child born of this union would be legally considered the child of the deceased, bearing his name and retaining his property. Verses 7–10 contemplate the case in which the nearest relative refuses to perform this duty on behalf of his dead brother. The legal process affords the widow remarkable freedom of movement and influence in prosecuting the case. She appears before the elders and presents her complaint (v. 7b). The elders of the town summon the brother-in-law and speak to him (v. 8a). If he publicly refuses to do his duty (v. 8b), the widow then performs a ritual of public humiliation – removing her brother-in-law's sandal and, in a gesture of rudeness and humiliation,[43] spitting in his face (v. 9). By announcing, 'This is what shall be done to the man who will not build his brother's house', the widow shows that her response is neither impulsive nor idiosyncratic, but accords with established legal procedure. Although the woman expressly acts in the interests of her deceased husband, she also defends her own honour. This text therefore discourages a man with levirate responsibility from simply disregarding it and abandoning his widowed sister-in-law. The elders of the city are to stand by the woman against a potentially callous male.

Conclusion

In the past three decades feminist scholars have rightly alerted readers of the Scriptures to misogynistic elements in the biblical texts. It is clear that the documents were all written from an androcentric perspective. It is also clear that household heads were just as prone as other community leaders to twist positions of responsibility into positions of power, and to exercise that power in brutal self-interest. It is tempting to assume that the narratives of such abuse reflect the Israelite norm and demonstrate that the system itself is fundamentally flawed. The stories do indeed prove the fulfilment of the prediction made by God at the fountainhead of human history: 'I will greatly increase your pangs in childbearing; in pain you shall bring forth children; you shall crave the power of your husband, but he will *rule* over you' (Gen. 3:16).

---

43. Cf. Num. 12:14; Job 17:6; 30:10; Matt. 26:67; 27:30; Mark 10:34; 14:65;
    Luke 18:32.

Because of humanity's sin, a woman's role became not only painful but also frustrating. And because of the ongoing sins of men, women are all too often treated as subjects rather than as co-regents in the exercise of dominion over the earth. It is easy to forget that this represents neither the biblical ideal nor the covenantal norm. According to the standards signalled by the Decalogue and developed in greater detail in the Deuteronomic Torah, the role of the 'father' in the 'father's house' involved primarily care and protection of all those under his charge. However, this care and protection often degenerates to exploitation and abuse of women as if they are nothing more than household property, as disposable as sheep or oxen. Contemporary efforts to determine and re-establish biblical ethical norms must pay attention not only to accounts of the way it was, but especially to texts that outline the way it should have been. In this and many other respects the book of Deuteronomy offers a glorious gospel, setting a trajectory of male–female relations that leads ultimately to Paul's statements in Ephesians 5:25–33:

> Husbands, love your wives, as Christ loved the church and gave himself up for her, that he might sanctify her, having cleansed her by the washing of water with the word, so that he might present the church to himself in splendor, without spot or wrinkle or any such thing, that she might be holy and without blemish. In the same way husbands should love their wives as their own bodies. He who loves his wife loves himself. For no one ever hated his own flesh, but nourishes and cherishes it, just as Christ does the church, because we are members of his body. 'Therefore a man shall leave his father and mother and hold fast to his wife, and the two shall become one flesh.' This mystery is profound, and I am saying that it refers to Christ and the church. However, let each one of you love his wife as himself. (ESV)

The seeds of this perspective were planted long ago in God's covenant with Israel. May they sprout and may this plant flourish anew among God's people today.

© Daniel I. Block, 2017

2. ORDERED RELATIONSHIPS IN LEVITICUS

Katherine Smith

From beginning to end, the book of Leviticus envisions a people who live in ordered relationships as a community belonging to their covenant God. The social structure of Israel's life in the land depends upon this relational order. When offence endangers relational order, overcoming the fracture in relationship is critical if there is to be life and not death.

For the past two decades, revisionist theologians have argued that the meaning of Leviticus 18 – 20 is plain, but its relevance must be confined to ancient Israel in the land.[1] One writer has even stretched the argument so far as to say that to take Scripture seriously requires resisting the plain sense of particular texts.[2] Sadly, the evangelical church is not immune from also doubting the relevance of Leviticus as Christian Scripture. This chapter will explore why ordered relationships are critical to Leviticus, then reaffirm the relevance of its understanding of relational order for the church today.

---

1. For example, D. T. Stewart, 'Leviticus', in D. Guest, R. E. Goss, M. West and T. Bohache (eds.), *The Queer Bible Commentary* (London: SCM, 2006), p. 81; R. Treloar, '"On Not Putting New Wine into Old Wineskins" or "Taking the Bible Fully Seriously": An Anglican Reading of Leviticus 18:22 and 20:13', in *Five Uneasy Pieces: Essays on Scripture and Sexuality* (Adelaide: ATF, 2011), pp. 13–30.

2. Treloar, 'Anglican Reading', pp. 26–28.

Ordered relationships in the framework of Leviticus

Ordered relationships are a priority in the opening chapters of Leviticus. The first speech opens in 1:2 with an Israelite wishing to approach Yahweh through the bringing of gifts. The first gift, the whole burnt offering (1:3–17), teaches that the life which is acceptable in God's presence is one of wholeness and integrity.[3] The second gift, the cereal offering (2:1–16; 6:14–15), is where both the offerer and Yahweh remember the covenant relationship. The third gift, the fellowship offering (3:1–16), represents wholeness of relationship between a household and Yahweh.[4] The order of these first three gift instructions is critical. First, the offerer affirms wholeness of relationship with Yahweh, from which wholeness of relationship within the family is then derived. After this emphasis upon approaching Yahweh in relational order, the final two gifts, the purification and reparation offerings, address the problem of when relationship is fractured. In the case of the purification offering (4:1 – 5:13), when unintentional offence fractures the relationship between the offender and Yahweh, there is a means for atonement that leads to reconciliation.[5] When an offender breaks faith with his neighbour, which is the case of the guilt offering (5:14 – 6:7), the offender is to make peace. This involves making reparation for his offence with his neighbour, after which he then offers a guilt offering to Yahweh for atonement and forgiveness. So when unintentional offence breaks ordered relationships, it is imperative that the offender submits to a ritual process where reconciliation is the outcome, thus restoring relational order.

---

3. L. M. Trevakis, *Holiness, Ethics and Ritual in Leviticus* (Sheffield: Sheffield Phoenix, 2011), p. 206, observes that in the very act of presenting and surrendering a burnt offering, a gift that is without blemish, 'he or she could probably not help but come to the conclusion that the life God finds acceptable is one that is *tāmîm*'. When applied to humans, *tāmîm* can be rendered 'whole, blameless'. The offerer is therefore motivated to embody human integrity.

4. The use of *šĕlāmîm* (same stem as *šālôm*, 'peace, wholeness') to describe the ritual affirms the wholeness of (covenantal) relationship, irrespective of whether the term specifically envisages the food offering to Yahweh, the portion given to the priests, or the family feast.

5. J. Milgrom, *Leviticus 1–16: A New Translation with Introduction and Commentary*, AB 3 (New York: Doubleday, 1991), p. 245, and J. Watts, *Leviticus 1–10*, HCOT (Leuven: Peeters, 2013), p. 346, helpfully note that *sālaḥ*, usually translated 'forgiveness', encompasses the relational aspect of reconciliation.

The concluding chapters also emphasize relational order, but now in the context of living in the land. Leviticus 25 makes explicit two theological ideas which have been implied from the beginning of chapter 17. The first is that the land belongs to Yahweh, and that the Israelites dwell in the land without ownership (25:23). For this reason, how Israel relates to the land reflects how the nation relates to the land-giver (25:2–24). The second idea is that the Israelites belong as servants to Yahweh, their covenant God who redeemed them (25:38, 42, 55). For this reason, no Israelite may mistreat or enslave another Israelite (25:25–55). The covenant blessings then accentuate that wholeness of relationship is marked by Israel hearing and doing Yahweh's command, which leads to life and flourishing (26:3–13). The goal of these covenant blessings is the statement, 'I will put my dwelling-place among you, and I will not abhor you' (26:11 NIV).[6] This use of tabernacle language is deliberate. In Exodus 40, the tabernacle reaches completion (Exod. 40:33), the Israelites having obeyed Yahweh's earlier command (Exod. 25:2–9). Its purpose is also now fulfilled – God's glory fills the tabernacle (40:34–35). Thus what is expressed as a future action in Leviticus 26:11 is to a degree a present reality. However, the goal is also for Yahweh not to abhor the nation as he dwells among them.[7] This is not only the goal of Israel's obedience, but also the goal of Leviticus. The book's purpose is to persuade Israel to be Yahweh's servants in whole relationship with their covenant God, and to dissuade the nation from walking contrary to him. Otherwise, as the covenant curses warn, death and exile will be the consequence (26:14–45).

Thus relational order with Yahweh frames the book of Leviticus. Relational order is where wholeness of relationship exists between Yahweh and his people, from which wholeness of relationship then extends to relationships within families and between neighbours. The consequence of whole

---

6. Unless otherwise indicated all biblical translations in this chapter are the author's.

7. Lev. 26:11–12 points to a restoration of Edenic order, 'nothing less than the restoration, in Israel, of the relationship between God and man that existed before the flood', so C. Nihan, *From Priestly Torah: A Study in the Composition of the Book of Leviticus* (Tübingen: Mohr Siebeck, 2007), p. 108. Similarly J. Hartley, *Leviticus*, WBC 4 (Dallas: Word, 1992), p. 463; J. Milgrom, *Leviticus 23–27: A New Translation with Introduction and Commentary*, AB 3b (New York: Doubleday, 2001), pp. 2302–3; J. Sklar, *Leviticus* (Downers Grove: IVP, 2014), p. 316. However, there is also a present dimension to 26:11–12: that God's glory may continue to dwell among Israel and that the people may live.

relationship between Yahweh and Israel will be God dwelling in the midst of his people and for him not to abhor them. For this to be a reality, however, Leviticus motivates Israel to pursue an obedience reflective of their identity as servants of Yahweh.

Relational order and offence in Leviticus 18 – 20

Leviticus 18 – 20 are the core chapters that address family and community relationships in the land. Each begins and concludes with paraenesis (urgent exhortation) giving the reason for why Israel is to reflect relational order. Since these paraenetic frames are just as critical as the lists of commands and prohibitions, we will explore the frames of each chapter before moving to the substance of the commands.

Leviticus 18

The paraenetic frame of Leviticus 18 addresses the situation of Israel at Sinai, a newly-formed nation standing between two cultures. Israel has left Egypt with its customs and is preparing to journey to Canaan with its different practices. The opening frame in verses 3–5 unambiguously prohibits Israel from continuing with practices from Egypt and from adopting the behaviour of Canaan. In verse 4, the direct objects 'my ordinances' and 'my statutes' come before the verbs 'you shall do' and 'you shall keep', highlighting that the instructions they are to follow are those of Yahweh their God. Verse 5 repeats this, adding that there is life in living the commands. The repetition of 'I am Yahweh' (v. 5), shortened from 'I am Yahweh your God' (vv. 2, 4), is critical: Israel is to keep Yahweh's statutes because he is their covenant God.

The concluding paraenetic frame in verses 24–30 reiterates that Israel must not reflect the behaviour of the nations of Canaan. The pronoun 'these' (twice in v. 24) refers back to the prohibitions just listed (vv. 6–23):[8] if they defile themselves in these ways, then the land will vomit them out as it did to its previous inhabitants. The nation will be exiled. No one is exempt. Verses 24–28 underline communal responsibility, including both Israelites ('native-born', NIV) and foreigners (v. 26), while verse 29 (in the singular) highlights individual accountability. The penalty for individuals is exile from their

---

8. See also J. Milgrom, *Leviticus 17–22: A New Translation with Introduction and Commentary*, AB 3a (New York: Doubleday, 2000), p. 1578.

people.[9] Thus the paraenetic frame emphasizes that participating in prohibited behaviour will lead to relational breakdown between Israel and the land, which is symptomatic of relational breakdown between Israel and Yahweh. The penalty of exile for the nation and for the individual accentuates the seriousness of the offence in the eyes of the law-giver.

The structure and substance of the commands in 18:6–24 are straightforward. Verse 6 provides the basic principle,[10] literally: 'No man is to approach any flesh of his flesh to uncover nakedness: I am Yahweh.' The nature of the offence is clear: a man exposes the nakedness of a close family member with the intent of sexual activity.[11] The following prohibitions in verses 7–18 then apply this principle to cases of family relationships in descending order of proximity, from the closest to the more distant relative.[12] Again, there is no ambiguity. A man must not uncover the nakedness of someone with whom he shares a kinship relationship. Statements such as 'he is your father', 'she is your mother', or 'she is your sister', highlight why uncovering their nakedness is prohibited. Moreover, uncovering the nakedness of a close relative may also cause dishonour to another family member because of their relational proximity. For example, a man uncovering the nakedness of his father's wife (v. 8) reveals not only her nakedness but also that of his father. Thus uncovering the nakedness of someone of the

---

9. This takes 'cut off' (kārat in niphal, 18:29) to mean exile rather than death. See also Milgrom, Leviticus 17–22, p. 1582. The passive niphal implies that this penalty is executed by God, but this does not preclude physical exile. As B. A. Levine, Leviticus (Philadelphia: JPS, 1989), p. 242, observes, 'The policy that a person, family, or tribe would be "cut off" and banished from the larger community . . . translated itself into the perception that God would similarly "cut off" those who offended Him, if human agencies had allowed such offenses to go unpunished'. Sklar, Leviticus, p. 136, proposes that 'cutting off' refers to both exile and premature death: 'In either case, the sinner was removed from the covenant community and regarded as the Lord's enemy.'

10. So G. Wenham, Leviticus, NICOT (Grand Rapids: Eerdmans, 1979), p. 253. By contrast, Milgrom, Leviticus 17–22, p. 1533, proposes that v. 6 encompasses offences 'ostensibly missing from the following list'.

11. See most scholars, e.g. Hartley, Leviticus, pp. 293–5; N. Kiuchi, Leviticus (Nottingham: Apollos, 2007), pp. 333–4; Levine, Leviticus, pp. 119–20; Milgrom, Leviticus 17–22, pp. 1533–4; Nihan, From Priestly Torah, pp. 430–1; Sklar, Leviticus, p. 231; Wenham, Leviticus, pp. 253–4.

12. Wenham, Leviticus, p. 254, helpfully clarifies that vv. 6–18 prohibits sexual activity 'between people who are consanguineous to the first and second degree'.

same flesh breaks relational order not only within the family but also with the law-giver (vv. 2, 4, 5, 6).

The prohibition in verse 19 is a transition to cases outside family relationship where sexual activity is prohibited. The first two occur between a man and a woman (vv. 19–20), the others do not (vv. 22–23). Verse 19 prohibits a man 'uncovering the nakedness' of a woman during her menstrual uncleanness (defined in 15:19–20), while verse 20 forbids sex with a neighbour's wife. Verse 21 then interrupts the list of sexual offences by condemning the giving of children (literally 'seed') to Molech. This shifts the topic from male–female cases (vv. 6–20) via an offence related to the outcome of sexual activity. Verses 22–23 then prohibit two situations: when a man has sex with another man (v. 22) and when either a man or a woman has sex with an animal (v. 23).[13] Homosexuality is described as detestable (*tôʿēbâ*), and bestiality as a confusion or perversion (*tebel*), since it confuses the distinction between humanity and animals.

In summary, the Israelites must desist from the behaviours of Egypt and not repeat the offences of Canaan; they must not have sex within the 'prohibited degrees' of family relationships or outside marriage, or practise child-sacrifice, homosexuality or bestiality. Such acts break relational order and cause offence to others and to Yahweh their God, resulting in personal or communal exile.

Leviticus 19

While the paraenetic frames in chapter 18 stress that Israel's actions reflect their allegiance to their covenant God, the pithy opening frame in chapter 19 affirms that how Israel lives must reflect who Yahweh is: their God is holy, so Israel must be holy (19:2). The concluding frame then affirms that Israel must keep all Yahweh's statutes and ordinances (v. 37). Who they are and to whom

---

13. Most scholars accept the traditional reading of 18:22, but some now question various aspects. Nihan, *From Priestly Torah*, pp. 437–8, argues that the prohibition 'is aimed primarily not at the active partner but at the *receptive* one . . . a man should not behave [sexually] like a woman does'. See also S. M. Olyan, '"And with a Male You Shall Not Lie the Lying Down of a Woman": On the Meaning and Significance of Leviticus 18:22 and 20:13', *Journal of the History of Sexuality*, 5/2 (1993), pp. 179–206; J. Walsh, 'Leviticus 18:22 and 20:13: Who Is Doing What to Whom?', *JBL* 120 (2001), pp. 201–9. B. Wells (unpublished paper, following Walsh) suggests that the phrase normally translated 'lie as one lies with a woman' indicates not manner but location, i.e. 'lie on a lying place (bed) of a woman'. However, *contra* Nihan, the verse addresses the active not the receptive partner; and *contra* Wells, the focus of the chapter (and presumably this verse) is on people, not place.

they belong, informs how they must act and live. The commands and prohibitions between these two frames then inform Israel how they are to embody being holy (19:3–36). Intriguingly, the opening command to revere one's mother and father (19:3, alluding to the fifth commandment) comes before those addressing the Israel–Yahweh relationship more directly.[14] The placing of the two commands to respect parents and to keep the Sabbath before the declaration 'I am Yahweh your God' suggests that obedience to these key commands is an acknowledgment in practice that Yahweh is their covenant God. Two other commands in the chapter concern family matters. In verses 5–8, following a fellowship sacrifice, the offerer's household who participate in a fellowship meal must not eat the sanctified food beyond the second day, otherwise they desecrate what belongs to Yahweh and thus rupture relational order. The actions of the family influence whether the sacrifice is accepted by Yahweh. Then in verse 29, profaning one's daughter by making her a prostitute affects the purity of the whole land, which hints at communal exile. In summary, Israelites who respect parents and daughters, and who honour what is holy, reflect relational order and acknowledge that Yahweh is their covenant God.

Leviticus 20

Unusually, the paraenetic frames in Leviticus 20 (vv. 7–8, 22–26) are themselves enclosed by an *inclusio*, one that bans Molech worship and necromancy (vv. 1–6, 27). The frame in verses 7–8 first highlights the Israelites' responsibility to sanctify themselves because Yahweh is their covenant God, balancing Israel's responsibility with Yahweh's work of sanctifying Israel.[15] The closing paraenetic frame begins by repeating yet again the imperative to obey Yahweh and avoid local customs (vv. 22–23). Verses 24–26 are then arranged in a chiasm, with Yahweh's work of separating Israel from the nations (vv. 24b, 26) enclosing the command to make a distinction between clean and unclean animals (v. 25).[16] Significantly, verse 26 associates God's act of separating Israel from the nations

---

14. Scholars discuss whether Leviticus 19 has been shaped by the Decalogue (Exod. 20:2–17) or is composed from two separate decalogues (see Milgrom, *Leviticus 17–22*, pp. 1600–2). The Decalogue by nature presents general principles, so Leviticus 19 could be applying those principles to specific situations.

15. See also Milgrom, *Leviticus 17–22*, p. 1739. Israel's sanctification is both Yahweh's work of redemption in their past and his continuing work of sanctification in their present (20:8).

16. Ibid., p. 1761.

with the command for Israel to imitate his holiness. Israel's holiness is being set apart *from* the nations solely *for* Yahweh.[17]

The instructions in Leviticus 20:9–21, however, are distinctively outcome-oriented. They no longer prohibit behaviour, but rather communicate the penalty for offences prohibited in chapters 18 – 19. Leviticus 20 starts with addressing relational order in families, notably where a man curses his father and his mother, for which the penalty is death; the offender bears his own blood-guilt. As Milgrom notes

> dishonoring parents – that is, the breakdown of obligations to one's father or mother – is able to lead to the breakdown of relationships with the other members of the familial chain, including sexual taboos . . . without respect for parents, all other family relationships are liable to collapse.[18]

Verses 10–21 then progress to sexual offences, in turn those leading to the death penalty (vv. 10–16), to being cut off (vv. 17–18), and to remaining childless (vv. 20–21).[19] However, the order of verses 10–16 does not follow that of chapter 18, as we might expect. Burnside plausibly suggests that successive offences depart further and further from the norm of sexual relationship between husband and wife:[20]

Verse 10	Departs from the norm in that the woman is married to another man.
Verse 11	Departs further here, since the woman is a family member.
Verse 12	Further still, the woman is in the next generation.
Verse 13	Even further, it is now a man with another man.
Verse 14	Yet further, it is a man and two sexual partners.
Verses 15–16	Finally, it is sexual relations between people and animals.

---

17. Milgrom, ibid., p. 1762, argues that Israel's holiness is both the imitation of God and separation from the nations. He rightly observes that 'being holy' is to be set apart not only *from* something but also *for* something or someone.

18. Milgrom, *Leviticus 17–22*, pp. 1744–5.

19. See also Milgrom, ibid., p. 1743; Sklar, *Leviticus*, p. 254. Verses 17–21 also use the language of (uncovering) nakedness.

20. J. Burnside, *God, Justice, and Society: Aspects of Law and Legality in the Bible* (New York: Oxford, 2011), p. 363; adapted here by combining vv. 15–16.

In summary, sexual acts that depart from the norm of a husband–wife relationship are culpable of relational offence and thus bear a penalty. Just as culpable is cursing one's father and mother. The fact that there is no means of atonement for any of these offences highlights their seriousness in the eyes of the law-giver. There is no means by which the offenders can make reparation or seek a restoration of the relationship with Yahweh once they have cursed their parents or committed a sexual offence that departs from relational order.

Summary of Leviticus 18 – 20

The central sections of these chapters deal with relational order within families and the community. Offence breaks relational order not only between Israelites, but also with Yahweh their covenant God, and the penalty can be exile or death. Moreover, each chapter frames the commands and prohibitions within paraenetic instruction stressing that Yahweh has set apart Israel from the nations for himself. He sanctifies them, and they must also sanctify themselves, which requires living distinctively. This distinctiveness is relating to Yahweh and to one another in wholeness. If they do this, then Yahweh – who lives in their midst – will delight in them and not abhor them.

Leviticus and the gospel

The paradox of the gospel is that Jesus fulfilled the pattern of the law so that believers are free to live in obedience. While there is no condemnation in Christ, we cheapen God's grace if we continue in patterns of behaviour that we know break relationship (Rom. 6; Heb. 10:26–31). The church is still a covenant community called to live as a holy people set apart from the world and for Christ (1 Pet. 1 – 2). So those who are in Christ must distinguish between pure patterns of living that glorify Christ and impure ones that do not (Rom. 8:1–4; Gal. 5:19–24). The wholeness of our relationship with God must be reflected in whole relationships within our families. Thus revering our fathers and mothers, whatever their imperfections, remains the norm for believers in Jesus (Eph. 5:1 – 6:9; Col. 3; 1 Pet. 2:11 – 3:7). Respecting the dignity of our parents, our children and our extended family reflects relational order. Respecting that sexual acts are reserved for a covenant relationship between a husband and wife reflects God's desire for relational order within families. Leviticus links its commands and prohibitions to Israel's identity as a covenant people who must reflect the character of their covenant God who redeemed them. So we the church must link our obedience to our identity as a new covenant people, reflecting the character of our covenant God who has redeemed us. If we separate the command from the gospel, then the command is futile. But if we accept that we belong to Christ and our lives are not our own, then living the command is truly life.

3. 'WHO IS THIS COMING UP FROM THE WILDERNESS?' IDENTITY AND INTERPRETATION IN THE SONG OF SONGS

Rosalind Clarke

The identities of the central male and female characters in the Song of Songs are critical in the interpretation of the book. They continue to be variously identified as Solomon and his wife,[1] God and Israel,[2] Christ and the church,[3] Christ and the individual Christian soul,[4] an everyman and everywoman.[5] In some cases, more than one of these is recognized as present in the Song, and of course some interpreters have identified multiple male and female characters.[6] This chapter will present a brief investigation into the questions of identity raised within the Song itself in the context of its literary unity, canonical

---

1. E.g. James M. Hamilton Jr, *Song of Songs* (Fearn: Christian Focus, 2015).
2. E.g. Luis Stadelmann, *Love and Politics: A New Commentary on the Song of Songs* (New York: Paulist Press, 1992); Ellen F. Davis, *Proverbs, Ecclesiastes and the Song of Songs* (Louisville: Westminster John Knox, 2000).
3. E.g. Robert Jenson, *Song of Songs* (Louisville: John Knox, 2005).
4. E.g. Richard Brooks, *Song of Songs* (Fearn: Christian Focus, 1999); Edmée Kingsmill, *The Song of Songs and the Eros of God* (Oxford: OUP, 2009).
5. Many commentators follow this interpretation, including Tremper Longman III, *Song of Songs* (Grand Rapids: Eerdmans, 2001).
6. E.g. Iain Provan, *Ecclesiastes/Song of Songs* (Grand Rapids: Zondervan, 2001).

status and unique genre.[7] It will show that the Song of Songs honours human love and human marriage, but constantly points beyond the potential of human marriage. The Song presents an intimate portrait of an idealized human marriage as a metaphor for the marriage between God and Israel. As the Song participates in the messianic and eschatological hope of the prophetic books, it invites readers to fall in love with the longed-for Messiah, the bridegroom who will lead his people out of the wilderness.

The final, canonical form of the Song is a carefully, intentionally constructed book, making use of repetition and refrains throughout, and so it should be interpreted as a literary whole, rather than as an anthology of unconnected or loosely connected poems.[8] As a literary unity the Song is *sui generis*. That is to say, while individual poetic units in the Song can be recognized as having the form of a *wasf*,[9] or having a wisdom form,[10] there simply is no comparable text which draws those different forms together into a single unit. Nor is there a comparable text with the same internal setting – that is to say, the woman's

---

7. The date, authorship, genre, theme, unity, structure and purpose of the book are all disputed. See e.g. Richard Hess, *Song of Songs* (Grand Rapids: Baker Academic, 2005), pp. 17–36 for a good, relatively brief, overview of the issues, or Marvin Pope, *Song of Songs* (New York: Doubleday, 1977), pp. 17–229 for a more comprehensive discussion.

8. M. Timothea Elliott, *The Literary Unity of the Canticle* (Frankfurt am Main: Peter Lang, 1989) is a careful and thorough study of the literary features of the Song which demonstrate its internal unity. See also Michael Fox, *The Song of Songs and the Ancient Egyptian Love Songs* (Madison: University of Wisconsin Press, 1985), pp. 218–22, and D. Phillip Roberts, *Let Me See Your Form* (Lanham: University Press of America, 2007), p. 396.

9. A *wasf* is a love poem which describes the features of the loved one from head to toe by means of a series of metaphors and similes. Song 4:1–7; 5:10–16; 6:4–9; 7:1–8 all take this form.

10. For Katharine Dell, the refrain addressed to the daughters of Jerusalem (2:7; 3:5; 5:8) is a wisdom element in the Song; Dell, 'Does the Song of Songs Have Any Connection to Wisdom?', in Anselm C. Hagedorn (ed.), *Perspectives on the Song of Songs* (Berlin/New York: De Gruyter, 2005), p. 15. Song 8:6–7 is also commonly viewed as a wisdom interpolation; e.g. Michael Sadgrove, 'The Song of Songs as Wisdom Literature', in E. A. Livingstone (ed.), *Studia Biblica 1978* (Sheffield: JSOT Press, 1979), 1:246. Sadgrove also suggests that 1:6 and 8:11–12 together function as a riddle or test of wisdom (p. 246).

instruction of the daughters of Jerusalem.[11] With respect to genre, all that can be said with certainty is that the Song brings together various poetic forms in a unique way to reflect on an intimate relationship between a man and woman. However, the Song is distinct from other ancient Near Eastern love poetry, since it exists only as part of the Jewish and Christian Scriptures. The rest of the canon must be taken as its primary literary context,[12] so allusions and references to other canonical texts should be taken seriously in its interpretation as a canonical text.

The strength of an allusion depends upon its proximity, its thematic links and its verbal links. With respect to proximity, the Song has been included in various different canonical groupings: the Writings and the Megilloth in the Hebrew Bible, and the Wisdom and poetic books in the Christian Bible.[13] These groups of texts thus provide the immediate context for interpretation.

Identity and interpretation

There is a high degree of ambiguity surrounding the identity of the central characters in the Song which has contributed to the wide diversity in its inter-pretations. It is tempting to rush to resolve the ambiguity, but it should be noted that it appears to have been deliberately created in the Song, and thus it is an important part of the way in which it engages with its readers.

---

11. Kenton Sparks argues that this was the *Sitz im Leben* for the Song in 'The Song of Songs: Wisdom for Young Jewish Women', *CBQ* 70 (2008), p. 278. It is hard to say with any certainty, given the absence of any external evidence for female wisdom schools. Nevertheless, the internal setting is clear: the woman addresses the daughters of Jerusalem on the nature of love, using examples from her own experience to make her point.

12. John Barton has argued persuasively that neither Jewish nor early Christian communities called for the Song to be excluded from the canon, and later attempts have not gained significant support. See John Barton, 'On the Canonicity of Canticles', in Hagedorn (ed.), *Perspectives*, pp. 1–7.

13. See Lee Martin McDonald and James A. Sanders (eds.), *The Canon Debate* (Peabody: Hendrickson, 2002), pp. 585–90, for extensive evidence of the various orders of the Christian canon. In almost every case, the Song directly follows Proverbs and Ecclesiastes.

The problem with the pronouns

The book proper begins in 1:2 without any introduction of the characters, simply: 'Let *him* kiss *me* with the kisses of his mouth.'[14] Neither the 'him' nor the 'me' are identified in any way before the reader is thrust into the action of the Song by, as Cheryl Exum describes it, 'a disembodied voice'.[15] This style continues through most of the book, with speakers and actors identifiable only by the pronouns used for and by them. In several places in the Song, there are insufficient pronominal indicators to be sure which character is speaking, male or female,[16] and on other occasions the wrong pronoun appears to have been used.[17]

Names and ambiguity

The usual way of overcoming the ambiguity inherent in pronouns is to name characters. Unfortunately, the Song includes very few personal names, of which Solomon is the most prevalent, with seven references to him throughout the book.[18] However, the varied uses of his name only add to the ambiguity of the male character's identity. The first mention of Solomon is in the superscription of the book, but it is not clear what the preposition is intended to convey here: 'by', 'for' or 'about' Solomon are all possibilities. Perhaps it is simply an indication that the poem is in some way connected to the other Solomonic wisdom books.[19] The superscription does not exclude the possibility of Solomon appearing as a character in the Song, but neither does it require that interpretation. The next reference to Solomon comes in a simile in Song 1:5, likening

14. All biblical translations in this chapter are taken from the NIV.

15. Cheryl Exum, *Song of Songs* (Louisville: Westminster John Knox, 2005), p. 92.

16. E.g. Song 3:6–11; 5:1e; and 6:11–12.

17. Song 2:7; 3:5; 8:4 all use the masculine plural form for the verbs addressed to the presumably female group of the daughters of Jerusalem. That may be a deliberate choice, to indicate that the identity of that group is not straightforward. There is also some difficulty with the choice of the feminine demonstrative pronoun in 3:6 apparently used with a male referent. See 'Questions of identity' below, p. 44.

18. Song 1:1, 5; 3:7, 9, 11; 8:11, 12.

19. Gianni Barbiero thinks that the superscription undoubtedly intends to convey authorship, but fictional authorship only, as in Proverbs, Ecclesiastes and the Wisdom of Solomon; *Song of Songs: A Close Reading*, tr. Michael Tait (Leiden: Brill, 2011), p. 45. The comparison with the same attribution in Psalm 72 is not as helpful as Barbiero suggests, since that is undoubtedly a psalm about Solomon, even if it is also ascribed to Solomon.

the woman to the curtains of Solomon. This is a reference to the temple and a reminder of Solomon's role as temple-builder. Chapter 1 thus suggests a Solomonic backdrop to the setting of the Song, but gives no indication that Solomon is an active participant in the narrative.[20]

This changes in Song 3:6–11, where Solomon is named three times in the context of a wedding procession. The daughters of Jerusalem are urged to go out and look at him. He is now present in the internal world of the Song, and celebrated on his wedding day. However, the final references to Solomon in the riddle of 8:11–12 portray the woman repudiating Solomon and distinguishing him from her lover. The dramatic school of interpretation tends to take this as evidence that there are two male characters: Solomon and not-Solomon. The extent to which the central male character in the Song can be identified as Solomon will be discussed below.[21]

The female character is also named, possibly, in Song 6:13. It is not clear whether the term Shulammite is intended to designate her name, her tribe or her place of origin. Some scholars have even suggested that Shulammite should be read as a feminized version of Solomon.[22] The woman is literally a 'Solo-moness', a term which might indicate a connection to King Solomon, or more likely her role as a wisdom-teacher, or as a peace-bringer.[23] The one thing that the term does not do is settle the question of her identity.

Questions of identity

Several explicit questions of identity punctuate the book:

'Who is this coming up from the wilderness like a column of smoke, perfumed with myrrh and incense made from all the spices of the merchant?' (3:6)
'Who is this that appears like the dawn, fair as the moon, bright as the sun, majestic as the stars in procession?' (6:10)
'Who is this coming up from the wilderness leaning on her beloved?' (8:5)

---

20. These indirect references to Solomon contribute to Jan Fokkelmann's reading of Solomon as a 'fairy-tale character' in the Song, rather than a historical figure; *Reading Biblical Poetry* (Louisville: Westminster John Knox, 2001), p. 190.

21. See sections 'King Solomon', p. 46, and 'Not Solomon', p. 47.

22. Sparks describes her as 'the feminine counterpart of Solomon' ('Song of Songs', p. 287).

23. See Exum, *Song of Songs*, pp. 226–7 for a discussion of these possible readings. The terms Solomon, Shulammite and peace share the same Hebrew stem.

The inquiry in Song 5:9 could also be added to this list, since the daughters of Jerusalem ask the woman how they can identify her beloved. They are not asking his name, but what he is like so that he may be found. These questions indicate that the problem of identity is an intentional feature of the Song. In the next two sections, these questions will be considered and answers sought from within the Song itself.

Who is this coming up from the wilderness?

The first explicit question of identity comes in Song 3:6: 'Who is this coming up from the wilderness?' The pronoun and the verb both have a feminine singular form, so the question expects the answer 'a female person'. The Hebrew interrogative *mî* (usually 'who?') is very occasionally used for a thing rather than a person,[24] and in this case it would fit the answer given by the immediate context: Solomon's carriage (*miṭṭâ*, a feminine noun).[25] Others take the feminine 'this' to indicate that the carriage brings the bride,[26] but since the rest of the passage only mentions the bridegroom Solomon, this is unpersuasive. It seems more likely that Solomon's carriage, correctly taking the female pronoun, implies the answer 'Solomon', correctly addressed as a person, rather than a thing. Who, then, is this bridegroom[27] coming out of the wilderness on his wedding day?

---

24. Paul Joüon and T. Muraoka, *A Grammar of Biblical Hebrew* (Rome: Editrice Pontificio Instituto Biblico, 2003), 144b, p. 535.

25. Exum takes this route, translating, 'What is that coming up from the wilderness' (*Song of Songs*, p. 138).

26. E.g. Davis, *Proverbs, Ecclesiastes and the Song*, p. 260. Pope argues that since there is no immediate answer in ch. 3, the answer can be assumed to be the bride, by comparison with the question and answer in 8:5a (*Song of Songs*, p. 424).

27. It has been argued that the wedding depicted in these verses is not the wedding of the central characters in the Song. This is prompted partly by the later negative reference to Solomon, and partly by the ceremonial aspect of this wedding, which contrasts with the personal, intimate nature of the relationship elsewhere in the book. However, there are at least two ways in which the text indicates that it is about those same characters. First, the question of Song 3:6 is repeated in 8:5. Repetition is a key feature of the Song and repeated words are always used in the context of the same characters. Second, the wedding signals a shift in the description of the woman to *kallâ*, bride). She is called *kallâ* six times between 4:1 and 5:1, when previously the term has not been used at all. After the wedding, as we would expect

He is described in two longer passages, Song 3:6–11 and 5:10–16, as well as in briefer comments throughout the book.

King Solomon (3:6–11)

The bridegroom comes out of the wilderness like a pillar of smoke perfumed with myrrh and frankincense, escorted by mighty warriors, in a carriage of cedar upholstered in royal purple, on a base of gold with pillars of silver. He is crowned on the day of his wedding. This passage paints a glorious picture of unalloyed splendour and celebration. Solomon's kingliness is demonstrated in his power and his wealth. The particulars of the luxury he commands are reminiscent of his role as temple-builder: the carriage is made of cedar wood, gold, silver and purple, but more than this, he carries with him the scents of the temple, the frankincense and myrrh, and all the spices. This Solomon coincides with the Chronicler's much more detailed depiction of him as an ideal king, an ideal bridegroom, an ideal Israelite, an ideal YHWH-worshipper.[28] There is no hint, at least not in these verses, of the historical Solomon's many flaws in each of these aspects. Rather, this wedding is a source of rejoicing for all the people, as the daughters of Jerusalem are encouraged to go out and look on him in praise and celebration.

The perfect bridegroom (5:10–16)

The questions of identity in Song 5 prompt the female lover to describe her beloved to the daughters of Jerusalem. She tells them that he is outstanding, one among ten thousand; he is radiant, ruddy and beautiful; his appearance is like jewels, precious metals, lilies and cedars. He is altogether lovely. To the woman he is perfect to look at, to smell, to touch and to kiss. He is utterly desirable in every way and not just to his own beloved – the other women acknowledge his superiority as well. In 1:4 they praise him 'more than wine' and in 6:1 they agree that he is worth seeking.

The shepherd-king (1:2–4, 12–17; 2:3–13)

In the opening chapters of the Song, the male character is the subject of a whole range of metaphors and similes: oil, apple tree, gazelle, and so on. Some of

---

(note 27 *cont.*) if it were her wedding, her status shifts and the terminology used for her shifts correspondingly. See Andre LaCocque, *Romance She Wrote* (Harrisburg: Trinity Press International, 1998), p. 108.

28. See Raymond Dillard, 'The Chronicler's Solomon', *WTJ* 43 (1981), pp. 290–1. The divine name is usually translated 'the LORD', and sometimes vocalized by scholars as 'Yahweh'.

these metaphors have a human counterpart: king and shepherd. There is no *a priori* reason to presume that these signifiers are intended any more literally than descriptions of him as flora and fauna. He is a king, desired by his lover and praised by all women in 1:2–4, but in 1:7–8 the woman speaks to her beloved as if he is a shepherd, asking where he grazes his flocks and rests his sheep. He replies in kind, giving her directions as to where she should graze her goats. She seeks out a shepherd, but the lover she finds in 1:12 is a king. This king is fragrant and handsome – like the bridegroom described in 5:10–16. He is like the apple tree: he protects, he provides, he cares for his bride. He is like a shepherd who protects, provides and cares for his flock. There is no contradiction between his shepherd status and his royal status, since to be an Israelite king is to be a shepherd.[29]

Not Solomon (8:11–12)

The Song ends with a brief parable in which Solomon is depicted as a vineyard-owner who rents out his vineyard to tenants. The woman, by contrast, is also a vineyard-owner, but she keeps her vineyard her very own, until she chooses to give it freely. The parable appears to be a condemnation of Solomon's sexual promiscuity with many hundreds of wives and concubines,[30] by contrast with the woman's hard-won sexual purity, which she can choose to give freely, presumably to her lover, who surely cannot be the Solomon condemned by the parable. Thus, this parable does what the rest of the Song has avoided, by distinguishing the Solomon of history, whose actions with respect to marriage are not condoned, and the Solomon of the rest of the poem, who is an idealized king and bridegroom. The king in the Song both embodies the Solomonic ideal and is better than the Solomonic reality. What a man this must be: as glorious as Solomon, one in ten thousand, an altogether lovely shepherd-king who protects, provides and cares for his beloved bride. An ideal husband indeed.

Who is this coming up from the wilderness, leaning on her beloved?

The remaining questions of identity concern the woman who is the focus of the book. She is a woman who embodies all the glories of the heavens in Song 6:10: sun, moon and stars. The question from Song 3:6 is repeated in 8:5, this

---

29. See 2 Sam. 5:2 and Ps. 78:71. The concepts are commonly paired in the ancient Near East.

30. See Barbiero, *Song of Songs*, pp. 485–9 for a more detailed exploration of these verses.

time with a much clearer answer, 'Who is this coming up from the wilderness, leaning on her beloved?'[31] The female lover is described throughout the Song, but detailed descriptions are given in the three *wasfs* dedicated to her: Song 4:1 – 5:1; 6:4–9; 7:1–9a.

The vineyard-keeper (1:5–6)

In 1:5 she introduces herself as black and beautiful, dark and lovely. She is like the tents of Kedar, woven from black wool, but also like the beautiful temple curtains of Solomon, made from purple, scarlet and gold thread.[32] Her darkness is not genetic, nor her own fault, but rather a sign of her oppression, being forced to tend her brothers' vineyards and in so doing to neglect her own (1:6). The parable in 8:11–12, together with the vineyard imagery in the rest of the book, suggests that in fact the woman's vineyard is herself, to be given or withheld as she chooses; to be enjoyed by her lover but withheld from other men. As she tends her brothers' vineyards in the sun, so she neglects to care for herself.

The rose of Sharon (1:9 – 2:7)

Reunited with her shepherd-king-lover, the woman exchanges compliments with him. Together they praise each other and themselves. He calls her a mare among Pharaoh's chariots, perhaps because she rouses men to a sexual frenzy of desire, or perhaps merely because he views her as a coveted possession.[33] She is also the rose of Sharon, a species of flower mentioned only in Song 2:1 and Isaiah 35:1.[34] She is a lily of the valleys and a lily among thorns, an indication that she is better than the other women, prized above them by her beloved.

The body as a landscape (4:1–7)

The male lover describes his beloved using the form of the *wasf*. From top to bottom, each part of the body is described by means of a metaphor or simile. These are predominantly connected with the land in different ways: general flora and fauna, and specific landmarks such as Mount Gilead and the tower of David. Similar *wasfs* in chapters 6 and 7 also refer to the produce of the land: honey,

---

31. The pronoun and verb are both feminine singular in 8:5 as in 3:6.

32. 2 Chr. 3:14.

33. See Exum, *Song of Songs*, pp. 108–9.

34. Although in Isaiah the term is translated 'crocus' in the NIV, it is the same Hebrew word: *ḥăbaṣṣelet*.

wheat, wine and fruit, and introduce many more named landmarks. The metaphors are notoriously difficult to interpret as expressions of the male lover's admiration for and attraction to the woman's physical features. In fact, the use of extended similes deliberately draws the reader's attention away from the woman's appearance and towards the land. The simile in Song 4:4, for example, is extended three times beyond the initial comparison of her neck to the tower of David: first it is built in rows (or 'with elegance'), then it holds a thousand shields, finally the shields belong to warriors. This extension of the tower imagery ensures that it dominates in the reader's imagination over that of the girl's neck. The whole section gives the impression that the woman's body is viewed by her lover as a landscape, a lush vista of a beautiful country where he is free to roam.

The bride as a garden (4:12 – 5:1)
From the wide panorama of a whole land, the imagery in the second half of chapter 4 narrows to that of a precious garden. Unlike 4:1–7, Song 4:12 – 5:1 contains no direct mention of any bodily part. Only the garden is described: the fountain, the orchard, the well, and all the fruits and spices grown therein. Even in the mind of the male lover, by 5:1 his love is first his garden, and only secondly his sister-bride.

The darling Jerusalem (6:4–9)
The second *wasf* concerning the woman, in Song 6:4–9, repeats the metaphors for hair, teeth and temples from Song 4. In addition, the woman is compared to the cities of Tirzah and Jerusalem, and to their armies striking awe into their enemies with waving banners. This makes it clear that her identification is not with just any landscape or lush garden, but specifically with that of Israel.[35] That is one reason why Ellen Davis insists that 'this is not universal love poetry; the "historical geography" of Israel belongs to the poem in an essential way'.[36] The woman is identified not only with Israel's natural landscape but also with its cities and its armies: '[She] is identified not only with the holy land, with the geography of Israel, but also with its history which is indissolubly bound up

---

35. Barbiero notes that Tirzah and Jerusalem represent respectively the northern and southern kingdoms of Israel (*Song of Songs*, p. 329).

36. Ellen F. Davis, 'Romance of the Land in the Song of Songs', *AThR* 80 (1998), p. 538, *contra* Daniel Grossberg who claims that the many geographical references 'evoke an extensive "everywhere"'; 'Nature, Humanity and Love in the Song of Songs', *Interpretation* 59 (2005), p. 237.

with its geography.'[37] This woman is represented by – and represents – Israel the nation, as well as Israel the place.

The promised-land princess (7:1–8)

This last extended description of the woman portrays her as a prince's daughter who is like Heshbon, Bath Rabbim, the tower of Lebanon, Damascus and Mount Carmel. She is fertile with wheat and wine, fragrant like apples and bearing fruit like a palm tree and a vine. The poem lingers lovingly over the contours of the land, it delights in the fruitfulness of the land, it points out the landmarks of the country.[38] It is a place, at least as much as a person, which the reader is invited to admire.

The woman in the Song is a vineyard, albeit a neglected one, a rose of Sharon and a lily of the valleys, a landscape, a garden, a beloved Jerusalem and a promised-land of a princess. What a woman this must be, to bring all the blessings of the Promised Land to her beloved. What delight must she bring him! What fertility! What satisfaction! The woman tells us she has stored up all her choice fruits for her lover to enjoy (7:13) – what enjoyment must that be!

Some thoughts on interpretation of the Song of Songs

Identifying the Song's male and female protagonists and their major character-istics has significant implications for interpretation. It has already been seen that the Song is firmly situated within the culture, geography and history of Israel. It should not be surprising that such a highly poetic text is deeply allusive and that these allusions are part of the way in which it generates its meaning. Thus the importance of reading the Song as a canonical text can be seen in the allusions and parallels identified with other canonical texts. Reading the Song as a literary unity allows the possibility of an overarching structural metaphor governing the whole text as well as the details of individual words and phrases. It is the nature of metaphor to allow meaning to exist at multiple levels, so the Song as a whole could sustain more than one layer of interpretation. It is concerned with many things: it is about sexuality and redemption, wisdom and women, marriage and kingship. But the descriptions of the characters in the Song consistently push us to admit meanings beyond these. The male character

---

37. Barbiero, *Song of Songs*, p. 330.
38. See Harold Fisch, *Poetry with a Purpose* (Bloomington: Indiana University Press, 1988), p. 89.

is an idealized Solomon-bridegroom-shepherd-king, who is distinguished from the historical Solomon. The female character is a vineyard-rose-landscape-garden-Jerusalem-promised land-princess. These descriptions compel an interpretation which gives due weight to the effect of reading the Song in its canonical context where the theological weight of its language can be fully appreciated.

The Song of Songs is about human sexuality

In Israel, the king and his queen should demonstrate what it means to be Israelite: how to be obedient to God in all aspects of life, including marriage, love and romance. The Song of Songs gives a uniquely personal, intimate insight into a royal marriage. If the royal bridegroom admires, protects, cares for, seeks out, listens to and above all loves his bride, so should all Israelite bridegrooms. And if the royal bride asserts her equality and mutuality with her bridegroom, so too may all Israelite brides. Thus the Song of Songs honours human love and human marriage. Love is said and shown to be powerful and important. It is to be treasured and sought out. Marriage is to be celebrated joyfully and gloriously. The hyperbole of the metaphors puts high value on human marriage, human love and human sexuality. There is much here to learn, for men and women alike, about how to value, desire, care for, stay faithful to and love one's spouse.

The Song of Songs is about God and Israel

While the Song has much to say about human marriage, it also constantly points beyond the potential of human marriage. The male lover is not only a king who is an exemplar for his people, he is a shepherd-king-bridegroom who embodies the idealized Solomon. The female lover is not merely a beautiful princess-bride, she is a landscape, a garden, a darling Jerusalem, the Promised Land. These descriptions in the Song form a matrix of metaphors coherent with the use of the marriage metaphor in the prophetic books, illustrated here by reference to use of the metaphor in Isaiah.

The love song of the vineyard in Isaiah 5:1–7 is an explicit metaphor for Israel and YHWH, as seen in verse 7: 'The vineyard of the LORD Almighty is the nation of Israel.' There is no mention of marriage in Isaiah 35, but the chapter makes an important metaphorical link between the redeemed people of Israel and the revived land of Israel. As noted above, it has an important verbal link to the Song through the mention of the rose of Sharon. As the redeemed people return to Zion, so the neglected land is revived with blossom and rejoicing. The two metaphors of love and redemption are linked with the land and the people in Isaiah 62:4–5:

No longer will they call you Deserted,
  or name your land Desolate.
But you will be called Hephzibah,
  and your land Beulah;
for the LORD will take delight in you,
  and your land will be married.
As a young man marries a young woman,
  so will your Builder marry you;
as a bridegroom rejoices over his bride,
  so will your God rejoice over you.

In Isaiah three related sets of metaphors can be identified for the female figure:

BELOVED is the VINEYARD is ISRAEL
REVIVED LAND is REDEEMED ISRAEL
BRIDE is the LAND ISRAEL is the NATION ISRAEL

Direct verbal links to each of these three texts are found in the Song, through the vineyard terminology, the rose of Sharon and other flora and fauna, and through marriage and land terminology. However, it is not necessary to depend on these links in order to see significant elements of the female metaphors in the Song itself:

BRIDE is VINEYARD (Song 1:6; 7:8; 8:12)
BRIDE is REVIVED LAND (Song 2:1; 4:11; 7:2–9)
BRIDE is LAND ISRAEL is NATION ISRAEL (Song 4:1–7, 12–16; 6:4–7; 7:2–9)

Two related sets of metaphors can be identified for the male figure:

LOVER is the VINEYARD OWNER is YHWH
BRIDEGROOM of the LAND ISRAEL is YHWH

The connection between the Song's male character and YHWH is not made directly in the Song. However, this identification is supported by the use of worship and praise language for the male lover that elsewhere is reserved mainly for YHWH.[39] Further, the references to him bringing his bride out of the

---

39. The women exalt (*gyl*) and rejoice (*śmḥ*) in him, and commemorate (*zkr, hiphil*) his love, or possibly his lovemaking. While *śmḥ* has a wide range of uses, *gyl* is almost

wilderness[40] are coherent with the wider prophetic metaphor of marriage between God and his people. For the prophets that metaphor is used to structure the history of God's relationship with Israel, from betrothal and marriage covenant, bringing the bride home and settling with her in the land, through to adultery, divorce and restoration.[41] The metaphors in the Song relate to the final stage, recapitulating the betrothal and marriage in its redeemed and restored context.

There is sufficient internal evidence to suggest that the Song intends the lovers to be read as a metaphor for God's relationship with Israel. The intimate, passionate depiction of an idealized human marriage provides a deeper under-standing and experience of the divine–human marriage. The Song demonstrates the power and depth of sexual desire in the context of marital love, and thus, the power and depth of God's love for his people can begin to be partially grasped. This metaphorical interpretation lends even greater honour to human marriage by making marriage an appropriate analogy for God's love for his people. It also reminds us of the limits of human marriage: the shadow can never offer the ultimate satisfaction found only in the reality. The cycles of longing and separation in the Song, and especially in its ending, are a reminder that God's people are still longing for the heavenly bridegroom to make haste to return.

The Song of Songs is about Christ and the church

Christ was portrayed as a bridegroom, marked by the gifts of gold, frankincense and myrrh on his arrival, just as the bridegroom of Song 3 on his wedding day. He frequently refers to himself as a bridegroom in parables and other teaching. He invoked the language of the kingdom and was from his birth to his death recognized as 'the king of the Jews'. In Matthew 12:42, Jesus tells his hearers, 'and now something greater than Solomon is here'. Matthew is not the only New Testament writer to identify Jesus as the ideal bridegroom, the good

---

exclusively used with respect to YHWH. Of its 44 uses outside the Song, only the three found in Prov. 23:24–25 approve another object of such rejoicing. *zkr* is a common verb but used just 41 times in the *hiphil*, as it is here, where it can carry the idea of public record or announcement. The only person so commemorated, and the only object positively commemorated, is YHWH.

40. For Davis, mention of the wilderness is key to interpreting the Song. It 'exerts pressure just because it does not seem to fit the love story at all' ('Romance', p. 237).

41. See Seock-Tae Sohn, *YHWH, the Husband of Israel* (Eugene: Wipf and Stock, 2002) for a detailed exploration of this metaphor.

shepherd, the glorious king and the one greater than Solomon. The church is described as Christ's bride in Ephesians 5:23–32 and again in Revelation 21:2. She is the holy city, the new beloved bride, the darling Jerusalem, where God will once more walk among his people: 'They will be his people, and God himself will be with them and be their God.'[42]

The Song of Songs, written long before the birth of Christ, nonetheless participates in the messianic and eschatological hope of the prophetic books. The bridegroom who will lead his people out of the wilderness is the longed-for Messiah. The land will be redeemed and the sanctuary of Eden restored when the Messiah comes to renew all creation. The beloved will belong to her lover and he to her when God claims his people as his own, and himself as theirs. Just as the bride ends the Song of Songs calling for her lover to come to her, so the Bible ends with the bride calling out to her lover to return: 'Come away, my beloved,' she cries in the last verse of the Song.[43] The church agrees, 'Amen. Come, Lord Jesus'.[44]

© Rosalind Clarke, 2017

---

42. Rev. 21:3.
43. Song 8:14.
44. Rev. 22:20.

4. THE SEXUALITY OF GOD INCARNATE

Andy Angel

I want to ask the question: how did God experience human sexuality? Churches are divided over issues of human sexuality today just as they have been in other times. The debates are significant and help to inform Christian understanding and teaching. However, they can seem to lack humanity. Many of us who have experienced difficulties over our sexuality and traditional Christian teaching (in e.g. marriage, divorce, singleness, homosexuality, bisexuality, transsexuality, freedom of sexual expression or lack of it – the list could be endless) have sometimes wondered where the teachings of the faith coincide with our basic humanity. The justifications of Christian viewpoints (and they can be many, varied and conflicting) can lose credibility as sometimes they do not seem to take into account what it feels like to be human. Many of the moral questions we ask are important. However, most of us find it much easier to listen to someone who understands what we are going through than we do a moral argument. Hence my question. How did *God* find living out *his* human sexuality?

———————

This article is an abridged version of chapter three of Andy Angel, *Intimate Jesus: The Sexuality of God Incarnate* (London: SPCK, forthcoming) and is printed here by kind permission of the publisher. Fuller engagement with contemporary scholarship over some of the more disputed matters of textual interpretation on which this article touches may be found in the book, with full references and bibliography.

I realize that I am not the first to ask this question. The churches and the Christian creeds have asserted for roughly two millennia that God became man in the person of Jesus. So God in Christ experienced human sexuality, and male sexuality in particular. This is obvious really, and has not escaped the notice of some down the centuries who have asked the questions which follow on from the observation. There are artists, novelists and dramatists who have explored the subject of Jesus' sexuality in various ways over the years – primarily by exercising their imaginations often well beyond anything written in the Gospels or any other ancient texts which purport to tell us something of Jesus' life or person.[1]

New Testament critics seem to have been more reticent about asking how God experienced human sexuality. In the twentieth century, William E. Phipps raised the question in his *Was Jesus Married?* but his ideas have not met with widespread acceptance.[2] Scholarly studies of Jesus tend to focus on his teaching and mission. Much of what has been written on the subject has centred on the *Secret Gospel of Mark* and the Coptic fragment, the *Gospel of Jesus' Wife*. The former suggested a possible homoerotic liaison between Jesus and a young man.[3] The latter contains a line in which Jesus says 'my wife'.[4] However, many scholars view both these texts as modern creations rather than genuinely ancient texts and as not giving us any reliable information about Jesus' sexuality or marital status.[5] As Dale Martin laments, very few professional theologians discuss the sexuality of Jesus at all.[6] Even fewer ask how God experienced human sexuality in Christ.

---

1. For example, D. H. Lawrence, *The Escaped Cock* (Isle of Skye: Aquila, 1982); Terrence McNally, *Corpus Christi* (New York: Grove Press, 1998); and most famously Nikos Kazantzakis, *The Last Temptation of Christ*, tr. P. A. Bien (New York: Simon and Schuster, 1960).

2. William E. Phipps, *Was Jesus Married? The Distortion of Sexuality in the Christian Tradition* (New York: Harper & Row, 1970).

3. Morton Smith, *Clement of Alexandria and the Secret Gospel of Mark* (Cambridge, MA: Harvard University Press, 1973), p. 185.

4. Karen L. King, 'Jesus said to them, "My wife . . .": A New Coptic Papyrus Fragment', *HTR* 107 (2014), p. 133.

5. On *Secret Mark*, see Peter Jeffery, *The Secret Gospel of Mark Unveiled: Imagined Rituals of Sex, Death and Madness in a Biblical Forgery* (New Haven: Yale University Press, 2007). On the *Gospel of Jesus' Wife*, see Leo Depuydt, 'The Alleged *Gospel of Jesus' Wife*: Assessment and Evaluation of Authenticity', *HTR* 107 (2014), pp. 172–89.

6. Dale B. Martin, 'Sex and the Single Saviour', in idem, *Sex and the Single Saviour: Gender and Sexuality in Biblical Interpretation* (Louisville: Westminster John Knox, 2006), pp. 91, 94.

John asserts unequivocally that God the Word became human in Christ (John 1:14). So I shall pose my question to John first as this Gospel assumes that Jesus' experience is at least in some sense God's experience. I am going to read the Gospel as a narrative, making the assumption that John writes as a storyteller who is at least to some extent familiar with the cultures and narrative techniques and plot lines of the ancient Jewish, Greek and Roman worlds. I will read the text as written for a Christian community which was already familiar with at least some of the life and teaching of Jesus, such that to understand the Gospel we may need to presume some knowledge which the Gospel itself does not provide. I am going to read the text in its final form. I will also read the text as deliberately in dialogue with the reader and open to playing with the reader's expectations.[7] I will speak as if the Gospel were written by John the apostle but believe that all I say of the author/narrator could equally be said of an unknown author from the first-century Christian church and/or the implied author of the text.

Despite that, nobody asked . . .

> At that moment his disciples came and were astonished that he was talking with a woman. Despite that, nobody asked, 'what are you after?' or 'why are you talking with her?' (John 4:27)[8]

Worn out from his journey, Jesus had sat down by a well. A few moments earlier he had sent his disciples into town to buy food, too tired to accompany them himself. A woman came to the well and they struck up a conversation. While Jesus and this Samaritan woman were still talking the disciples arrived back at the well. John does not tell us whether they said anything at this moment but he does note that none of them asked the questions that were clearly on their minds. Possibly there was an awkward silence. Possibly there was an embarrassing conversation or exchange of greetings in which the disciples avoided verbalizing their thoughts. Not only did the disciples keep their thoughts from Jesus but they did not tell each other what they were thinking either. John does not tell us explicitly whether the disciples knew what each other was thinking.

---

7. Not unlike Jeffrey Lloyd Staley, *The Print's First Kiss: A Rhetorical Investigation of the Implied Reader in the Fourth Gospel*, SBLDS 82 (Atlanta: Scholars Press, 1988), pp. 95–6.

8. Unless otherwise indicated all biblical translations in this chapter are the author's.

But as he writes up this scene later in life he clearly believes that they had all been drawing the same kind of conclusion. They all thought that Jesus was after something.

Don Carson suggests that the first question, 'what are you after?' was addressed (albeit silently) to the woman rather than Jesus. The Greek text can be interpreted this way.[9] But this interrupts the flow of the text. The disciples are amazed that Jesus is talking with the woman, not that she is talking with him. So why would they want to ask her anything? They want to know what *he* is up to and so both questions are most naturally addressed to him. Moreover, codices Sinaiticus and Bezae (amongst other manuscripts) spell out that the disciples were addressing their questions to Jesus by adding the Greek word *autō* after *eipen* in verse 27. There does not seem to be a variant which adds *autē* ('to her').

Rudolph Schnackenburg argues that the second question must mean 'what are you talking about with her?' rather than 'why are you talking with her?' because the Greek word *ti* is used in both questions (*ti zēteis* and *ti laleis met' autēs*) and their being in parallel suggests that *ti* must mean the same in both questions.[10] However, *ti* also occurs in a question and statement in parallel in John 18:21 where *ti* means 'why?' in the question and 'what' in the statement, as Schnackenburg himself recognizes.[11] So parallel usage of *ti* even in the same verse is no guarantee of the same meaning. Given that the disciples question Jesus' motives in asking 'what are you after?', it makes most sense to translate the parallel question '*why* are you talking with her?', as this gets to the heart of the matter, Jesus' motives.

So what exactly was it that so concerned the disciples about Jesus talking to this woman? That she was Samaritan may have been of some concern but neither John nor the disciples draw any attention to this. John states that they were astonished at his talking to a *woman* and the disciples ask 'why are you talking with *her*?' Nobody says anything about her being a Samaritan at this juncture. In explaining the disciples' reluctance to ask either question going

---

9. D. A. Carson, *The Gospel According to John*, Pillar New Testament Commentaries (Eerdmans: Grand Rapids, 1991), p. 227.

10. Rudolph Schnackenburg, *The Gospel According to John, volume 1: Introduction and Commentary on Chapters 1–4*, tr. Kevin Smyth, HThKNT (New York: Herder, 1968), p. 443.

11. Rudolph Schnackenburg, *The Gospel According to John, volume 3: Commentary on Chapters 13–21*, tr. David Smith and G. A. Kon, HThKNT (New York: Crossroad, 1982), p. 228.

around their heads, commentators tend to point to wisdom literature and rabbinic sayings discouraging men from talking to women.[12] For example, Rabbi Yose'ben Yohanan of Jerusalem taught (m. 'Abot 1:5),

A. (1) Let your house be wide open. (2) And seat the poor at your table. (3) And don't talk much with women. B. (He spoke of a man's wife, all the more so is the rule to be applied to the wife of one's fellow. In this regard did sages say, 'So long as a man talks too much with a woman, (1) he brings trouble on himself, (2) wastes time better spent on studying Torah, and (3) ends up an heir of Gehenna.')[13]

This advice was well known if not always heeded as evidenced by the story of Beruriah, wife of Rabbi Meir, who berated Rabbi Jose the Galilean for using too many words in asking directions to Lydda: 'Foolish Galilean, did not the Sages say this, "do not engage in much talk with women"' (b. 'Erub. 53b).

However, the majority of contemporary commentators prove deafeningly silent when it comes to explaining at all clearly *why* the rabbis or Jesus or any other men might wish to avoid talking to women or what kind of trouble they thought this might bring upon them.[14] Those that do tend to give incomplete

---

12. Between them commentators who remark on Jesus not talking to a woman draw attention to the following texts by way of explanation: Sir. 9:1–9; m. 'Abot 1:5; m. Sot. 3:4; b. 'Erub. 53b; b. Qidd 70a; 'Abot R. Nat. 2.1d; and more generally the book of Proverbs. See e.g. Raymond E. Brown, *The Gospel According to John 1–12*, AB 29 (New York: Doubleday, 1966), p. 173; Schnackenburg, *John 1–4*, pp. 442–3; C. K. Barrett, *The Gospel According to St John: An Introduction with Commentary and Notes on the Greek Text*, 2nd edn (London: SPCK, 1978), p. 240; Carson, *John*, p. 227; J. Eugene Botha, *Jesus and the Samaritan Woman: A Speech Acts Reading of John 4:1–42*, NovTSup 65 (Leiden: Brill, 1991), p. 160; Francis J. Moloney, *The Gospel of John*, SP 4 (Collegeville: Liturgical Press, 1998), p. 134; Craig S. Keener, *The Gospel of John: A Commentary*, 2 vols. (Peabody: Hendrickson, 2003), pp. 596–7; John F. McHugh, *A Critical and Exegetical Commentary on John 1–4*, ICC (London: T&T Clark, 2009), p. 289.
13. Translation taken from Jacob Neusner, *The Mishnah: A New Translation* (New Haven: Yale University Press, 1988), p. 673.
14. E.g. Brown, *John 1–12*, p. 173; Schnackenburg, *John 1–4*, pp. 442–3; Barrett, *St John*, p. 240; R. Alan Culpepper, *Anatomy of the Fourth Gospel: A Study in Literary Design* (Philadelphia: Fortress, 1983), p. 116; Botha, *Samaritan Woman*, p. 160; McHugh, *John 1–4*, p. 289.

or unconvincing answers.[15] Perhaps the disciples were keen that Jesus avoid scandal.[16] Perhaps, as Rabbi Yose ben Yohanan taught, they were concerned that Jesus was wasting time that could have been more profitably spent, e.g. studying Torah.[17] But neither of these explanations accounts for the disciples not asking Jesus 'what are you *after*?' This question implies that at least part of the problem lies in Jesus' intentions towards the woman. Besides, John is hardly likely to suggest that Jesus ought to have spent more time studying Torah (see e.g. John 1:17). Possibly then, the disciples do not ask these questions because they admire his moral character and know he cannot be up to no good.[18] However, this fails to answer the obvious counter question of why these questions entered their heads in the first place. So, for example, Augustine asserts that the disciples were marvelling at a good thing and not suspecting an evil thing (Augustine, *Tractates on the Gospel of John* 15.29). However, his very denial indicates he was aware of the possibility. His protest gives the game away – that he too realized that Jesus seems to have put himself in a compromising position.

A minority of commentators are less coy, commenting to the effect that 'sexual innuendo is not far from the surface of the disciples' unspoken questions'.[19] This would seem likely. Rabbi Yose ben Yohanan probably had this in mind when he warned that conversing with women can lead a man into trouble and land him in Gehenna (m. 'Abot 1:5). This is very much the message of Proverbs 7:1–27. The same message was alive and well in Jewish wisdom literature around the turn of the eras as illustrated by these words of the Jewish teacher Ben Sira (Sir. 9:3–9, NRSV):

> Do not go near a loose woman, or you will fall into her snares. Do not dally with a singing-girl, or you will be caught by her tricks. Do not look intently at a virgin, or you may stumble and incur penalties for her. Do not give yourself to prostitutes, or you may lose your inheritance. Do not look around in the streets of a city, or wander about in its deserted sections. Turn away your eyes from a shapely woman, and do not gaze at beauty belonging to another; many have been seduced by a

15. For a cryptic statement, see e.g. Jo-Ann A. Brant (*John*, Paideia (Grand Rapids: Baker Academic, 2011), p. 87) who states that 'what the disciples witnessed is unspeakably shameful' but without explaining why.

16. So Bruce Milne, *The Message of John*, BST (Leicester: IVP, 1993), p. 86.

17. Andreas J. Köstenberger, *John*, BECNT (Grand Rapids: Baker Academic, 2004), p. 159.

18. Keener, *John*, p. 621.

19. E.g. Moloney, *John*, p. 134.

woman's beauty, and by it passion is kindled like a fire. Never dine with another man's wife, or revel with her at wine; or your heart may turn aside to her, and in blood be plunged to destruction.

Rabbi Yose ben Yohanan, Proverbs and Ben Sira all agree that carelessly associating with women can bring trouble on a man and plunge him into destruction on account of leading him into sexual misdemeanours (Prov. 7:21–27).[20] So as George Foot Moore put it, 'the rabbis, in their endeavour to "keep a man a long way from sin", took manifold precautions against the excitement of lustful thoughts through the senses, and administer their warnings with liberal threats of damnation'.[21] Amongst his precautions for avoiding adultery, Ben Sira recommends not walking around the deserted parts of any town and avoiding communication with any woman who may be off limits. He advises further that men avert their eyes from beautiful women as female beauty can have an unhelpfully intoxicating effect on a man. Jesus does not seem to be acting according to this code. He seems to be alone in a deserted place outside of town when a woman turns up. Rather than avoiding communicating with her, Jesus initiates conversation. By the time the disciples get back from town, he is doing things which the disciples would expect a righteous man to avoid. It is little wonder that they are astonished. They suspect him of putting himself at the risk of exciting lustful thoughts and not being able to resist the ensuing temptations.

But why does John draw attention to these unspoken questions at this point in the narrative? How does this insight from the narrator help us to understand any of the subsequent utterances or actions?[22] Despite the lively conversation amongst commentators about the reason for and significance of the woman leaving her water jar, John provides something of an explanation for her action. He links her action back to the disciples' unspoken questions by means of the

---

20. The similarities between Proverbs and Ben Sira are probably due to Ben Sira drawing on Prov. 7. See Patrick W. Skehan and Alexander A. di Lella, *The Wisdom of Ben Sira*, AB 39 (New York: Doubleday, 1987), pp. 218–9.

21. George Foot Moore, *Judaism in the First Centuries of the Christian Era: The Age of the Tannaim*, vol. 2 (Cambridge, MA: Harvard University Press, 1927), p. 269. Moore cites various passages in support of this view and, along with Strack-Billberbeck (*Kommentar zum Neuen Testament aus Talmud und Midrasch*, 6 vols. Munich: Beck, 1922–61), is one of the two sources generally used by commentators to find their rabbinic texts to explain why rabbis ought not to talk to women.

22. Similarly, Botha, *Samaritan Woman*, p. 161.

word 'therefore' or *oun* (John 4:28). But this only raises more questions. How can unspoken words prompt actions? Was it their silence? Was it the few words they did speak (if they did speak at this point)? Was it their tone of voice? Or facial expressions? Or general body language? Or something entirely different? And can we know? Well, probably not, because John supplies just enough information to suggest she had a motive, but not enough to leave us anything but guessing as to what the motive was.

And the very act of writing down these unspoken questions raises still further questions. Does not the text identify the author or narrator as or closely with the beloved disciple (John 21:24)? Does not this suggest that he was there by the well? So why was he unable to ask these questions at the time? And why is he able to ask them now? And not simply ask them of Jesus but write them down for who knows who to read and hear? What has changed for this disciple? John Chrysostom puts it down to a more intimate knowledge of the love of Christ which casts out all fear.[23] But if so, what was this disciple afraid of before?

Narrative critics have noted that sometimes an author makes a statement intended to disrupt the flow of the narrative in order to get the audience to look more deeply into the text. Writing of this Gospel, Alan Culpepper suggests that the evangelist indicates to the audience that they need to look beneath the surface of the text 'by means of various nods, winks or gestures'.[24] John 4:27 is one such wink. By offering this comment on the disciples' unspoken thoughts, John draws the (possibly unsuspecting) audience into the process of the disciples making value judgments.[25] Moreover, John does something the audience does not expect or, to use Jeffrey Staley's term, John victimizes the audience.[26] At the point in the narrative where the audience expects the spiritual marriage of Jesus and his Samaritan bride to take place, John draws their attention to the subject of Jesus' sexuality.

The Jewish Messiah and his Samaritan bride

John sets the Gospel audience up for the expectation that Jesus the bridegroom-messiah will take the hand of his bride, the Samaritan people, in spiritual marriage. In the prologue, John writes that his own did not accept him but the

---

23. Chrysostom, *Homilies on John*, 33.3.

24. Culpepper, *Anatomy*, p. 151.

25. Botha, *Samaritan Woman*, p. 160.

26. See the discussion in Staley, *First Kiss*, pp. 95–118.

Word gave the right to become children of God to all who believed in him (John 1:11–12). At the wedding of Cana Jesus told the slaves to fill the jars with the water which changed into wine. He was responsible for this miracle and so for the provision of wine, traditionally the role of the groom.[27] Using the figure of a bridegroom, John the Baptist explains to his disciples why people are flocking to Jesus. John the Baptist compares his joy to that of a bridegroom's friend rejoicing at the voice of the groom on his marriage. The Baptist then comments that he must decrease and Jesus must increase (John 3:26–30). John the Baptist not only implies that Jesus is the Messiah, but uses the figure of marriage to identify Jesus as the bridegroom and people flocking to him as the marriage of the Messiah to the covenant people.[28] Soon after John moves the action to Samaria.

Within biblical narratives there are types of story or typical plot lines which would have been readily recognizable to ancient audiences. One of the typical patterns of biblical narratives is the betrothal-type narrative. The groom or his surrogate travels to a foreign land. There he meets a girl by a well. Often at this point one or other of them draws water from the well. The girl rushes home to announce the arrival of the stranger. The stranger is normally invited to eat and then becomes betrothed to the girl.[29] The well makes good sense as a meeting place for these soon-to-be-betrothed couples as in biblical poetry it can symbolize fertility and sexuality (e.g. Prov. 5:15). Examples of this betrothal narrative form are found in the stories of how Isaac and Rebekah (Gen. 24:1–27), Jacob and Rachel (Gen. 29:1–12) and Moses and Zipporah (Exod. 2:15–21) got betrothed.

Storytellers would have followed these typical patterns creatively rather than slavishly. By and large they would have followed the form of the particular kind of story they were telling but sometimes they would add twists or change the plot where it helped them to make the points that they wished to make as narrators of their particular tale. So the story of Isaac and Rebekah seems to follow quite typical plot lines where the groom's surrogate meets a girl of

---

27. So, e.g. Staley, *First Kiss*, pp. 89–90; Jocelyn McWhirter, *The Bridegroom Messiah and the People of God: Marriage in the Fourth Gospel*, SNTSMS 138 (Cambridge: Cambridge University Press, 2006), p. 49; McHugh, *John 1–4*, p. 193.

28. Similarly, McHugh, *John 1–4*, pp. 191–4.

29. Robert Alter, *The Art of Biblical Narrative*, 2nd edn (New York: Basic Books, 2011), pp. 62–3; Lyle Eslinger, 'The Wooing of the Woman at the Well', in Mark W. G. Stibbe (ed.), *The Gospel of John as Literature: An Anthology of Twentieth-Century Perspectives* (Leiden: Brill, 1993), p. 167.

impeccable credentials (beautiful, hospitable, hard-working and a virgin, Gen. 24:15–20) and the marriage is swiftly arranged (Gen. 24:28–51). On the other hand, Jacob has to work hard to marry Rachel the woman he really loves despite the fact that his seven years' labour for him seems but a few days (Gen. 29:20). Tellingly, when he meets her at the well he rolls the stone away from the mouth of the well so that her father's flocks can be watered. This detail suggests that opening his well (marriage with Rachel) will involve working for Laban (Gen. 29:10).[30]

John has Jesus arrive in the foreign country of Samaria where he meets a woman by a well. These three details (foreign country, woman and well) alone suggest that John is using the betrothal narrative form. The way he has set up the narrative confirms this impression. He made Jesus the true bridegroom at the wedding of Cana. John the Baptist has proclaimed Jesus the bridegroom-messiah of the covenant people. By placing his narrative of Jesus meeting a woman at a well in a foreign country John the Apostle signals that his story of the bridegroom-messiah is about to reach a significant moment: the one where the groom meets his girl.[31] The audience need not be wholly surprised

---

30. Alter, *Biblical Narrative*, pp. 61–70. On John 4:1–42, Staley, *First Kiss*, pp. 100–01.

31. Following the many scholars who read this story as playing with the betrothal narrative form, e.g. Culpepper, *Anatomy*, p. 136; Staley, *First Kiss*, pp. 98–103; Eslinger, 'Wooing', pp. 165–82; Jo-Ann A. Brant, 'Husband Hunting: Characterization and Narrative Art in the Gospel of John', *BibInt* 4 (1996), p. 211; McWhirter, *Bridegroom*, p. 59; Michael W. Martin, 'Betrothal Journey Narratives', *CBQ* 70 (2008), pp. 505–23; McHugh, *John 1–4*, p. 267. Gail R. O'Day (*Revelation in the Fourth Gospel: Narrative Mode and Theological Claim* [Philadelphia: Fortress, 1986], pp. 131–2 n.49) argues that while John 4 may allude to betrothal narratives it is not modelled on them because two key elements (the drawing of water and the betrothal) are missing. This argument misses the point. John deliberately has the woman given 'living water' (i.e. salvation) and the betrothal happens in the conversion of the citizens of Sychar. Teresa Okure (*The Johannine Approach to Mission: A Contextual Study of John 4:1–42*, WUNT 31 [Tübingen: J. C. B. Mohr, 1988], pp. 87–88) admits 'no real parallels' between OT betrothal narratives and John as it now stands. This is an unacceptable claim given that: (a) Jesus travels to a foreign land; (b) he meets a woman by a well; and (c) he asks for a drink. Rather, as Jo-Ann A. Brant (*Dialogue and Drama: Elements of Greek Tragedy in the Fourth Gospel* [Peabody: Hendrickson, 2004], pp. 247–8) notes, the dialogue is 'a comic treatment of the [betrothal] type-scene that plays with the elements of marriage' rather than slavishly imitating them.

either that Jesus meets a *Samaritan* and so an unsuitable bride, as John has prepared us for the idea that those not from his people will be given the right to become children of God (John 1:11–13).

Given that the Baptist has already indicated that the marriage of the bridegroom-messiah consists in people coming to the Messiah Jesus, the audience may be forgiven for suspecting at this point that John will use the ensuing narrative of Jesus meeting a Samaritan woman by a well to suggest the spiritual marriage of the bridegroom-messiah and the Samaritans – and they are not disappointed.[32] John has already pictured John the Baptist declaring to his disciples 'I am not the Messiah' (*ouk egō eimi ho christos*, John 1:20; 3:28). The Samaritan woman knows the Messiah called the Christ (*christos*, John 4:25) is coming and Jesus replies, 'I am he' (*egō eimi*, John 4:26). As narrator John uses the same string of words (*egō* + *eimi* + *christos*) for John the Baptist denying that he is the Messiah and for Jesus declaring that he is the Messiah. John most recently denied being the Messiah in the same breath as describing Jesus as the bridegroom (John 3:28–29). Jesus now confesses that he is the Messiah to the Samaritan woman at a well in a betrothal narrative.

John develops the theme further. Jesus' words of response are 'I am he, the one talking to you' (*egō eimi ho lalōn soi*, John 4:26). These words seem to echo words of the Lord God Almighty through the prophet: 'I am, I am the Lord speaking' (*egō eimi egō eimi kyrios lalōn*, Isa. 45:19 LXX) and especially 'I am he who speaks' (*egō eimi autos ho lalōn*, Isa. 52:6 LXX). Most obviously and as with all the other 'I AM' sayings the *egō eimi* recalls the name God gives to Moses: 'I am who I am' (*egō eimi ho ōn*, Exod. 3:14 LXX). John intends the audience to hear that Jesus is the Lord God Almighty.[33] So not only has the bridegroom-messiah courted the Samaritan woman at the well, but the Word of God who is one with the Father. John develops the prophetic motif of the Lord God courting Israel here as God invites the rejected Samaritans back into his covenant marriage. As McHugh notes, this seems to recall prophecies of the return of the northern kingdoms (e.g. Hos. 2:14–23).[34]

The narrative has been building to this point from the moment Jesus offered the Samaritan woman his 'living water', by which he was referring to the Spirit of God which gives life (cf. John 7:37–39) or salvation, as in the 'water of life' of Jeremiah 2:13 (LXX).[35] For whatever reason, the woman refuses Jesus' offer

---

32. Similarly, McHugh, *John 1–4*, p. 193.

33. E.g. McHugh, *John 1–4*, p. 288.

34. So McHugh, ibid., pp. 267, 288–9.

35. So e.g. Barrett, *St John*, p. 233.

of 'living water' until verse 15, where she seems more open to it. Conversation continues through the topics of husbands and worship centres until we reach the point at which Jesus announces that he is the Messiah she and her people await. John has Jesus make his announcement in language that signals that he is not only the bridegroom-messiah who offers the Samaritan bride marriage into salvation but the Lord God Almighty who opens up the way back into covenant marriage for the Samaritan people.

At this climactic point in the narrative, the audience expects this spiritual marriage to take place, but instead they get Jesus' disciples casting silent sexual aspersions. John goes against audience expectations in two respects here. First, he fails to deliver the expected spiritual marriage – although he does this later – and instead indicates the disciples' concern that Jesus may be nurturing unwholesome sexual intentions towards this woman. Second, rather than cast blame in the direction of the woman who for whatever reason has had five husbands before the man with whom she is now living unmarried, John has the disciples cast aspersions on the wholesomeness of *Jesus'* sexual intentions. In doing so, John not only draws attention to Jesus' sexuality but provides serious motivation for the (possibly now disturbed) Christian audience to go back over the narrative to check that Jesus has not behaved inappropriately. So John invites us to look back over the whole narrative with sex in mind.

Looking over the narrative with sex in mind

Like Lyle Eslinger and others, I believe that the key to unlocking the flow of this narrative lies in the various connotations of 'living water'.[36] *Hydōr zōn* could simply mean 'running water' or 'spring water'. Hagar finds a well of spring water (*phrear hydatos zōntos*, Gen. 21:19 LXX). Similarly, Isaac's servants find a well of spring water (*phrear hydatos zōntos*, Gen. 26:19 LXX). Spring water was used in various cultic rituals: the ritual cleansing of a leper (Lev. 14:5–6 LXX); the ritual atonement of a house that had previously had a leprous disease (Lev. 14:50–52 LXX); the testing of a woman accused of adultery (Num. 5:17 LXX); and the cleansing of people who have touched a dead body (Num. 19:17 LXX). So 'living water' might bear cultic connotations. One prophecy has rivers of living water flowing from Jerusalem on the day when God comes to rescue the covenant people (Zech. 14:8 LXX) and in another God identifies himself as the fountain

---

36. E.g. Eslinger, 'Wooing', p. 180.

of living water (*pēgē hydatos zōēs*, Jer. 2:13 LXX).[37] So 'living water' might symbolize the salvation God brings. However, like 'spring' and 'well' the phrase 'living water' could also carry sexual connotations. The lover speaks of the channel of his beloved as a well of 'living water' (*phrear hydatos zōntos*, Song 4:15 LXX).[38] Given that there are no further references to 'living water' or *hydōr zōn* in the Septuagint, a first-century AD Jewish author working in a Greek environment, like John, would understand these words to connote running water, possibly with connotations of salvation, purity rituals or sex.

Extrabiblical Jewish and early Christian literature evidence most of these connotations. Philo refers to the use of living water in the ritual testing of a woman suspected of adultery (*Spec. Laws* 3.59). In the ancient Jewish novel *Joseph and Aseneth*, an angelic visitor commands Aseneth to wash her face and hands with living water in preparation for her marriage to Joseph (*Jos. Asen.* 14:12, 15). The angel associates this preparation with repentance and finding refuge in God. So the action of washing with living water bears connotations of salvation and purification. In the Prayer of Levi, Levi washes his whole body in living water, washes his clothes in clean water and makes his ways straight before praying (Pr. Levi 7:2). The action associates living water with cultic purity ritual. These connotations are also present in early Christian literature. The Didache instructs that ideally candidates should be baptized in living water (Did. 7:1). Its use in baptism associates living water with ritual, purity and salvation.[39] Ignatius of Antioch uses living water as a metaphor of salvation and the Holy Spirit (Ign. *Rom.* 7:2).[40] The Latin version of the Epistle of Barnabas identifies

---

37. On the life-giving nature of the waters of salvation in Zech. 14:8, see Carol L. Meyers and Eric M. Meyers, *Zechariah 9 – 14*, AB 25C (New York: Doubleday, 1993), pp. 434–5. On living waters as symbolic of salvation in Jer. 2:13, see William L. Holladay, *Jeremiah 1*, Hermeneia (Philadelphia: Fortress, 1986), p. 92.

38. On living water bearing sexual connotations here, see Roland E. Murphy, *The Song of Songs*, Hermeneia (Minneapolis: Fortress, 1990), pp. 160–1. For a useful discussion of some of the connotations of 'living water', see McHugh, *John 1–4*, pp. 273–9.

39. For the association with ritual and purity, see Kurt Niederwimmer, *The Didache*, Hermeneia (Minneapolis: Fortress, 1998), pp. 126–7. The association of baptism and salvation in Christ seems fundamental to early Christian thinking; see e.g. Rom 6:4–11.

40. William R. Schoedel, *Ignatius of Antioch*, Hermeneia (Minneapolis: Fortress, 1985), p. 185. Schoedel points out that Ignatius is probably dependent on the Gospel of John here.

Christ as the fountain of living water, associating his living water with baptism, forgiveness and salvation (Barn. 11.2). So the wider Jewish and Christian literature understands living water to be running water which may be used in purity rituals and may bear connotations of salvation.[41]

I suggest that 'living waters' and their various connotations provide the golden thread that holds the whole narrative together and explain the otherwise abrupt changes of subject so often noted by commentators. When Jesus first asks for a drink, he really would like cool, refreshing water but when he offers 'living water' to the woman in verse 10 he means life and salvation. Being beside a well with a man who has already asked for a drink and failed to hear her first brush off, in verse 11 she replies more or less 'where's your bucket?', as quite understandably she hears his offer of 'living water' as some kind of sexual advance.[42] This misunderstanding continues until verse 15 where she decides that she would like to try this water. Hearing her response to what she thinks are sexual advances, in verse 16 Jesus tells her to find her husband and the conversation about her previous relationships ensues. (Assuming that 'living waters' has been misheard as sex rather than salvation makes sense of this otherwise abrupt change of topic.)[43] After the conversation about husbands and her current man, the woman changes the topic of conversation to places of worship. This change of topic makes sense if the woman assumed that sex was the wrong subtext and that this man was religious and really talking about cultic matters.[44] Jesus takes this cue to steer the conversation in the direction of salvation and true worship (vv. 22–24). John draws on all the various connotations of 'living water' (spring water, sex, cult and worship) in this conversation until Jesus finally gets to the point of making what he is really offering her clearer in verse 26 when he is rudely interrupted by the disciples' return and complete misunderstanding of what is going on. It seems too much of a coincidence that

---

41. An electronic search of the LXX, the Greek OT Pseudepigrapha and the Apostolic Fathers turned up only these references to *hydōr zōn*.

42. So Eslinger, 'Wooing', pp. 168–70; Brant, 'Husband Hunting', p. 214.

43. Commentators note the disconnect between vv. 15 and 16, e.g. Carson, *John*, p. 220; Moloney, *John*, p. 131; J. Eugene Botha, 'John 4.16: A Difficult Text Speech Act Theoretically Revisited', in Stibbe (ed.), *The Gospel of John as Literature*, pp. 183–4. I follow those who see the various connotations of 'living waters' as supplying the connection (e.g. Eslinger, 'Wooing', p. 166).

44. Again most commentators note a disjunction in the conversation, generally explaining it as the woman trying to change the topic in embarrassment or to save face (so e.g. Eslinger, 'Wooing', pp. 180–1; Köstenberger, *John*, p. 153).

the four LXX connotations of 'living water' all appear in this text and provide a key to understanding its narrative flow. Rather than assuming John has written a bumpy narrative which moves clumsily from living water to husbands (vv. 15–16), and equally clumsily from husbands to worship centres (vv. 18–20), before morphing slightly more smoothly from worship centres to salvation, I prefer to read John as deftly using the various LXX connotations of 'living water' to provide a smooth narrative which sparkles with humour as the characters talk at cross-purposes.

With betrothal narrative motifs and 'living water', sex has been in the air from more or less the start of the scene. As the audience goes back over the narrative with this in mind, they may find that their attitudes towards characters in the narrative (and indeed in real life) change. Craig Keener is probably right that ancient audiences would have judged the Samaritan woman to be sexually immoral.[45] But reading her opening response to Jesus in verse 9 ('how do you a *Jew* ask me for a drink given I am a *Samaritan* **woman**?') in the light of the disciples' disapproval of *his* actions and with her personal history in mind, she looks more like a woman who knows what men can be like and who wishes to protect herself from the kind of man who hangs around wells asking women for drinks at times of day when others are unlikely to be around. She continues to brush him off through verses 11–12 and possibly she attempts to put him down. She drops her resistance at his persistence. Later in the narrative, she leaves because of the disciples' disapproval (again, the *oun* in v. 28), although ironically they are disapproving of *him* rather than *her*, and if they did disapprove of her John says nothing about it. This makes the scene in which Jesus talks with her of her husbands and the man she is now living with all the more remarkable. It is unlikely that she is now living with a man as protector with whom she is not in a sexual relationship as John uses the same language (*echō* and *anēr*) for her current man and former husbands, which if anything suggests these relationships are all sexual. Whatever the reasons for the endings of her marriages (and the reasons offered by commentators are many and varied), Jesus clearly does not make this woman feel like running away – at least not enough to motivate her to actually do it, as she does in verse 28. Jesus' words about her relationship history are somehow less threatening than the disciples' saying nothing (at least that John records). Jesus does not make her feel like 'a specimen of matrimonial maladjustment' as one commentator somewhat indelicately judges her.[46] Instead, although she finds it hard to believe he could be the

---

45. Keener, *John*, p. 607.

46. I do not give the reference quite deliberately.

Messiah (note the *mēti* in v. 29b), his talking to her about her relationship history somehow becomes so important to her that she wants everyone to meet this 'prophet' (John 4:29). Clearly her relationship history is central to her identity, as her claim to have met 'a man who told me everything I ever did' must be an exaggeration. Although John does not specify what it was, there must have been something about the way Jesus spoke to this woman that left her affirmed and accepted. Her actions suggest this. She shows no shame in telling her fellow townsfolk that Jesus told her all about her relationship history, and she wants to return to Jesus (implied by v. 29). Whatever she has experienced of salvation has to do with her sex life and Jesus has spoken words (seemingly experienced as healing words) into this part of her life. Not only this but John notes that these words bring the Samaritans to believe in him (v. 39) rather than her struggles over whether he was the Messiah or not. Jesus' talking into her sex life has become the locus of salvation and vehicle of witness. John presents a significant challenge to any who would over-spiritualize salvation, not least by presenting Jesus as not only comfortable talking into the difficult and messy sexual relationships of another but able to do so in ways which the other finds both acceptable and healing.

The Samaritan woman's responses also tell us something of the sexuality of Jesus himself. Although she brushes him off initially, he must have been sufficiently attractive as a man (who was, it seems, a complete stranger to her) for her to change her mind and accept what she thought were his sexual advances. After all, not all men are this attractive to all women. He must also have come across as 'safe' to this woman. If he had not done, she would have disappeared soon after he started talking about her past relationships (as she did in v. 28 in response to the disciples' reaction). This combination says something quite remarkable about Jesus' sexuality: that he could come across as attractive, sufficiently sexual to make what could come across as plausible advances, and safe all at the same time. Some of this may have something to do with the abstinence Jesus exercises in the narrative. John makes a point of his going without food and drink – or indeed, sex. He has no drink because the woman refuses him and he has no bucket. He has no food because his food is to do the will of the Father (v. 34) which he has been doing in offering salvation to this woman. He has no sex because he refuses her offer in verse 15. John presents Jesus as putting the salvation of the woman (which she experiences in her sex life) before his own sexual fulfilment. But this is not to suggest that Jesus has little or no sex drive. John leaves us in no doubt that both the woman and the disciples were pretty sure that he did. However, Jesus' self-control may not be put down to his being divine. John clearly presents Jesus as frail flesh at the start of this narrative. While the disciples have the energy to go shopping in town, Jesus is shattered and needs to sit down by the well (vv. 6, 8). This is possibly the most remarkable aspect of John's portrait of Jesus' sexuality here – that Jesus lived out his sexuality in ways that put the interests of others first without any more access to reservoirs of self-control than any other human being. In the light of John's use of the ascription 'saviour', this seems to be a point John is underlining for his audience. The gods, heroes and emperors who were hailed as saviour in Greek, Roman and Jewish writings hardly exercised the self-control that Jesus did when the opportunity for sex presented itself. It is also noteworthy, in the light of Sjef van Tilborg's thesis (that the Johannine Jesus shows signs of being homosexual), that the disciples and the Samaritan woman clearly thought he was straight or at least capable of enjoying straight sex.[47]

In telling this story, John does not leave the audience alone either (and here I include in the audience all of us who read his Gospel). In commenting on the disciples' unspoken thoughts in verse 27, he draws us into exploring the theme of sexuality in the narrative and so initiates a process of reflection which may unmask some of our own sexual attitudes and prejudices.

First, he sets us up to read the story in the purely spiritual terms of people outside the current covenant people finding salvation in Christ and by verse 42 we find that such people have indeed believed in him. However, he upsets our expectations in verse 27 and so disrupts any reading of this text which might allow us to desexualize and over-spiritualize salvation. Not only does he focus our attention on Jesus' sexuality but he makes somebody's sex life the locus and vehicle of salvation in this story.

Second, when John focuses our attention on the disciples' disapproval of Jesus' sexual intentions, any of us who focus on the woman's sexual misdemeanours are suddenly unmasked. There is no small debate about the reason for the woman being married five times and I offer no comment on what led to her five marriages ending – except to note that neither John nor Jesus says anything about this in the narrative. Her past is past. However, in reading the story we make it ever present by supplying reasons like divorce, levirate marriage, patriarchal oppression, serial adultery, and so on. This may say more about us than it does about the Samaritan woman. The ancient Greek, Roman and Jewish novels suggest that they were no less interested in sexual gossip and titillation than we are today. I suspect that John remains silent on so much of her personal history in order to leave us to victimize ourselves, and perhaps learn from our fears, hatreds, self-justifications and self-defences.

---

47. Sjef van Tilborg, *Imaginative Love in John*, BibInt 2 (Leiden: Brill, 1993).

Third, John plays a final joke on us as audience. Sex and romance were major themes in ancient Greek, Roman and Jewish novels. John sets up a betrothal narrative and hints at a budding relationship, but instead offers a story of chastity and sexual healing. But surely that is the point. This is a story for grown-ups: one in which God in Christ shows himself sufficiently comfortable in his human sexuality that he can lay his own desires aside to show genuine love to the sexually broken – and so meet their real needs.

© Andy Angel, 2017

5. DEVELOPING A BIBLICAL THEOLOGY OF SINGLENESS

Barry Danylak

Introduction

Since 1970 the Western world has experienced a precipitous drop in the pro-portion of married adults. In the UK in 1970 more than two-thirds of eligible adults were married. This has declined to less than 50% today, and is projected to continue to decline to about 42% within the next twenty years.[1] Some but not all of this is attributed to an increased acceptance and occurrence of co-habitation. It is also the result of greater delay in first marriage and a decline in the number of people who choose to be in a committed relationship at all. To put the shift in perspective, consider that, of those born in 1931, 51% of men and 75% of women were married by age 25, compared with less than 6% of men and 12% of women born in 1985.[2] This pronounced shift has created in

---

1. Office for National Statistics, *Population Trends*, Report No. 136 (Summer 2009), p. 82, Table 1.5; pp. 114–5, Table 1. See also Office for National Statistics, *Statistical Bulletin: Marital Status Population Projections, 2008-based* (24 June 2010), p. 2, Table 1.
2. Office for National Statistics, *Statistical Bulletin: Marriages in England and Wales 2010* (29 February 2012), p. 9.

most Western nations a marriage-minority culture,[3] and has brought with it a range of lifestyle complexities including a marked increase in divorce, cohabitation, gay/lesbian relationships and gender dysphoria. Effective engagement with this demographic shift and its accompanying lifestyle complexities merits a response grounded in a solid biblical theology of singleness based in turn on careful exegesis of the relevant biblical texts. First Corinthians 7 is the most extended discussion of singleness and marriage in the New Testament. Yet given its highly contextualized discussion it presents numerous exegetical challenges.

Just as sound exegesis is necessary for sound theology, so too, sound theology is necessary for sound exegesis. This paper is a case study of how an exegetical problem may spur broader biblical-theological reflection as a means of aiding its resolution. The net result is a more robust theological understanding of singleness as a whole, which provides insight for more effectively engaging with contemporary challenges.

The exegetical problem

The problem in this case concerns the strange assertion that launches Paul's discussion on marriage and singleness in 1 Corinthians 7:1, 'It is good for a man not to touch a woman' (NASB). The statement comes as first among a series of apparent responses to questions which the Corinthians have raised in a previous letter. Ascetically-minded Patristic exegetes generally took the statement as Paul's response to ascetic concerns raised by the Corinthians, although they disagree over whether the issue was primarily sexual relations or marriage, whether they were motivated by maturity or naivety, and whether the ascetic concern came from the Corinthians or external false teachers. John Chrysostom, for example, writes of Paul:

> He introduces also the discourse concerning virginity: 'It is good for a man not to touch a woman.' 'For if,' says he, 'you enquire what is the excellent and greatly superior course, it is better not to have any connection whatever with a woman:

---

3. Based on marriage statistics for those of legal age to marry (usually 16 years and older). Data for a wide spectrum of European countries is available in: Office for National Statistics, *Statistical Bulletin: Population Estimates by Marital Status and Living Arrangements: England and Wales 2002 to 2014* (8 July 2015), p. 13. Similar marriage patterns are present in the USA, Canada and Australia.

but if you ask what is safe and helpful to your own infirmity, be connected by marriage.'[4]

By contrast, most modern exegetes think that Paul is quoting ascetically-minded Corinthians before proceeding to offer his reservations on their excessive ascetic ideals. They read the text as saying: 'Now concerning the things about which you wrote, namely: "It is good for a man not to touch a woman" . . .' In this case the statement represents a Corinthian perspective that Paul proceeds to correct.

There is a related point of disagreement over whether the essential issue raised by the Corinthians concerns marriage itself or sexual relations within marriage. How we navigate these two points substantially colours how we read the chapter as a whole. On the one hand, if it is Paul's pronouncement affirming the celibate state, it reinforces his emphasis on the legitimacy of a celibate calling, which he then proceeds to qualify. On the other hand, if it represents the view of ascetic Corinthians advocating sexual abstinence within marriage, then it sets the stage for Paul's subsequent effort to mitigate a peculiar Corinthian predilection for 'celibate marriage' and to uphold more traditional views of marriage and sexual relations within it.

The recent consensus is that the statement reflects the Corinthians advocating abstinence within marriage.[5] The most compelling arguments for this are: (a) the vocabulary of 'touch' (*haptō*) connotes sexual contact and rarely occurs in reference to marriage; (b) the statement stands directly against Paul's Jewish heritage which regarded marriage as a covenantal blessing; (c) the statement nearly contradicts Genesis 2:18 'it is not good for the man to be alone' (NASB), of which Paul was surely aware; and (d) there is no corroborating evidence to suggest that Paul was ascetically oriented. In short it seems most unlikely a statement that could be attributed to Paul. One recent commentator states:

> On his own authority, Paul could not have advocated celibacy for everyone, for he would be contradicting God's utterance: 'It is not good for the man to be alone' (Gen. 2:18). Then Paul would be against procreation (Gen. 1:28), God's covenant blessings from generation to generation (Gen. 17:7), and the growth of the church.[6]

---

4. *Hom.* 19 (1 Cor. 1 – 2).

5. See Gordon Fee, '1 Corinthians 7:1–7 Revisited', in Trevor J. Burke and J. Keith Elliot (eds.), *Paul and the Corinthians: Studies on a Community in Conflict* (Leiden: Brill, 2003), pp. 197–213; and Fee, *The First Epistle to the Corinthians*, rev. edn (Grand Rapids: Eerdmans, 2014), pp. 303–5.

6. Simon J. Kistemaker, *1 Corinthians* (Grand Rapids: Baker, 1993), p. 209.

But the alternative, that the statement reflects the Corinthians' perspective, is also not without difficulties. A wide number of contemporary influences have been proposed to explain the Corinthians' marriage-denigrating asceticism, including Gnostic dualism, Jewish sectarian movements, Sophia worship, Cynic or Stoic philosophy, Isis or other Egyptian cults, and medical practitioners. But none has proved compelling.

Textual evidence for an ascetic movement in Corinth is also scant. In 1 Corinthians, Paul refers to their sexual struggles in four different ways in chapter 7 alone (vv. 2, 5, 9a, 9b); in 5:1–13 he castigates them for allowing a type of immorality (*porneia*) 'that is not tolerated even among pagans' (5:1 ESV); in 6:9–10 he lists four types of sexual sinners who will not inherit the kingdom of God; in 6:15 he emphatically condemns the culturally acceptable use of prostitutes ('May it never be!' NASB), before exhorting his readers to 'flee immorality' (6:18 NASB); and in 10:1–13 he further condemns sexual immorality, implicitly relating it to cultic feasting in pagan temples.[7] Paul warns of further discipline for those still unrepentant of immorality (*porneia*) in 2 Corinthians 12:21. There is also a later reference in 1 Clement upbraiding the Corinthians for 'impure embraces' along with 'detestable lusts' and 'abominable adultery'.[8] Nor do the Corinthians exhibit typical corroborating signs of asceticism. They appear socially integrated, having dinner-parties with their non-Christian associates (1 Cor. 10:27), and boast of their right to eat anything in good conscience. Their mantra appears to be that 'all things are lawful' (1 Cor. 6:12; 10:23 NASB). Their claims, boasts and behaviour show anything but an ascetic disposition toward sexual renunciation.

Perhaps the most viable interpretation is that this asceticism was not representative of the whole church, but rather of a group of pneumatic enthusiasts – perhaps, as Gordon Fee has proposed, a group of women espousing a brand of over-realized eschatology with roots in Hellenistic dualism.[9] But evidence in 1 Corinthians for such a group of women is meagre. The statement 'it is good for a man not to touch a woman' (7:1 NASB) is male-oriented, and hardly reads like a female mantra, while Paul's direct address to men in 7:28 strongly suggests that he is responding to men, not women. Nor do we have substantive indication that those Paul addresses in chapter 7 are suddenly a different group from those he upbraids for going to prostitutes in chapter 6. In addition, the

---

7. Brian Rosner, 'Temple Prostitution in 1 Corinthians 6:12–20', *NovT* 40 (1998), pp. 336–51.

8. 1 Clement 30.1. Translation courtesy of Michael W. Holmes, *The Apostolic Fathers*, 3rd edn (Grand Rapids: Baker, 2007), p. 85.

9. Gordon Fee, '1 Corinthians 7:1 in the *NIV*', *JETS* 23 (1980), pp. 313–14.

advice he gives in chapter 7 fits poorly with the idea that 7:1b represents an ascetic viewpoint propagated by eschatologically-minded Corinthian women. Neither his qualification that the divorced wife should remain unmarried or become reconciled to her husband (7:11) nor his eschatological argument promoting singleness (7:29–31) makes logical sense if the *problem* lies in ascetic women abandoning their husbands to fulfil a new eschatological existence.

So we need to revisit the possibility that the statement in 7:1b is that of Paul, not of the Corinthians. In support of this, Paul repeats 'it is good' language later in the chapter: '*it is good* for them [the unmarried and widows] if they remain even as I' (7:8 NASB, emphasis added); and 'I think then that *this is good* in view of the present distress, that *it is good* for a man to remain as he is' (7:26 NASB, emphasis added). All three uses begin new sections of the discourse, and all three give variants of a common theme: it is good for the unmarried to remain so. At the same time, there is no doubt that Paul was well aware of the language of Genesis 2:18, that it was '*not good* for the man to be alone' (NASB, emphasis added). In fact, just five verses earlier he directly quotes from Genesis 2:24 that 'the two [they] shall become one flesh' (1 Cor. 6:16 NASB).

What would move Paul to make a seemingly ascetic assertion that in its very language stands in direct conflict with the Genesis creation story? The answer may well lie in how Paul interprets what happens between the Genesis account and his first-century response to the Corinthians. And it is here that a full-canon, diachronic biblical theology on marriage and singleness may shed insight on Paul's perspective, especially as it relates to an equally central biblical-theological thread, the provision of offspring as the vehicle of God's blessing.

Theological background

Genesis

The importance of offspring is impossible to miss in the Genesis account. 'Be fruitful and multiply' is, after all, the first commandment of the Old Testament, given initially to birds and sea creatures on the fifth day of creation (Gen. 1:22 NASB), and then reiterated to humans on the sixth day (Gen. 1:28). It is given twice again to Noah and his family after the flood (Gen. 9:1, 7). Beyond the first humans and the 'new Adam' of Noah after the flood, the only other individual directly commanded to 'be fruitful and multiply' is Jacob (Gen. 35:11 NASB), the physical father of the Israelite nation who has twelve sons from four different women. In each case the command is associated directly with blessing, explicitly in the first two instances and implicitly in the third.

The Hebrew word for 'seed' or 'offspring' (*zera*') appears in Genesis 3:15 in the first messianic reference, as part of God's judgment on the serpent: 'I will put enmity between . . . . your *offspring* and her *offspring*; he shall bruise your head, and you shall bruise his heel' (ESV, emphasis added). In Genesis 4 it appears again as a possible messianic reference, illuminating a marked contrast in the birth accounts of Cain and Seth. On the birth of Cain in Genesis 4:1, Eve says, 'I have produced a man with the help of the LORD' (ESV). But after Cain kills Abel, Eve gives birth to Seth in Genesis 4:25 and says, 'God has appointed for me another *offspring* instead of Abel' (ESV, emphasis added).[10] Eve credits the birth of Cain to her own human initiative, but the birth of Seth she credits to divine provision. In the birth account of Seth, 'offspring' is modified by 'another', which as in English can be taken as 'another' in sequence or 'another' in kind. One Hebrew tradition regarded 'another seed' to mean 'a seed from another source or parentage',[11] hinting that the Messiah would share in non-Jewish ancestry (i.e. through Ruth the Moabitess).[12] But the text here does not specify the nature of the other kind of birth that the Messiah represents.

The central drama of the book of Genesis, the call of Abraham and the establishment of the covenant, again points to the central importance of offspring. The promises of the covenant (established in several episodes) fall into three categories: (a) God will bless Abraham with exceedingly numerous offspring, including a great nation, kings, and many nations. (b) God will give Abraham and his descendants a tract of land occupied by Canaanite nations, with victory over them. (c) God will make Abraham's name great, and he himself will be Abraham's reward. All these promises depend on Abraham having a physical son and heir. Hence the story soon gravitates toward the human–divine drama of how God will provide a son, since Abraham's wife Sarah was barren. Like Eve's descriptions of Cain's birth versus Seth's, Abraham and Sarah have two sons – one through the human contrivance and the other through divine provision. And it was Abraham's response of faith in trusting God to provide a child that Paul later recognized as the faith credited to him as righteousness (Rom. 4:3).

---

10. The terms 'produced' ('gotten' in the US edition) and 'appointed' have similar sounds to the names Cain and Seth.

11. Genesis Rabbah 23.5 (on Gen. 4:25).

12. Max Wilcox, 'The Promise of the "Seed" in the New Testament and the Targumin', *JSNT* 5 (1979), p. 14.

The Sinai covenant

If offspring in the Abrahamic covenant is a marker of God's unilateral provision, in the Sinai covenant it is a marker of God's blessing for obedience to the covenantal stipulations. This is evident in the blessings and curses in Deuteronomy 28, but is also prominent in the stipulations in Deuteronomy 7:12–14:

> And because you listen to these rules and keep and do them, the LORD your God will keep with you the covenant and the steadfast love that he swore to your fathers. He will love you, bless you, and multiply you. He will also bless the fruit of your womb and the fruit of your ground, your grain and your wine and your oil, the increase of your herds and the young of your flock, in the land that he swore to your fathers to give you. You shall be blessed above all peoples. There shall not be male or female barren among you or among your livestock. (ESV)

Here again, physical offspring are the fundamental marker of God's covenantal blessing. God will bless them with fruitfulness in three different ways: their children, their crops and their animals. Conversely, no humans or animals will be barren – barrenness is a mark of divine disapproval of human disobedience. Covenantal blessing of abundant progeny presumes the context of marriage, and it is not surprising that we find no old covenant figures who voluntarily choose to remain unmarried. Marriage is the prerequisite of covenantal blessing.

As for Abraham, so for the individual Israelite, physical progeny was critical for retaining the family's land and for preserving its name beyond death. Hence various legal provisions such as the exception for Zelophehad's daughters (Num. 27:1–11) and the institution of levirate marriage (of a childless widow to her brother-in-law, Deut. 25:5–10) ensure the preservation of the family's land and its name. Having one's name 'blotted out of Israel' was a judgment worse than death, because it entailed not only physical death but also the lack of offspring to 'remember one's name'. Moreover, every individual Israelite was accountable to the covenant. Deuteronomy 29:20 warns that *any individual* apostate will be subject to 'every curse which is written in this book', and 'the LORD will blot out his name from under heaven' (NASB). This threat is dramatically illustrated in the account of Naomi. With the deaths of her husband and sons, Naomi cries in utter despair that 'the Almighty has brought calamity upon me' (Ruth 1:21 ESV). Conversely Boaz, who serves as both kinsman-redeemer and brother-in-law, later expresses his intentions in marrying Ruth as 'to perpetuate the name of the dead in his inheritance, that the name of the dead may not be cut off from among his brothers and from the gate of his native place' (Ruth 4:10 ESV).

In the Sinai covenant, marriage and physical progeny were fundamental markers of covenantal blessing. To be unmarried in ancient Israel was to be unblessed, and implied God's judgment for disobedience. It is as a portent of judgment on the people that God calls Jeremiah not to take a wife, since children would soon die of disease, unlamented and unburied (Jer. 16:1–4). But with the prophets we also see a new phase in the anticipation of a new work of God himself. The prophet Isaiah is especially illustrative of this new phase.

Isaiah

The term *zera'* occurs frequently in the book of Isaiah. On the one hand, it refers to the sinful nation, the physical seed of Jacob. The book's opening words pronounce judgment on the 'sinful nation, a people laden with iniquity, offspring of evildoers, children who deal corruptly!' (Isa. 1:4 ESV). A later lament alludes to both Abrahamic and Mosaic covenants in asserting that, but for disobedience, 'your offspring would have been like the sand, and your descendants like its grains; their name would never be cut off or destroyed from before me' (Isa. 48:19 ESV).

On the other hand, we have a most unusual reference to 'holy seed' (*zera' qōdeš*) at the end of Isaiah's commission (6:13 ESV). This concluding line gives a note of hope to the catastrophic judgment that Isaiah is commanded to prophesy. The 'holy seed' is read by most exegetes as the post-exilic remnant of the Israelite nation. One difficulty with this interpretation is that the term 'holy' is usually associated in Isaiah with the holy God of Israel, and seldom with the unregenerate people.[13] And as elsewhere, 'seed' could be taken here as singular or collective. So it is interesting that following 6:13 there are numerous prophetic signs linked to divinely provided progeny. In 7:14 a virgin shall conceive and 'bear a son' (ESV), in 8:3 the prophet has children that are then described in 8:18 as 'signs and portents in Israel from the LORD of hosts' (ESV), in 9:6 'a child is born' (ESV), and in 11:1 'there shall come forth a shoot from the stump of Jesse' (ESV). We see in Isaiah an implicit parallel with the two types of offspring in Genesis, one symbolizing human effort and the other divine provision.

The word *zera'* occurs again at the climax of the fourth Servant Song (Isa. 53:10): 'when his soul makes an offering for guilt, he shall see his *offspring*' (ESV). But what kind of offspring does the servant see here following his death? The most plausible view is that they are spiritual rather than physical.[14] Elsewhere

---

13. Isaiah does speak of an eventual renewed people who will be holy (4:3; 62:12), and 63:18 suggests that they were once holy in the past.

14. Alec Motyer, *The Prophecy of Isaiah: An Introduction and Commentary* (Downers Grove: IVP, 1993), p. 440; John N. Oswalt, *The Book of Isaiah, Chapters 40–66* (Grand Rapids: Eerdmans, 1998), p. 402; Edward J. Young, *The Book of Isaiah* (Grand Rapids:

in the Old Testament, blessing associated with *seeing* rather than *having* progeny generally refers to grandchildren or great-grandchildren rather than immediate offspring.[15] One is blessed in *having* one's own offspring, and in *seeing* one's offspring's offspring. But here the servant *sees* his own offspring. Moreover, Isaiah 53:8 says of the servant, 'as for his generation [or progeny][16] . . . he was cut off out of the land of the living' (ESV). The language here parallels that of being 'blotted out'.[17] The servant has died without children or hope – yet in his death he suddenly sees his offspring.

It is telling that, in the chapters following the servant's death, two unmarried and barren figures are restored – the barren woman in Isaiah 54 and the eunuch in Isaiah 56. Just three verses after the account of the servant's death, we read of the barren woman who will have more children than a married woman and whose descendants 'possess the nations' (54:3 ESV). But these children are supernaturally birthed, for she has not been in labour (54:1) and is without human husband (54:5). As Alec Motyer concludes, 'the *barren woman* sings, not because she has ceased to be barren but because the Lord has acted in his Servant with the effect that his "seed" become her *children*/"sons"'.[18] The picture is of a woman once barren who now gives birth, not to physical children but to innumerable spiritual children.[19]

Isaiah 56 gives similar hope to the eunuch, who should no longer regard himself as a 'dry tree', since God would give him in the temple 'a monument and a name better than sons and daughters' (56:5 ESV). It is a picture of restored communion and remembrance for those once considered cursed and therefore cut off from God's people. Acts 8 records an amazing fulfilment of this passage in the Ethiopian eunuch's encounter with Philip. It is intriguing that he was

---

Eerdmans, 1972), vol. 3, p. 355; Jan Leunis Koole, *Isaiah Three* (Leuven: Peeters, 1997), p. 324; August Pieper, *Isaiah II [Yeshaʿyah 2]: An Exposition of Isaiah 40–66* (Milwaukee: Northwestern, 1979), pp. 450–1.

15. Gen. 50:23 (Joseph); Job 42:16 (Job); Ps. 128:6; so Koole, *Isaiah Three*, p. 324.

16. For reading this as 'progeny', see Oswalt, *The Book of Isaiah*, p. 395.

17. Cf. the Dead Sea text 4Q219 where God will 'cut you off [from the earth] [and your seed from] beneath heaven . . . Then your name and memory will perish from [the] enti[re earth]', 4Q219 2:26,27; Donald W. Parry and Emanuel Tov (eds.), *The Dead Sea Scrolls Reader, Vol. 3: Parabiblical Texts* (Leiden: Brill, 2005), p. 59.

18. Alec Motyer, *Prophecy of Isaiah*, p. 445, italics original.

19. The figure of the barren woman had a more immediate application as the sterile unproductive nation that God would restore in their return from exile. Our focus here, however, is on the woman as a figure of spiritual birth in the new covenant.

reading Isaiah 53:8 on the suffering servant not having descendants. One may wonder what his reaction was when he read of the restored eunuch only a few chapters later.

Paul

Paul too seems aware of the distinction between the two kinds of offspring in Genesis and Isaiah. This first becomes apparent in his claim that the promises given to Abraham were fulfilled in his singular seed rather than his collective seed (Gal. 3:16). The move is theological more than grammatical – it is the unique divinely provided seed, i.e. Christ (for whom Isaac serves as a type), to whom the promises are given and through whom they are realized. Paul reroutes the fulfilment of the Abrahamic promises from the multitudinous physical progeny of Abraham to the divinely provided offspring who is Christ. He can then declare that all those who are 'of Christ', who are offspring of Christ not physically but spiritually, are the true offspring of Abraham and heirs according to the promise (Gal. 3:29).

While Paul's opponents could concede that, as a Jew, Jesus was a physical descendant of Abraham and therefore Abraham's seed, they would not possibly concede that the Galatian Gentiles were also Abraham's seed. After all, the historical record was undeniable. Abraham had two sons: Isaac the father of the Jews, and Ishmael the father of the Gentiles. But only Isaac received the promises and therefore only the Jews could inherit them. Paul responds with an allegorical interpretation of the Hagar and Sarah account (Gal. 4:21–31), which is not an interpretive sleight-of-hand but a theological 'listening to the law' (as he puts it in Gal. 4:21), with an awareness of the two kinds of birth typified by Isaac and Ishmael. The fundamental difference was that Hagar bore Ishmael as a result of human contrivance, while Sarah bore Isaac as a result of divine provision. Insofar as the Jews are Abraham's physical descendants through conventional human means while the Galatian Christians are Abraham's spiritual descendants through the divinely provided offspring, i.e. Christ, it is the Galatians rather than the Jewish legalists who are the true descendants of Isaac. The text Paul then cites to confirm this is Isaiah 54:1: the barren woman now sings (Gal. 4:27). The barren woman parallels Sarah in that both women conceive children supernaturally as the result of divine provision.

Paul never mentions himself either being married or having physical progeny. Is there evidence to suggest that he sees himself in the pattern of the barren woman bearing spiritual children on behalf of the suffering servant? Just prior to the Hagar–Sarah allegory Paul describes the Galatians as 'my little children, for whom I am again in the anguish of childbirth . . .' (Gal. 4:19 ESV). He tells the Corinthians, 'I became your father [begat you] in Christ Jesus through the gospel' (1 Cor. 4:15 ESV). To the Thessalonians he describes himself as both a nursing mother and a father with his children (1 Thess. 2:7, 11). To Philemon Paul appeals 'for my child, Onesimus, whom I have begotten in my imprisonment' (Phlm. 10 NASB). He addresses both Timothy and Titus as his 'legitimate' (*gnēsios*) child (1 Tim. 1:2; Titus 1:4) or simply his 'child' (2 Tim. 1:2; 2:1). Paul is a spiritual father to his converts – begetting them in Christ through the gospel.

If having physical offspring was a fundamental expression of God's blessing under the Sinai covenant, it no longer functioned in the same capacity under the new covenant. All the covenantal blessings are realized through union with Christ, as expressed in Ephesians 1:3: God has blessed us with every spiritual blessing *in Christ*. The single life thus testifies to the essence of the gospel itself. Not even the sweet blessings of marriage and family, children and grandchildren are necessary to be fully blessed in the new covenant – Christ, the offspring of God, is completely sufficient.[20]

Resolution of the exegetical problem

Returning now to the statement of 1 Corinthians 7:1b, it is clear that Paul's theology of a singleness fully sufficient in Christ informs his counsel on the question of marriage. Paul is not affirming *universally* that it is good for a man to be alone, which would be a contradiction of Genesis, but that it is good *in some circumstances* for a man to refrain from marriage and sexual union. This is not a singleness lived alone, for Paul recognizes that in the new family of God (in which he is father, mother and brother of his converts) life is not lived alone.

But we must also address the lexical objection raised by Gordon Fee and others.[21] If Paul's statement here is about marriage, why does he use the strange verb 'touch' (*haptō*) that seems to indicate sexual relations rather than marriage?

---

20. For a fuller presentation of this biblical theology of singleness, see Barry Danylak, *Redeeming Singleness: How the Storyline of Scripture Affirms the Single Life* (Wheaton: Crossway, 2010).

21. Fee, 'I Corinthians 7:1 in the *NIV*', pp. 307–9; Fee, *First Corinthians*, p. 305. Numerous others follow suit, e.g. Roy E. Ciampa and Brian S. Rosner, *The First Letter to the Corinthians* (Grand Rapids: Eerdmans, 2010), pp. 272–5; Kistemaker, *1 Corinthians*, p. 210; Richard Hays, *First Corinthians* (Louisville: John Knox, 1997), p. 113.

In other words, isn't the issue really sexual relations in marriage rather than marriage itself? Perhaps the right answer is, Yes and No. First, everything in verses 8–40 has to do with marriage itself and not just sexual relations. So it is most likely that the matter addressed in verses 1–7 also concerns marriage. Graeco-Roman society tended to dissociate marriage, which had to do with social duty and responsibility, from sexual activity. What Paul must do before addressing their questions on marriage is to make clear that sexual expression as God intended belongs in marriage and only in marriage. How can Paul communicate this point, while also acknowledging a legitimate calling and life of singleness? He responds to their question concerning the necessity of marriage with a surprising choice of language: 'It is good for a man not to touch a woman.' In other words, it is good for a man not to marry if and only if he is also ready to commit himself to sexual abstinence. With such language the point could not be confused. Marriage and sexual expression are a package as God intended – neither should exist without the other. Conversely, singleness is a legitimate and good option, but only when lived with sexual abstinence.

Conclusion

Paul's response to the Corinthians' view that 'it is good for a man not to touch a woman' is grounded in his understanding of the new covenant, the sufficiency of Christ and the new spiritual family of God.

As Western society becomes increasingly single and increasingly post-Christian, it presents a new range of challenges. A robust biblical theology of singleness provides a foundation for effectively engaging with some of these. First, it clarifies that singles are not unblessed or second class within the new covenant. In Christ alone we are all full participants in all the spiritual blessings of the kingdom of God. Having Christ alone is sufficient to be fully blessed in the new covenant, irrespective of whether God also grants wealth, property, marriage or children. Second, a theology of singleness shows us the power of the new spiritual family to supersede the biological family as the locus for intimate relationships. It reminds us that our union with Christ is corporate, as together we become the perfected bride of Christ. We will live forever neither marrying nor giving in marriage (cf. Matt. 22:30), but simply being corporately the bride of Christ. Finally, it clarifies that neither marriage nor sexual relationship is fundamentally necessary to be a complete and fully realized male or female human being. Rather, our fundamental identity is grounded in the *imago dei* as fully expressed in the incarnate Christ. Jesus Christ has fully expressed the image of God and is the basis for our identity as fully complete human beings.

We can thus fully affirm with Paul in Colossians 1:28 that: 'We proclaim him admonishing everyone and teaching everyone with all wisdom that we may present every person *complete in Christ*.'[22]

---

22. Author's translation.

6. 'LET EVEN THOSE WHO HAVE WIVES BE AS THOUGH THEY HAD NONE' (1 COR. 7:29)

Sarah K. Whittle

Introduction

Discussions of what if any relationship we might have with a spouse in the resurrection are challenging and potentially distressing. From the Gospel tradition we find that in the world to come there will be no marriage as we know it (Luke 20:35; Matt. 22:30; Mark 12:25).[1] But closely related and not as widely addressed is the question of what influence that future might have on our present. For Paul, there is no doubt that the shape of the world to come has a powerful impact on the way one should live now; his eschatology means that this future perspective is brought into the present and profoundly affects his ethics. On this basis, John Barclay has recently proposed that Paul presents some strikingly negative aspects of marriage, of which he observes we seem to have lost sight.[2] Paul's instruction in 1 Corinthians 7:29 is certainly radical: he would

---

1. Unless otherwise indicated all biblical translations in this chapter are from the NRSV.
2. For John M. G. Barclay, 'the decision of many early Christians shaped by "apocalyptic" convictions, to choose singleness over marriage, poverty over wealth, and martyrdom over life, remains a challenge which modern Western Christians are all too eager to forget' ('Apocalyptic Allegiance and Disinvestment in the World: A Reading of 1 Corinthians 7:25–35', in Ben C. Blackwell, John K. Goodrich and

prefer believers remain single, but even those who are married should live as though they are not. Assuming Scripture still speaks to our situation, how might we be faithful to Paul's instruction to the Corinthians? What was the 'present distress'? And were the specific ways in which Paul calls the Corinthians to live in the present distress intended for all time? Importantly, and a question not adequately addressed by Barclay, since Paul assumes that the *parousia* (the return of Christ) was imminent, to what extent are his practical instructions about marriage still valid?[3] Rather than issues of singleness or celibacy, as are often tackled with this text, this chapter will focus on marriage, specifically, Paul's plea 'let even those who have wives be as though they had none' (7:29) – the first in a series of five 'as not' statements.[4]

Anthony Thiselton represents a more pastoral approach to the text, according to which Paul assumes people will continue to marry, raise families and participate in the world. For Thiselton, Paul's main point is that each has a particular *gift* from God. 'It is important to note that *Paul freely honors both states*, commending one over the other only on the basis of different callings and gifts (v. 7), and sometimes a pragmatic opinion (v. 25) about what may be a better alternative for a specific situation or time (vv. 26, 29).'[5] Thiselton alludes to the 'present or impending crisis' but believes that this is a situational and secondary concern.

Jason Matson (eds.), *Paul and the Apocalyptic Imagination* (Minneapolis: Fortress Press, 2016), pp. 257–74, here p. 265, emphasis added). Anthony C. Thiselton reads Paul as much more positive towards marriage: 'Paul does not suggest that marriage is a second-class fallback arrangement for those who cannot otherwise control their sexual desires . . . He simply paints a scenario of a couple whose desire for each other is so strong that it constantly distracts them from the centrality of the gospel' (*First Corinthians: A Shorter Exegetical and Pastoral Commentary* (Grand Rapids/ Cambridge: Eerdmans, 2006), p. 105).

3. Barclay stresses that the issue is reprioritization, not simply imminence. But he does not deal with the problem of imminence.

4. For Will H. Deming, *Paul on Marriage and Celibacy: The Hellenistic Background of 1 Corinthians 7*, SNTSMS 83 (Cambridge: Cambridge University Press, 1985), Paul is not 'a champion of sexual asceticism'. Rather, he is 'a cautious and measured proponent of the single lifestyle, a form of celibacy characterized by freedom from the responsibilities of marriage, and for which the absence of sexual fulfilment was no more than an unintended consequence and an inconvenience, never an end in itself', p. 4. Deming deals with apocalyptic but does not see Paul as strongly influenced by it.

5. Thiselton, *First Corinthians*, p. 116, author's emphasis.

Consequently, 'Christians may still with good conscience enter marriage, [and] remain in their married state with all that this implies (7:2–7)'. For Thiselton, Paul does introduce an eschatological dimension, but this is for the purpose of 'relativizing worldly things'.[6] On the 'as not' statements, he concludes that the focus is on 'the single theme of the need to avoid whatever distracts the Christian from single-minded service of the Lord'.[7] According to Thiselton, Paul urges 'Go for what will best empower you to serve Christ without anxiety and distraction'.[8]

Rather than setting a more general eschatological scenario in which the present distress is situational and concluding that Paul is merely relativizing arrangements, Barclay focuses on interpreting the phrase in an 'apocalyptic' context and the expectation of a consequent shift in *allegiance*. Barclay also challenges contemporary followers of Christ to take seriously Paul's 'as not' statements, but from a different perspective. Barclay's apocalyptic starting point does not at first appear to make a huge difference – many authors mention apocalyptic as a frame of reference for these sayings. But Barclay's trajectory and end result are different: what is at stake is a proper understanding of the *time*. 'Paul calls for adjustment to a present "apocalyptic" reality, in whose light marriage seems an unnecessary form of exposure to the death-soaked conditions of the present evil age.'[9]

A resurgence in interest in apocalyptic

There has been a resurgence in interest in apocalyptic in recent decades. In particular, a recent study in Pauline theology has claimed that 'fascination with apocalyptic has reached new heights'.[10] The volume of essays brought together as *Paul and the Apocalyptic Imagination* is one result of this. As is evident in this collection of essays, there remains a good deal of discord regarding exactly what is in view in the use of the terminology. John Collins' *Semeia* 14 article is still regularly cited in definitions of 'apocalyptic Literature'. In Collins' view, there is a corpus of texts which 'share a significant cluster of traits'

---

6. Ibid., p. 119.

7. Ibid., p. 118.

8. Ibid., p. 119.

9. Barclay, 'Apocalyptic Allegiance', p. 265.

10. John Goodrich, 'After Destroying Every Rule', in Blackwell *et al.* (eds.), *Paul and the Apocalyptic Imagination*, pp. 275–96, here p. 276.

distinguishing them from other works. An apocalypse is 'revelatory literature within a narrative framework, in which a revelation is mediated by an other-worldly being to a human recipient, disclosing a transcendent reality, which is both temporal, insofar as it envisages eschatological salvation, and spatial insofar as it involves another, supernatural world'.[11]

Barclay is rather confident about ascertaining Paul's engagement with apocalyptic. While acknowledging that 'what counts is constantly negotiable and inherently malleable', he claims that we can trace 'deployment of themes, motifs and patterns of thought' that are characteristic of apocalyptic literature without the requirement of claims that they come as a collection or are adopted unmodified.[12] In terms of modification, there is general agreement on the sense of continuity and innovation, not least in the idea of 'apocalyptic eschatology': history is coming to an end, and a series of eschatological events will climax in a final judgment and era of justice along with a new created order.[13] Of course, Christian apocalyptic differs from its Jewish counterpart on the basis of the significance of the Christ event. As Collins puts it, 'the Christians believed that the Messiah had already come and that the firstfruits of the resurrection had taken place'.[14] For Barclay, 1 Corinthians is 'shot through' with motifs from Jewish 'apocalyptic tradition'. He categorizes these as revealed knowledge, oppressive powers, determinate times and cosmic

---

11. John J. Collins (ed.), *Apocalypse: The Morphology of a Genre*, Semeia 14 (1979), p. 9. Collins has addressed what he calls the 'semantic confusion' around the use of the word apocalyptic, pressing for a distinction between apocalyptic as literary genre, apocalypticism as social ideology and apocalyptic eschatology. John J. Collins, *Apocalyptic Imagination: An Introduction to Jewish Apocalyptic Literature*, 3rd edn (Minneapolis: Fortress Press, 2016), p. 2.

12. Barclay, 'Apocalyptic Allegiance', p. 257.

13. Loren T. Stuckenbruck claims that Paul's thought is 'both continuous with and distinct from Jewish "apocalyptic eschatology"'; 'Some Reflections on Apocalyptic Thought', in Blackwell *et al.* (eds.), *Paul and the Apocalyptic Imagination*, pp. 137–56, here p. 142.

14. Collins, *Apocalyptic Imagination*, p. 337. However, Collins highlights the fact that Paul's revelation is *not* given in the form of an apocalypse, pointing out that Paul himself labels it as a 'mystery', and 'presents himself as "steward of the mysteries" (1 Cor 4:1)'. Therefore, he finds that Paul's revelatory experience 'embraced some of the media that we have found to be typical of the apocalypses', p. 330. For Collins, the most important element is 'the affirmation of another world and life beyond this one', p. 332.

events.[15] The point is that a correct estimation of these aspects of apocalyptic will lead to a rather different and more challenging reading of Paul's instructions on marriage. First, the evidence from elsewhere in the letter.

Evidence for apocalyptic

In 1 Corinthians 1:18–32 Paul sets out the foolishness of the message of the cross. There is a wisdom that is 'of the world', which is set over against the wisdom 'of God'. The world cannot know God through its wisdom, which is also categorized as 'human wisdom' and 'the wisdom of the wise'. By contrast, Paul's knowledge is selectively disclosed only to those who are being saved. It turns out that *Christ* is this wisdom from God (vv. 23, 30). The wisdom is not 'of this age' or 'the rulers of this age, who are doomed to perish' (1 Cor. 2:6). The phrase 'this age', a motif clearly concerned with time, is used elsewhere by Paul to indicate the present world as an 'evil age' (Gal. 1:4).[16] And here Paul departs from Jewish apocalyptic with a distinctive claim that the Christ event means that the long-anticipated 'new age' has now been inaugurated; the decisive act of God was in the past.[17] Consequently, believers live in two ages: the present age and the age to come. In this section alone we can see several motifs of Pauline apocalyptic: counter-intuitive wisdom with selectively-revealed knowledge; the distinct ages; the world, i.e. the present, old order; and the world's rulers, the cosmic powers, who have been defeated in Christ's resurrection and are 'doomed to perish'.

A later section of the letter (1 Cor. 15:15–28) has similar motifs, with temporal constructs as well as the language of power and resurrection. The setting is a discussion about the resurrection of Christ and subsequent resurrection of those in Christ. Christ is the 'first fruits' of those who have died and been raised (v. 20); at Christ's coming, those who belong to him will be raised. 'Then comes the end', Paul says. The events are described as having cosmic significance. Christ will destroy 'every ruler and every authority and power'. Then he will destroy death, 'for God has put all things in subjection under his feet'.

---

15. Barclay, 'Apocalyptic Allegiance', p. 258. According to J. C. Beker, Paul's gospel is an apocalyptic gospel 'because it looks forward to the final triumph of God in Christ over all those powers in the world that resist his redemptive purpose'; *Paul's Apocalyptic Gospel: The Coming Triumph of God* (Philadelphia: Fortress Press, 1982), p. 15.

16. For 'this age' or 'this world' see 1 Cor. 1:20; 2:6; 3:18–21; 5:9–13.

17. Elsewhere, Paul's 'new creation' motif is well established: 2 Cor. 5:17; Gal. 6:15.

Regarding 1 Corinthians 7 and Paul's marriage discourse, Barclay finds that what emerges out of this apocalyptic setting is Paul's 'policy of detachment' and 'disinvestment'. 'The alteration to the structures of the cosmos effected by the resurrection', Barclay claims, has 'reconfigured human allegiances'.[18] His emphasis is important: marriage should be understood to be included in such reconfigured allegiances.

The context of the 'as not' phrases

In 1 Corinthians 7 Paul turns to 'the matters about which you wrote' (v. 1). In a reciprocal arrangement, he concedes rather than commands: 'each man should have [sexual relations with] his own wife, and each woman [with] her own husband' (v. 2). Paul's logic is based on the avoidance of sexual immorality (v. 2); sex is *either* with a spouse *or* it is immorality. Abstinence is permitted temporarily (v. 5). In fact, Paul wishes that 'all were as I myself am' (v. 7); that is, single and celibate. Yet, he affirms that both single and married are gifted: the former, to manage passion and self-control; the latter, to deal with the additional distress and anxieties concerning the affairs of the world (vv. 28, 31). Both the unmarried and the married should remain in their current state; making changes will not enhance one's life in Christ. The phrase 'remain with God' (v. 24) places the emphasis both on the idea that they are to remain and that they are to remain in Christ.

Paul then moves on to instructions to the unmarried: 'now concerning virgins' (v. 25); by common consent this section is the most difficult in the epistle.[19] Fortunately, for our purposes the identity of the virgins is not important. But the instruction to 'remain as you are' is based on the rationale of the present distress (v. 26). Following this, Paul makes a comment about the shortening of time – 'the appointed time has grown short' (v. 29). He then concludes with the statement about the passing away of the present form of *this* world (v. 31). So the context is clearly an eschatological one. The interpretation of these three points is not straightforward, however.

'The present distress'
Thiselton, along with many others, considers the influence of famine, or fear of impending famine, but stresses that this should not be seen as an alternative

---

18. Barclay, 'Apocalyptic Allegiance', p. 259.

19. Roy E. Ciampa and Brian S. Rosner, *The First Letter to the Corinthians*, Pillar New Testament Commentaries (Grand Rapids/Cambridge: Eerdmans, 2010), p. 328.

to an eschatological dimension, concluding that famine may be 'one possible indication among others of an eschatological question mark over the permanence of the present world order'.[20] Barclay translates the phrase as 'the present constraint, present necessity, or circumstance of constraint'.[21] Partly on linguistic grounds, Barclay rejects the explanation of impending famine in Corinth,[22] as well as that of an imperative to proclaim the gospel in the available time.[23] He also rejects the commonly-held idea of 'Messianic tribulations' or 'woes'.[24] Instead, Barclay claims the phrase refers to a feature of 'the present evil age' (Gal. 1:4); that is, 'slavery to decay ... an indelible feature of the present age' (1 Cor. 15:24–26, 42–44; Rom 8:20–21).[25] And marriage exposes one further to these forces of decay. Here Barclay introduces the point that, since the resurrection, the new reign of Christ is set against death, and the believer's new reality is oriented to the cross. Consequently, the present arrangement should be understood as provisional. For Barclay, the constraint is 'the inevitable mortality and decay of all things in "this age"'.[26]

'The appointed time'

Paul introduces the section as follows: 'I mean, brothers and sisters, the appointed time (*kairos*) has grown short' (v. 29).[27] But to what *time* is Paul referring, and what is the quality of this time?[28] There is a consensus that the reference is a period of time, and that it is the distinctive time between the death and resurrection of Christ and the revealing of Christ at his *parousia* and judgment. It is a

---

20. Thiselton, *First Corinthians*, p. 116.

21. Barclay, 'Apocalyptic Allegiance', pp. 260–2.

22. Bruce Winter, 'Secular and Christian Responses to Christian Famines', *TynB* 40 (1989), pp. 86–106.

23. Richard B. Hays, *First Corinthians*, Interpretation (Louisville: Westminster John Knox, 1997), p. 129.

24. Raymond F. Collins, *First Corinthians*, SP (Collegeville: Liturgical Press, 2006), p. 293.

25. Barclay, 'Apocalyptic Allegiance', p. 263.

26. Ibid.

27. This should not be collapsed into the previous point. Ciampa and Rosner, *First Corinthians*, p. 343.

28. Possible definitions of *kairos* include 'a point of time or a period of time'; 'a defined period for an event'; 'a period characterized by some aspect of social crisis'; Walter Bauer, William F. Arndt and F. Wilbur Gingrich, *A Greek–English Lexicon of the New Testament and Other Early Christian Literature* (Chicago: University of Chicago Press, 1957).

time when the powers of the world, or the old order, are defeated and yet remain active and malevolent. So this special time is characterized by both quantity and quality. Further, Ciampa and Rosner are quite right in their observation that this shortness of time 'radically affects how believers are to live their lives in the here and now'.[29] While not prepared to rule out the idea that the time of tribulation has been compressed, Thiselton prefers to read 'favourable moment of opportunity', on the basis of which 'Christians may still with good conscience enter marriage, [and] remain in their married state with all that this implies' (7:2–7).[30] For Barclay, on the other hand, this is the time where ages meet and overlap; Paul is referring to the life of believers 'mid-apocalypse'.[31]

The 'as not' phrases of verses 29–31

'From now on,' Paul says, 'let even those who have wives be as though they had none'. This is the first in a series of 'as not' phrases – the first of five parallel clauses all using an emphatic negative (*mē*). They move away from specifically marriage, broadening the issues: those mourning as though not mourning; those rejoicing as if not rejoicing. The final two phrases bring the section to a climax: 'Those who buy as though they had no possessions' and 'those who deal with the world as though they had no dealings with it'.[32] The reference to *the world* is clearly aligned with the concluding rationale of verse 31: 'for the present form of this world is passing away'. Attempts to find parallels in Jewish apocalyptic tradition and Stoic philosophy are largely inconclusive; Paul's usage appears to be unique.[33] One who has a wife should live as though he does not because the present cosmic arrangement is temporary: marriage belongs to the old order of the world and it is passing away.

We have already seen Paul instructs spouses 'do not deprive each other' (v. 5), so it is not sexual relations in view – Paul is not promoting asceticism. We have also seen that the sayings are framed by apocalyptic language. For Ciampa and

---

29. Ciampa and Rosner, *First Corinthians*, p. 345.

30. Antony C. Thiselton, *The First Epistle to the Corinthians: A Commentary on the Greek Text*, NICGT (Grand Rapids: Eerdmans, 2000), p. 583.

31. Barclay, 'Apocalyptic Allegiance', p. 266.

32. Ibid., p. 266. Though it is also possible that they refer to and explain the commitments required of marriage.

33. For the former, see Deming, *Paul on Marriage and Celibacy*. For the latter, the closest 'parallel' is often identified as *6 Ezra* (2 Esdras) 16.40–50.

Rosner, the five phrases cover the basics of human life: experiencing joy and sadness, buying goods and engaging with the world. They are 'in the same category as living as a married or single person, and like those experiences they are not to be treated as the ultimate significance in life'.[34] Thiselton's proposal is that the significance of the cosmic events relativizes and therefore should limit engagement in the world.[35] Barclay's emphasis, however, is on the fact that these activities *belong*, in one form or another, *to that which is passing away*: this world. Consequently, one's activities become a matter of allegiance. And here there are echoes of Ernst Käsemann's claim that the question raised in apocalyptic is: 'To whom does the sovereignty of the world belong?'[36] In this sense, one should not avoid investing because of the futility of investing in something which is due to pass away. Rather, one should not invest in this world 'because an alternative and more important investment is already required'.[37] In practical terms, Barclay finds that believers may participate in marrying, mourning, rejoicing, buying and dealing with the world, but 'without the normal practical and/or emotional attachments'.[38]

The world and allegiance to it

The section where Barclay's proposal for allegiance reveals its logic most fully is the discussion beginning with Paul's wish about being free from anxieties (vv. 32–35). On one hand, it is framed as Paul saving the Corinthians from unnecessary cares: a believer's interest, whether that of husband or wife, will be divided between the Lord and the spouse. According to David Garland, Paul does not mean that anxiety for one's spouse is inherently negative. 'Marriage means committing oneself in a special way to the existence of another by involving oneself with the spouse in a relationship of care and concern . . . Paul does not criticize the married for having these cares. He simply observes that marriage imposes demands that cannot be neglected.'[39] But Paul

---

34. Ciampa and Rosner, *First Corinthians*, pp. 348–9.

35. Thiselton, *First Corinthians*, p. 119.

36. Ernst Käsemann, 'On the Subject of Primitive Christian Apocalyptic', in *New Testament Questions of Today* (London: SCM, 1969), p. 109.

37. Barclay, 'Apocalyptic Allegiance', p. 268.

38. Ibid., p. 267.

39. David E. Garland, *1 Corinthians*, BECNT (Grand Rapids: Baker Academic, 2003), p. 333.

makes an interesting move. 'The unmarried man is anxious about the affairs of the Lord, how to please the Lord; but the married man is anxious about the affairs of the world, how to please his wife' (vv. 32–33). In fact, Paul lines up the spouse with the *world* and *over against the Lord*. This will be a surprising move for those who equate concern for the marriage relationship and spouse with service to the Lord. Again, the unmarried woman is concerned with 'the affairs of the Lord', but the married woman is 'anxious about the affairs of the world, how to please her husband' (v. 34). Thiselton does not see any great significance in Paul's use of 'world' here, beyond the idea of divided loyalties. According to Barclay, one option does not exclude the other, but they are not aligned. Pleasing one's spouse is not pleasing the Lord. Loving others, however, can be aligned with pleasing the Lord (Gal. 6:2) and is arguably the climax of Paul's instructions for the building up of community in Corinth (1 Cor. 12 – 13). This raises interesting questions about the relationship between allegiance to the community and allegiance to the family and/or household.

Barclay arrives at his position partly by means of a focus on Paul's 'apocalyptic' references to 'the world', a regular feature of Paul's letters. In 1 Corinthians, the term first appears in 1:20 in the section about human and divine wisdom. The debater of the age is paralleled with the wisdom of the world, where 'the world' is shorthand for a system hostile to God and characterized by arrogance and foolishness. Believers have received not the Spirit of the world but the Spirit who is from God (1 Cor. 2:12). Furthermore, 'the wisdom of this world is foolishness' (1 Cor. 3:19). The form of this world is passing away (1 Cor. 7:31). The God of this world has blinded the minds of unbelievers and prevented them from seeing the gospel (2 Cor. 4:4). Rejection and judgment of *the world* are common themes and constitute nearly half of all references (1 Cor. 1:20, 21, 27, 28; 2:12; 3:19; 6:2; 11:32).

There is no consensus, however, on the way Paul uses 'the world' in 7:31. According to David Garland, it is not the world that is negative, it is being enmeshed in it. And Paul does not advocate flight from it. Garland claims that we can ascertain from the 'as not' sayings that they presuppose involvement in the world – weeping, mourning, buying – it is a matter of the quality of engagement.[40] For Troels Engberg-Pedersen, these five imperative 'as not' sayings 'summarize Paul's view of the application of the gospel'.[41]

---

40. Garland, *1 Corinthians*, p. 331.

41. Troels Engberg-Pedersen, 'The Gospel and Social Practice According to 1 Corinthians', *NTS* 33 (1987), pp. 557–84, here p. 580.

> They concede to people that they live in this world and 'may' go on living according
> to its norms . . . they are certainly not meant to direct Christians away from the
> world of living with other human beings before God. Rather they are meant to
> direct the attention of Christians towards a different way of living with others in
> this world.[42]

It is true that Paul does not prohibit engagement with the world (explicit in
1 Cor. 5:10). Yet highlighting Paul's 'apocalyptic' language leads to interpreting
negatively Paul's reference here in verse 31, as participating in a system whose
time is ending because of the resurrection of Christ. And marriage – like
weeping, mourning and buying – belongs to this system that is passing away.
As Ciampa and Rosner observe: 'Clearly, marriage is of this world, since death
breaks the commitment (v.39; cf. Rom 7:2), and is one of the things that should
be assessed differently in the light of eternity.'[43]

Many demands on a believer belong in the category 'the world', notably the
emotional, social and financial demands of marriage, plus acquiring and maintaining a home. Barclay describes these as 'the goods of marriage'. We note that
Paul's instruction in 7:29 is addressed to a male: the *paterfamilias*, or household
head, would be responsible for maintaining the household, including property,
material goods, family, kin and slaves.[44] There is also a reminder that we should
not be thinking of the modern notion of marriage as romantic love, or even
of a nuclear family. As Margaret MacDonald observes, the modern concept of
family (a husband or wife along with children) does not have a precise parallel
in the ancient world. Moreover, in comparison to modern concepts of family,
'emphasis on property is especially striking'.[45] Limiting engagement with 'the
goods of marriage' and aspects of relationship that use the world helps with
our problem somewhat, but does not resolve it.

Given that we have established that marriage belongs to the present age,
which is passing away, so that even those who have a wife should live 'as though
they had none', what do we do about the problem of the *parousia*? While
revealing Paul's apocalyptic thinking, Barclay does not do justice to the problem.

---

42. Engberg-Pedersen, 'Gospel and Social Practice', p. 581.

43. Ciampa and Rosner, *First Corinthians*, p. 346.

44. Wives are addressed along with husbands in 7:34.

45. Margaret Y. MacDonald, 'Kinship and Family in the New Testament World',
    in Dietmar Neufeld and Richard E. Demaris (eds.), *Understanding the Social World
    of the New Testament* (Abingdon/New York: Routledge, 2010), pp. 29–43, here
    p. 30.

What was close in time for Paul is far distant from us, and we are well aware of the passage of time. As Beker pertinently comments, 'Christians today can no longer expect with Paul the imminent arrival of the kingdom, in the same manner, because "the appointed time" – which for Paul "has grown very short" (1 Cor 7:29) – has for us grown "very long"'.[46]

The problem of the *parousia*

Nancy Duff observes,

> The ongoing experience of time and history probably serves as a stronger hindrance to the appropriation of apocalyptic thought than any other problem we might have with the concept. How can we possibly take seriously Paul's admonition to 'stay awake' and to be alert when 1900 years have passed since Paul spoke them?[47]

Paul expected the end to come soon, probably in his lifetime. This is set out most explicitly in 1 Thessalonians 4:15–17: 'we who are alive . . . will be caught up in the clouds together with them to meet the Lord in the air' (see also 1 Cor. 15:24). And integral to Käsemann's understanding of 'apocalyptic' is that it includes 'expectation of an imminent parousia'.[48] For Käsemann, this is a historical claim. Rudolf Bultmann's project of 'demythologization' attempted to move from the cosmic to the internal or existential in order to deal with the problem.[49] But if it will not do to hold the position of the latter – as Barclay asserts – and we need to recapture the historic setting and cosmic nature of Paul's claims, how do we deal with the problem of the expectation of the

---

46. Beker, *Paul's Apocalyptic Gospel*, p. 115.
47. Nancy J. Duff, 'The Significance of Pauline Apocalyptic for Theological Ethics', in Marion L. Soards and Joel Marcus (eds.), *Apocalyptic and the New Testament: Essays in Honour of J. Louis Martyn* (Sheffield: Sheffield Academic Press, 1989), pp. 279–96, here p. 289.
48. Käsemann, 'Primitive Christian Apocalyptic', p. 109 n.1.
49. For Rudolf Bultmann, 'The real purpose of myth is not to present a picture of the world as it is. Myth should be interpreted not cosmologically but anthropologically, or better still, existentially' ('New Testament and Theology', in idem, *Kerygma and Myth*, tr. Schubert M. Ogden (Philadelphia: Fortress Press, 1984), p. 9).

imminent return of Christ? Beker recognizes this as 'a fundamental difficulty with Paul's apocalyptic gospel'.[50]

Thiselton's framework for the text is a discussion of 'theology of eschatological imminence' and 'chronology of eschatological imminence' – that is, the nearness of the end. Through engaging with the work of G. B. Caird, he challenges the idea that Paul's immanent eschatological imagery should be equated with the idea that the *eschaton* would come soon. He argues that Paul's end-of-the-world language metaphorically referred to that which was not the end of the world. This is not because the world will continue as it is indefinitely, but because the present world order has no future. The key point here is that the nearness of the end must be held in tension with the ethical instructions involving the ongoing state of affairs in the present order.

C. E. B. Cranfield captures something of the sense of tension between chronology and theology.

> The Parousia is near . . . not in the sense that it must necessarily occur within a few months or years, but in the sense that it may occur at any moment and in the sense that, since *the* decisive event of history has already taken place in the ministry, death, resurrection and ascension of Christ, all subsequent history is a kind of epilogue, necessarily in a real sense short, even though it may last a very long time.[51]

We have highlighted the fact that non-apocalyptic interpreters of Paul have an easier time with the problem of reading Paul's instructions nearly two thousand years later. The idea of a relativization of relationships is a common one – the marriage relationship should not come before the work of the Lord. So, for example, understanding the present distress as a local shortage of food, with Thiselton, means that Paul's plea not to marry – with all the additional responsibilities which that entails in a time of hardship – makes perfect sense. Barclay, however, along with other apocalyptic interpreters who see the present distress as the situation mid-apocalypse, has to deal with the emphasis on the imminent return of Christ, which of course failed to happen. The question

---

50. Beker, *Paul's Apocalyptic Gospel*, p. 44. For Beker, not only is the so-called primitive world view problematic, but 'Paul's emphasis on the imminent parousia is for all practical purposes either treated as peripheral, or existentially reinterpreted, or subject to development theories'.

51. C. E. B. Cranfield, 'The Parable of the Unjust Judge and the Eschatology of Luke–Acts', *SJT* 16 (1963), pp. 300–1.

seems to be whether we can hold on to the significance of apocalyptic for Paul as well as determine how Paul's instructions currently challenge the church.

Summary and conclusions

According to Barclay,

> marriage itself is not a sin, but the married believer has no investment in the 'goods' that marriage is thought to bring (financial; security; social honour; the generation of children; the continuance of one's name; the maintenance of one's property-line) and thus lives in marriage 'as not' having a spouse.[52]

But further, Barclay interprets Paul as calling those who are married to live 'without the normal practical and/or emotional attachments'.[53] This seems a particularly difficult statement when related to marriage. For the married, living as though one were not married is a consequence of the age in which one finds oneself, and the demands that have been made of followers of Christ, not just to leave behind the things of the world, but also to recognize that one is required to make a dramatic reorientation of allegiance in light of the resurrection and the hope of the world to come. The problem is not solved by relativization or even a recognition of the temporary nature of marriage. Rather, marriage *belongs* to the form of the world that is passing away. Believers should instead be oriented towards the new Lord of the world, raised and victorious over the powers. In this sense, it is clear that marriage belongs to the old order, the present evil age, and we know that death ends marriage. While bringing a great deal of insight to the apocalyptic Paul, Barclay's reading raises questions about the problem of the contemporary challenges of applying Paul's thought. This apocalyptic position is accompanied by the expectation of an imminent *parousia*.

Indeed, we continue to live in the same time-frame as Paul and with the same quality of time. However, for us, the shortness of time has become a very long time, and, as obvious as it sounds, singleness and celibacy is not really an option for all believers. Christian sects have tried to follow this instruction faithfully; they no longer exist. So it clearly will not do to simply transpose Paul's authority onto our situation. The other option would be to abandon an attempt to be

---

52. Barclay, 'Apocalyptic Allegiance', p. 270.

53. Ibid., p. 267.

faithful to Paul here. This seems to me to be the default, unacknowledged and unexplored position that many of us take on marriage. But Beker challenges us to hear Paul: 'The claim and power of the Pauline text over our present situation must be taken seriously so the horizon of the text, which so often threatens to become a frozen text, a text buried in the past, is kept open.' That we need to realize the eschatological tension inherent in the marriage relationship remains an important if unsatisfactory conclusion. Intentionally navigating a path between on the one hand avoiding 'the goods of marriage', and on the other loving and caring for a spouse, may go some way towards faithful living according to Paul – there is clearly an emphasis on property, household and kin, and inheritance. Acknowledgment of the cosmic change with the death and resurrection of Christ, including the passing away of the world in its present form, would be another place to begin. Still, it is hard to escape from the conclusion that Paul would prefer we remain single, as he was, and wholly focused on the world to come.

7. ARE WE SEXED IN HEAVEN? BODILY FORM, SEX IDENTITY AND THE RESURRECTION

Ian Paul

Introduction

The question of sex differentiation and its status in relation to human identity has become one of the most vexed and disputed questions in public discourse within contemporary Western culture. Though the presenting issues appear to be relatively straightforward and divide approximately into two areas of concern – that women and men should not be confined to predetermined roles within society, and that physical, bodily sex differentiation should not be emphasized – the underlying causes and concern turn out to be remarkably complex.[1] The first part of the complexity arises from careless use of terminology in much of the debate. Differences between male and female are often referred to as issues of 'gender', but this is incorrect, since 'gender' refers to the culturally constructed understandings of masculine and feminine identity in any culture. A good part of the debate actually focuses on biological sex identity – not the differences between masculine and feminine, but the differences between male and female – and this is the focus of my concern here.

---

1. Perhaps the best accessible guide to the complexities involved in the issues of transgenderism and intersex conditions is Mark A. Yarhouse, *Understanding Gender Dysphoria: Navigating Transgender Issues in a Changing Culture* (Downers Grove: IVP Academic, 2015).

There is, of course, a strong connection here, in that an assumption about the interchangeability of social roles between men and women gives rise to the question of the connection between social roles and bodily sex identity, and this in turn raises the question of the pliability of sex identity.[2] Those arguing that sex identity is to some extent pliable cite the existence of the intersex condition as evidence that binary sex differentiation is, in some sense, a secondary rather than primary human characteristic.[3] This has been countered both by feminists, who see the recognition of bodily sex difference as vital in the protection of women's safety, identity and contribution to society, and by those who highlight the ideological, rather than medical, forces at work in the debate.[4]

In response to this debate, Christians have often turned to the creation accounts in Genesis 1 and 2 as a resource for reflecting both on gender roles and on sex binaries.[5] But the other possibility is to focus not on origins but on

---

2. It is worth noting in passing that such debates can only take place in post-industrial societies. In any other context, physical strength for men and child rearing by women has such an obvious importance that these questions of interchangeability hardly arise.

3. For a Christian reflection on this issue in the context of a theology of creation, see Megan K. DeFranza, *Sex Difference in Christian Theology: Male, Female, and Intersex in the Image of God* (Grand Rapids: Eerdmans, 2015).

4. Germaine Greer has been the most prominent feminist to argue that post-operative transgender men are not women, on the grounds that surgery on their genitals does not change their chromosomal identity. See Steven Morris, 'Germaine Greer Gives University Lecture despite Campaign to Silence Her', *The Guardian*, 18 November 2015, <https://www.theguardian.com/books/2015/nov/18/transgender-activists-protest-germaine-greer-lecture-cardiff-university>. A recent report from the Tavistock Clinic highlights a new movement, Transgender Trend, formed by parents of transgender children who reject, on non-religious grounds, the current ideological direction of current practice. See 'Inside Britain's Only Transgender Clinic for Children', <http://www.thetimes.co.uk/article/inside-britains-only-transgender-clinic-for-children-pdtqcf9nk>, accessed 8 November 2016.

5. For examples of the first, see Richard Hess, 'Equality With and Without Innocence', in R. W. Pierce and R. M. Groothuis (eds.), *Discovering Biblical Equality: Complementarity Without Hierarchy* (Leicester: Apollos, 2005), pp. 79–95, and ch. 1 of Ian Paul, *Women and Authority: The Key Biblical Texts* (Cambridge: Grove Books Ltd, 2011). For an example of the second, see DeFranza's summary of evangelical and Roman Catholic teaching, particularly John Paul II's *Theology of the Body*, in DeFranza, *Sex Difference in Christian Theology*, pp. 154–172. It is disappointing that

destiny, on the *telos* of humanity in the biblical narrative – that is, to focus on heavenly perfection. I used the word 'heaven' in my title because of its prominence within Jesus' teaching, particularly within the Matthean tradition, and because of its presence in phrases such as 'like the angels in heaven'. However, I use the term 'heaven' to refer to the realm where God's just and perfect rule is exercised, that is, as a dimension of reality rather than a post-mortem destination, and with the assumption that the consistent perspective of the New Testament ('if not with one voice, certainly with a cluster of voices singing in close harmony'[6]) is that the Christian hope is of bodily resurrection in a renewed heavens and earth.[7]

So my interest here is whether, according to the New Testament, we will retain our sex identity (as male or female) in the resurrection, with a particular focus on Jesus' saying that 'they will be like the angels in heaven' (Matt. 22:30 = Mark 12:25, compare Luke 20:36).[8] This notion has become important, even for some of central importance, in the current debates about the church and same-sex marriage, particularly at the interface between Christian teaching and contemporary cultural debate. Is it the case that male–female marriage is part of the gospel that we have to share with the world, as some have claimed? Or (at the other end of the argument), is sex identity only a secondary, rather than primary human characteristic, so that in the resurrection, sex identity is something that we discard as part of the new creation? If that is the case, and we are now living the resurrection life (as Paul argues in Rom. 6, and elsewhere), then new life in Christ also means a radically new understanding of sex identity and sex differentiation in the new dispensation compared with the old.

Thatcher dismisses such readings as inadequate to the task because they do not give the answers about sexuality that he appears to want; Adrian Thatcher, *Redeeming Gender* (Oxford: Oxford University Press, 2016), pp. 137–41.

6. N. T. Wright, *The Resurrection of the Son of God* (London: SPCK Publishing, 2003), p. 476.

7. The best-known proponent of this view in contemporary discussion is, of course, N. T. (Tom) Wright, articulating this at a more popular level in N. T. Wright, *New Heavens, New Earth: The Biblical Picture of Christian Hope* (Cambridge: Grove Books Ltd, 1999) and Tom Wright, *Surprised by Hope* (London: SPCK, 2011), and in his academic work in Wright, *Resurrection of the Son of God*, pp. 372–4 and 450–79. It is worth noting that Wright is far from alone in this understanding of New Testament eschatology.

8. Unless otherwise indicated all biblical translations in this chapter are the author's. See appendix at the end of this chapter for a comparison of the three passages.

Two challenges

To provide a context for our discussion of the texts, it is worth considering two recent challenges to traditional Christian understanding of the importance of sex differentiation in creation. The first comes from Robert Song, a professor at the University of Durham, and outlined in his recent *Covenant and Calling*.[9]

In his exploration of 'Sex differentiation, sex and procreation' (pp. 38–61), at more or less the centre point of his argument (and its pivotal moment), Song reviews the range of different arguments about the significance of sex differentiation: sex hierarchy, which he dismisses, and sex complementarity in three different forms – biological difference, social functioning and difference as a theological signifier.[10] He is not persuaded by the theological arguments, and so concludes:

> Sexual differentiation is therefore justified within marriage, but it is only justified because marriage in creation is oriented to procreation. There are no other grounds that can provide the theological weight needed to require that marriage be sexually differentiated. However, this also implies that if procreation is no longer eschatologically necessary, then there are no grounds for requiring all committed relationships to be heterosexual. (p. 48)

Song makes two important logical errors here, which ultimately undo the shape of his argument. First, he elides marriage with 'all committed relationships' and fails properly to distinguish these things and, second, he mixes his categories of marriage in creation and the eschaton by assuming that, in the age to come (which we proleptically inhabit) there can be marriage without procreation, rather than there being neither. But the key thing to note for our discussion is that he is basing his logic on the key text about 'being like the angels in heaven', which is where he has in fact begun his discussion.

If Song is starting to bring questions about sex differentiation from the future of eschatology into the present, another important thinker (also a professor in

---

9. Robert Song, *Covenant and Calling: Towards a Theology of Same-Sex Relationships* (London: SCM Press, 2014).

10. It is worth noting that Song is here reflecting systematically, rather than doing textual exegesis – but his taxonomy of views here is much more nuanced and persuasive than Thatcher's assessment in *Redeeming Gender*, pp. 137–9.

Durham) looks in the opposite direction. In his chapter within the collection of essays *Thinking Again About Marriage*,[11] Mike Higton reviews the Church of England's two most important reflections on the nature of marriage, and makes some important observations:

> The aspects of this theology that I am most readily able to affirm are its insistences that to live well involves responding attentively to our bodiliness, and that we are not bodily in the abstract but always as particular sexed bodies. We receive that particularity, that differentiation, as a gift from God.
> (p. 20)

But he goes on heavily to qualify this affirmation. The terms he uses are concerned with redemption, but this must (at least implicitly) include the fall, since without the fall there is no need for redemption:

> We are not simply called . . . to live in attentive response to our bodiliness, but to live in attentive response to our bodiliness *in the light of God's love for the world in Jesus Christ*. Christian ethics, then, is not simply conformity to creation but about creaturely participation in redemption.[12]

Higton's point here – that we must read creation through the lens of redemption – is curiously confirmed by the fact that the two texts in Paul which are most contended in current debates about sexuality, in Romans 1 and 1 Corinthians 6:9, come in his discussion of the fallenness of humanity and its need for redemption, and the participation in the kingdom of God now as an anticipation of the eschaton, rather than where we might normally expect to find them, in the ethical injunctions which usually follow Paul's exposition of what God has done in Christ. Despite that, Higton's direction of travel appears to be different from Saint Paul's in heading towards a minimizing of the significance of sex difference within marriage.

But what these two arguments (of Song and Higton) do for us is to highlight the nature of the discussion – that the questions of sex identity and sex differentiation are held, like so many issues, in that tension between creation and new creation in which we are suspended.

---

11. John Bradbury and Susannah Cornwall (eds.), *Thinking Again About Marriage: Key Theological Questions* (London: SCM Press, 2016).

12. Ibid., p. 20, italics original.

The key text

This is strikingly true of our first and most important single text to consider: Jesus' saying in Mark 12:25 = Matthew 22:30 = Luke 20:36: 'they will be like the angels [in heaven]'.

Catholic theologian James Alison discusses this text at two different points in his writings, both of which focus on the Sadducees' theological failure in their understanding of God.[13] He offers a careful close reading of the texts, but what he fails to note is almost as interesting as what he observes. He highlights the significance of this episode within the Synoptics: the wording of the first half of the pericope is almost identical in all three accounts; the debate has a common shape to it in the three narrations; and the episode comes at the same point in all three as part of Jesus' teaching in the temple. Jesus has entered the temple precincts in the week of his passion; his authority has been questioned; he tells the parable of the vineyard (with a debt to Isaiah) and is nearly trapped on the payment of taxes before this episode; then goes on to discuss the greatest commandment. Matthew adds into this sequence the parable of the two sons and the parable of the marriage feast, while Luke moves the 'greatest command-ment' question to a much earlier point – but overall there is impressive agreement about the context of the 'angels in heaven' episode.

The Sadducees' strategy in questioning Jesus is to assume the truth of what he said, and then use the case of levirate marriage to create a *reductum ad absurdum*. The idea of bodily resurrection leads to an impossible contradiction, and must therefore be false. It is possible that the Sadducees have a problem with poly-androus relationships in particular, but there is more reason to suspect that the problem was with any kind of polygamous relationship, in a culture in which (notwithstanding exceptions amongst the social elite) monogamy was the norm.[14]

---

13. The first comes in ch. 2 'The Living God', in James Alison, *Raising Abel: The Recovery of the Eschatological Imagination* (New York: Herder & Herder, 1996), pp. 34–41, and the second articulation three years later as the essay 'Being Saved and Being Wrong', *Priests and People* (March 1999), pp. 111–15.

14. The question of the incidence of polygamy, prominent in narratives in the Hebrew Bible (OT), in Second Temple Judaism stands behind both this episode and the comment about elders in 1 Tim. 3:2. John J. Collins, 'Marriage, Divorce, and Family and Second Temple Judaism', in Leo J. Perdue, Joseph Blenkinsopp, John J. Collins and Carol Meyers, *Families in Ancient Israel* (Louisville: Westminster John Knox Press, 1997), pp. 104–62, offers a thorough review of the evidence. Despite noting the

What is more striking, and pertinent in the light of Jesus' response, is the assumption on the part of the Sadducees that, for those who do believe in resurrection life, the mundane realities of everyday life in this age will continue into the age to come. This follows the trajectory of Old Testament anticipations of even the most dramatic of God's interventions into history to renew the cosmos, which all include references to mundane aspects of life to express the significance of their hope. So 'they shall sit every man under his vine and under his fig tree' (Mic. 4:4; Zech. 3:10), and 'the one who fails to reach a hundred will be considered accursed . . . They will build houses and dwell in them; they will plant vineyards and eat their fruit' (Isa. 65:20–21). And this expectation is in line with most (though not all) of Second Temple Judaism's expectations, at least from the evidence of the Babylonian Talmud.[15]

A striking aspect of the exchange is the method of Jesus' response. Although elsewhere the Synoptics have Jesus citing the Writings[16] as well as the Latter Prophets,[17] in this debate he confines himself to citing the Torah, the only part of the Hebrew Bible believed to be authoritative by the Sadducees.

---

mention of polygamy in Josephus, Justin Martyr and the *Mishnah*, and its practice by elites such as Herod and his sons, Collins does not depart from the broad consensus that monogamy was the norm throughout this period. This is in line with the conclusion of the earlier S. Lowy, 'The Extent of Jewish Polygamy in Talmudic Times', *Journal of Jewish Studies* 9, no. 3–4 (1958), pp. 115–38.

15. David Werden notes the divergence of views in rabbinical Judaism between those who anticipate life in the age to come as devoid of bodily pleasures ('In the future world there is no eating nor drinking nor propagation . . .' TB *Berakoth* 17a; Rambam (Maimonides), *Hilchos Teshuvah* 8:2) and those who see mundane realities, including marriage, as persisting. In TB *Sanhedrin* 92b Ezekiel revives the dead who then go into Palestine, marrying and begetting children; *Seder Eliyahu Rabbah* 4:19 describes the 'world-to-come' with family in God's presence; in *Ketav Tamim* 91 Moshe Taku says, 'And [after the resurrection] the righteous will take wives in accordance with their deeds . . .'; in *Midrash Alpha-Betot, Batei Midrashot*, we find: 'Each righteous person will draw near his wife in the world to come . . .' David Werden, 'Eternal Marriage or Marriage in the Resurrection', <https://www.academia.edu/8286632/Eternal_Marriage_or_Marriage_in_the_Resurrection>, p. 3, accessed 10 November 2016.

16. Ps. 118:22 in Matt. 21:42; Ps. 110:1 in Matt. 22:43 and pars.

17. Isa. 61:1 in Luke 4:17–19; Hos. 6:6 in Matt. 9:13; Mic. 7:6 in Matt. 10:35; Mal. 3:1 in Matt. 11:10; Isa. 6:9 in Matt. 13:14 and pars; Jer. 7:11 in Matt. 21:13 and pars.

Some exegetical observations

Comparing Matthew's account with Mark's, we notice some minor differences. Jesus' (rhetorical) question to the Sadducees in Mark becomes a direct statement in Matthew, a change that Matthew is in the habit of making.[18] Matthew turns Mark's verbal phrase 'when the dead rise' to the near-equivalent noun phrase 'at the resurrection' (Mark 12:25; Matt. 22:30) and does the same again in the next verse. He personalizes and contemporizes the quotation of the Old Testament; this is no longer 'what God said to him' but 'what God said to you'.[19] And he omits Mark's emphatic conclusion ('you are badly mistaken!'), substituting instead the astonishment of the people. But in other respects the texts are very close – even to include the minor *anakolouthon* (represented as a dash in most English translations) as Jesus moves from the specific question of marriage to the wider question of God's relation with the dead.[20]

In contrast to these close parallels, Luke offers some significance differences. The account of the Sadducees' question remains the same, though slightly abbreviated by use of the adjective *ateknos*, 'childless' (Luke 20:29). But Jesus' response is significantly refigured.

---

18. See, for example, Mark 2:7 and Matt. 9:3; Mark 4:30 compare Matt. 13:31; Mark 9:33 omitted in Matt. 18:2; Mark 5:30 omitted in Matt. 9:22; Mark 6:24 omitted in Matt. 14:8; Mark 7:18 compare Matt. 15:11; Mark 10:3 omitted in Matt. 19:4; Mark 8:12 and Matt. 12:39; Mark 9:12 and Matt. 17:12 and so on. This seems to me to be significant evidence for Matthean redaction of Mark, which does not appear to have been noted elsewhere. Peter Head comes close to this observation in his exploration of the questions of Jesus, though his main interest is in the issue of the ignorance of Jesus and his need to ask (non-rhetorical) questions to elicit information. Peter M. Head, *Christology & the Synoptic Problem: An Argument for Markan Priority*, SNTSMS (Cambridge/New York: Cambridge University Press, 2008), pp. 111–16.

19. There is a clear theological-interpretive parallel here with Paul's claim in 1 Cor. 10:11 that 'these things were written as a warning for us' (compare Rom. 15:4: 'For everything that was written in the past was written to teach us') in that the purpose of the Scriptures is the contemporary formation of the people of God. The classic exploration of this phenomenon is Richard B. Hays, *Echoes of Scripture in the Letters of Paul*, new edn (New Haven: Yale University Press, 1993).

20. *Anakoloutha* are particularly characteristic of Mark, sometimes being followed in Matthew and Luke (as at Mark 2:10 = Matt. 9:6 = Luke 5:24) and sometimes being corrected and smoothed (as at Mark 11:32 = Matt. 21:26 = Luke 20:6).

First, Luke recasts the response in the more explicitly eschatological terms of 'this age' and 'the age to come' (vv. 34–35); this configuration echoes Jesus' comment in Matthew 24:38 suggesting that 'marrying and giving in marriage' distinctively belong to 'this age'. As part of this, Jesus links the age to come with judgment, since only those 'worthy' (v. 35) can participate. And in contrast to the other two accounts, he brings out the theological or philosophical reason behind this; marriage and procreation belong to the age of death, since it is only because we die that we need to have children to continue our line and our work.[21]

Commenting on Luke's version, James Alison picks this up with some rhetorical force. In the old dispensation, the way past the universal reign of death was having children, and in this context, levirate marriage was the man's passport to immortality of sorts. But, in sharp contrast to the Sadducees' failure of understanding and imagination (Alison declares), 'There is no death in God'.[22] Song also highlights this key observation.

> What happens in the resurrection, when death shall be no more? If there is no death, the sustenance of the people of God no longer requires future generations to be born; and if there is no need for future generations to be born, there is no need for marriage ... where there is resurrection, there is no death; where there is no death, there is no need for birth; where there is no birth, there is no need for marriage.[23]

Song then cites John Chrysostom: 'Where there is death, there is marriage.'[24]

In Luke, Jesus then extends the logic of this into an eschatological reconfiguration of familial belonging, parenting and childhood. Those who rise are 'children of the resurrection', presumably because it is their resurrection which has given birth to them in this new age, but since it is God who has brought about this resurrection, they are God's children, and this displaces any lines of heritage in 'this age'. This idea makes clear connections with Jesus' radical

---

21. Making the eschatological framework more explicit, and moving on to wider philosophical questions, could support the idea that Luke is making a Jewish discussion comprehensible to a largely non-Jewish readership.

22. Alison, *Raising Abel*, p. 38.

23. Song, *Covenant and Calling*, p. 15.

24. *On Virginity*, 14.6. The intimate connection between marriage and death is captured in the title of Dvora Weisberg's exploration: Dvora E. Weisberg, 'Between the Living and the Dead: Making Levirate Marriage Work', *AJS Perspectives* (Spring 2013), pp. 10–12. See also her book-length exploration, *Levirate Marriage and the Family in Ancient Judaism* (Waltham: Brandeis University Press, 2009).

reconfiguration of family relations at several points in the Gospels, and most explicitly and strikingly in Matthew 12:49 = Mark 3:34 = Luke 8:21: 'Whoever does the will of God are my mother, my brothers, my sisters.'

Before moving on from the detail of this text, it is worth noting that Luke's account includes a final comment from Jesus '. . . for to him all are alive' (v. 38). As Outi Lehtipuu points out, this echoes the description of the dead in 4 Maccabees, which gives expression to the possibility of some form of disembodied post-mortem existence.

> The phrase 'all live to him' has a close counterpart in 4 Maccabees, a writing that does not speak about resurrection but about immortality (*athanasia*) and that links 'living to God' both to the patriarchs long gone and the contemporary faithful: 'they believe that they, like our patriarchs Abraham and Isaac and Jacob, do not die to God, but live to God' (4 Macc 7.19) and 'those who die for the sake of God live to God as do Abraham and Isaac and Jacob and all the patriarchs.' (4 Macc 16.25)[25]

The question here is whether Luke is adapting his account to make sense to an audience with a wider philosophical outlook, or whether he is simply speaking into a minority position within Second Temple Judaism.

'Being like the angels'

Assuming that, overall, Jesus' comment here is consonant with the emphasis elsewhere in the New Testament on bodily resurrection as post-mortem destiny, what might the phrase 'they are like the angels in heaven' mean? As Lehtipuu highlights, the resurrection of the body came to be hotly contested in the early centuries of the church, and with it there was debate about precisely what the phrase meant. Origen took it to mean that at the resurrection the human body will be transformed into a celestial 'spiritual' body of a much finer and higher substance than the 'earthly' body.[26] But Methodius

---

25. Outi Lehtipuu, 'No Sex in Heaven – or on Earth?', in Anne Hege Grung, Marianne Bjelland Kartzow and Anna Rebecca Solevag (eds.), *Bodies, Borders, Believers: Ancient Texts and Present Conversations* (Eugene: Pickwick Publications, Wipf and Stock, 2015), p. 23.

26. Origen, *De Principiis* 2.2.2. Origen appears to be using the language of the 'spiritual' body here in a different way from Paul in 1 Cor. 15:44, where for Paul the resurrection body is animated by the Spirit but still clearly a physical body in some sense.

follows the teaching of Pseudo-Justin and Tertullian and argues against Origen, not least on the basis of the nature of analogies. To say 'the moon shines like the sun' does not mean that the moon is, in every regard, similar to the sun, and so the likeness between people in the resurrection and the angels offers only a partial parallel.[27]

Out of the debates about this text in the context of resurrection, five distinct questions emerge:

1. In the age to come, will we have bodies, that is, is our destiny bodily resurrection?
2. If we have bodies, will those bodies have the marks of sex difference, that is, will we be male and female?
3. If we have bodies which are sex differentiated, will we engage in sexual intercourse, that is, will our sexual organs have any utility?
4. If we have bodies with sexual organs which will have a use, will that lead to procreation?
5. If we have bodies which are sex differentiated, whether or not our sexual organs will have a use, and whether or not there is procreation, will marriage persist?

The importance of identifying these distinct questions is highlighted when we consider two alternative visions of the age in relation to Jesus' teaching here.

First, this Midrashic text (in written form from the eighth century but claiming to record the teaching of Akiva ben Yosef from the end of the first century) sets out one possibility:

All the orifices [of the body] will spew out milk and honey, as well as an aromatic scent, like the scent of Lebanon, as it is said: 'Milk and honey are under your tongue, and the scent of your robes is like the scent of Lebanon' (Song of Songs 4.11). And 'like seed' which will never cease [to flow from the bodies of the righteous] in the world to come, as it is said: 'He provides as much for His loved ones while they sleep' (Ps. 127.2), and friends are none other than women, as it is said: 'Why should my beloved be in my house?' (Jer. 11.15). Each righteous person will draw near his wife in the world to come and they will not conceive and they will not give birth and they will not die, as it is said: 'they shall not toil

27. Methodius, *Discourse on the Resurrection*, preserved in Epiphanius's *Panarion* 64.12–62. See Lehtipuu, 'No Sex in Heaven?', p. 30.

for no purpose' (Is. 65.23) . . . and they will come to the world to come with their wives and children.[28]

In this vision of post-mortem existence we have bodies, sex difference, sexual intercourse and marriage – but no procreation. This is the kind of 'mundane' view that Jesus appears explicitly to be refuting.

Second, Ben Witherington argues that the phrase 'they will neither marry nor be given in marriage' abolishes the sex difference in the process, suggesting that there are no new marriages in the resurrection, but that existing marriage bonds will persist. Jesus here is not arguing against the existence of marriage *per se*, but against the need for levirate marriage since this is an institution which specifically exists to counter the consequences of death.[29]

This is a surprising reading, since the Sadducees are in fact asking a question about existing marriages and not about marriages that might be conducted in the age to come. The pressing issue is precisely: this woman has been married to each of these men (bracketing out the issue of whether levirate marriages were considered to be full marriages in the usual sense); if marriage does indeed persist in the resurrection, what will it look like? And which of these marriages will persist?

Witherington's reading also goes against the understanding of marriage elsewhere in the New Testament; it is Paul who introduces the idea of conjugal rights in 1 Corinthians 7, arguing that marriage should naturally involve sexual intercourse. And this in turn is tied in with an expectation of procreation; it is the fruitlessness of sexual relations in Romans 1 which contrasts with the fruitfulness of Abraham and Sarah in Romans 4, the difference between idolatry and faith in God. In other words, across the New Testament the questions of marriage, sexual relations and procreation are bound closely together.

Virginity and resurrection life

We can confidently conclude, then, that Jesus' saying answers 'no' to the last three questions about resurrection life: there will be no marriage, sexual

---

28. *Midrash Alpha-Betot, Batei Midrashot*, II, ed. S. A. Wertheimer (Jerusalem: Mosad ha-Rav Kuk, 1980), p. 458, cited in David Nirenberg, 'Posthumous Love in Judaism', in Bernhard Jussen and Ramie Targoff (eds.), *Love After Death: Concepts of Posthumous Love in Medieval and Early Modern Europe* (Berlin: De Gruyter, 2015), pp. 55–70, here p. 60.

29. Ben Witherington, *The Gospel of Mark: Socio-Rhetorical Commentary* (Grand Rapids: Eerdmans, 2001), pp. 328–9.

intercourse or procreation in the age to come. This reading is confirmed by the majority of patristic interpretations of this text, which took it as a key text advocating virginity as an anticipation of the life to come – and it is striking how much interest there is on virginity in the fathers.[30]

Cyprian of Carthage is typical of the kind of discussion we find: virgins are living the resurrection life already, because they are exemplifying the pattern of existence that Jesus is setting out in these verses. 'What we shall be, already you have begun to be. The glory of the resurrection you already have in this world; you pass through the world without the pollution of the world; while you remain chaste and virgins, you are equal to the angels of God.'[31] But what is really fascinating in the patristic writers is the way that they frequently move from the question of resurrection life and virginal existence (encouraged not least by Rev. 14:4) to the question of the bodily organs, including sexual organs. They often appear to be responding to a very similar kind of *reductum ad absurdum* argument to the one that the Sadducees presented to Jesus: if we are to be raised bodily, and if we are going to do without sex in the resurrection, what is the point in having sexed, differentiated, sexual organs? The answers given are unambiguous. Lehtipuu summarizes the arguments of Pseudo-Justin and Tertullian in this way: 'If having sexual organs does not unavoidably lead to sexual intercourse in this world, it will certainly not do so in the world to come.'[32]

This conclusion has a direct impact on the relationship between questions 2 and 3 above. If there is no marriage, procreation and sexual relations in the resurrection, but virginity demonstrates that sex difference need not lead to sexual relations, that allows for the possibility that our resurrected bodies will indeed be sex differentiated. But is this necessary? The answer of Jerome (also an ardent opponent of Origen) is unequivocal: bodily resurrection must of necessity imply the continuance of sex identity. 'The apostle Paul will still be Paul, Mary will still be Mary.'[33] Since we only know ourselves as bodily persons with sex identity, then true continuity into the resurrection (whatever the

---

30. Although various reasons are often read back into the fathers on this issue, their interest is surprising not least because the socio-scientific evidence suggests that it was the Jewish commitment to marriage and family, carried over into the early Christian communities (rather than virginity) which set Christians apart from their pagan contemporaries. See Rodney Stark, *The Rise of Christianity* (San Francisco: HarperCollins, 1997), ch. 5.

31. Cyprian, *On the Dress of Virgins*, 22, cited in Lehtipuu, 'No Sex in Heaven?', p. 33.

32. Lehtipuu, 'No Sex in Heaven?', p. 26.

33. Jerome, *Letter 75 (To Theodora)* 2.

discontinuities) must involve retaining this. 'If the woman shall not rise again as a woman nor the man as a man, there will be no resurrection of the body for the body is made up of sex and members.'[34]

Jerome supports this by himself going back to Jesus' saying and noting that the phrase 'they will neither marry nor be given in marriage' in fact presupposes sex difference. If to be 'like the angels' implied losing sex difference, there would be no need to make explicit the absence of marriage, since that would not be a possibility.[35] If indeed 'Paul will be Paul and Mary will be Mary', then after the resurrection 'Jesus was Jesus'; since Jesus' body was sexed prior to his death and resurrection, and, following the resurrection, Jesus' body still bore the marks of his wounds, then it is hard to envisage Jesus' resurrection body not also being sexed.

Jerome's conviction has shaped the history of Christian art in this regard. A particularly good example of this is the series of frescoes of the Last Judgment in the cathedral of Orvieto in Umbria, central Italy, by the Renaissance artist Luca Signorelli, painted from 1499 to 1503. Men and women can be seen pulling themselves out of the earth and then helping others to do the same as they prepare to stand before the throne (Rev. 20:11–12). There is no doubting that their bodies bear the marks of sex differentiation!

This is the point at which new creation connects with first creation. As we noted at the beginning, Mike Higton observes that we experience our creatureliness in our bodiliness, and we experience this as male or female, receiving such differentiation as 'a gift' from God. It was not possible, for example, for Jesus to have been incarnated as a 'generic' human being; he needed to become either a man or a woman, and this historic particularity is expressed in recent decisions about the revision of the English versions of the Nicene Creed which have all

---

34. Jerome, *Letter 108 (To Eustochium)* 23.

35. At this point, it would be possible to enter a debate on whether angelic beings are envisaged in Scripture as being sexed. If the 'sons of God' in Gen. 6:4 are taken to be angelic, then they are not only sexed but oversexed; the angelic visitors to Abraham representing the presence of God in Gen. 18 appear to be 'men', as are the angels at the tomb after Jesus' resurrection. It is often thought that the seraphs covering their 'feet' in Isa. 6:2 is a euphemism for covering their genitals (compare Ruth 3:7); this could explain Paul's enigmatic 'because of the angels' in 1 Cor. 11:10; and in Zech. 5:9 we find angelic women. But Methodius' argument, that 'like the angels' suggests similarity in some regards rather than identity in every regard, means that such observations cannot settle whether our resurrection bodies will be sexed.

retained 'and he became man' and resisted change to the sex-inclusive 'he became human'.

We should note in passing that there is a parallel debate about sexual organs and digestive organs. If we cannot die in the resurrection, will we need to eat? If we cannot eat, why have digestive organs? The fathers make this connection, but so does Paul; in Romans 1 Paul associates a certain kind of sexuality as idolatry, but in Colossians 3:5 he calls greed idolatry. In the church in Corinth, problems with sex ran parallel with problems and questions about food and the stomach – and, Paul tells us, 'God will put an end to both' (1 Cor. 6:13).[36]

Sexuality, bodiliness and disability

There is a fascinating parallel between our question about sex differentiation and contemporary debates about disability – whether disabilities which are seen to shape self-understanding and identity will persist into the resurrection. This is especially important for those who wish to resist a 'medical' understanding of disability, which will then be 'healed' in the resurrection. Nancy Eiesland, in *The Disabled God*, comments: 'The resurrected Jesus Christ in presenting impaired hands and feet and side to be touched by frightened friends alters the taboo of physical avoidance of disability and calls for followers to recognize their connection and equality at the point of Christ's physical impairment.'[37]

But if Jesus takes his bodily wounds into the resurrection life, then by the same logic he surely takes his bodily organs (both sexual and digestive) into this life. Luke 24 tells us that he ate fish, and John 21 that he cooked some for others; Augustine's symbolic reading of these texts need not detract from their more obvious significance that resurrection is indeed bodily.[38]

---

36. I have argued elsewhere that the regular and frequent fasting related in the NT, contrasted with periodic fasting related in the OT, is symbolic of eschatological expectation, and so reflects a community which prizes both marriage (as an affirmation of this age) and virginity (as an affirmation of the life of the age to come). Ian Paul, 'How Often Did Jesus and His Followers Fast?', *Psephizo*, 1 September 2016, <http://bit.ly/2bUsien>.

37. Nancy L. Eiesland, *The Disabled God: Toward a Liberatory Theology of Disability* (Nashville: Abingdon Press, 1994), p. 100.

38. Augustine says the fish of Luke 24 represent the faith of the martyrs that have gone through the fiery trials of suffering, and of those in John 21 that '[t]he fish roasted is Christ having suffered' (Treatise 123).

Frances Young, in *God's Presence*, makes a similar argument in relation to her disabled son Arthur:

> Arthur's limited experience, limited above all in ability to process the world external to himself, is a crucial element in who he is, in his real personhood. An ultimate destiny in which he was suddenly 'perfected' (whatever that might mean) is inconceivable – for he would no longer be Arthur but some other person. His limited embodied self is what exists, and what will be must be in continuity with that. There will also be discontinuities – the promise of resurrection is the transcendence of our mortal 'flesh and blood' state. So there's hope for transformation of this life's limitations and vulnerabilities, of someone like Arthur receiving greater gifts while truly remaining himself.[39]

Wes Hill reflects on the significance of this dynamic – the transcendence of our bodily life which yet allows us to be more truly ourselves – in relation to sexual identity.[40] But he also warns us to draw a line on too specific speculation about the nature of resurrection life, and does so with a wonderful quotation from C. S. Lewis' *On Miracles*:

> I think our present outlook might be like that of a small boy who, on being told that the sexual act was the highest bodily pleasure should immediately ask whether you ate chocolates at the same time. On receiving the answer 'No', he might regard absence of chocolates as the chief characteristic of sexuality. In vain would you tell him that the reason why lovers in their carnal raptures don't bother about chocolates is that they have something better to think of. The boy knows chocolate: he does not know the positive thing that excludes it. We are in the same position. We know the sexual life; we do not know, except in glimpses, the other thing which, in Heaven, will leave no room for it.[41]

Indifference to sex identity

This sense in which we cannot actually envisage exactly what the resurrection life is like leads to a counter observation about the New Testament and

---

39. Frances Young, *God's Presence: A Contemporary Recapitulation of Early Christianity* (Cambridge: Cambridge University Press, 2013), p. 107.

40. Wesley Hill, 'Will I Be Gay in the Resurrection?', *Spiritual Friendship*, 10 March 2016, <https://spiritualfriendship.org/2016/03/10/will-i-be-gay-in-the-resurrection/>.

41. C. S. Lewis, *Miracles: A Preliminary Study* (Glasgow: Collins, 1960), pp. 166–7.

discussion of sex identity. Despite the evidence that sex identity and differentiation persists in the resurrection, the New Testament displays a decided indifference to sex identity. This is evident in several ways:

1. Paul's use of both Adam and Christ as archetypal humans, not archetypal male figures. In Romans 5 and 1 Corinthians 15, what matters is not their sex identity, their maleness, but their significance as archetypes of two ways of living. Paul is looking to the (undifferentiated) 'adam', the earth creature, rather than the male Adam, partner of Eve – as he makes clear in 1 Corinthians 15:47 when he makes a pun on Adam's name by describing him as 'from the dust of the earth'.

2. His similar use of Eve in 2 Corinthians 11:3, where she is *not* an archetype of susceptible women, but of all people in danger of being deceived.

3. Paul's language in Galatians 3:28, where he does not appear to be eliminating the differences between male and female, slave and free or Jew and Gentile, but downplaying the significance of such differences. John Barclay expresses this exquisitely:

> In baptism, at the moment when believers put on Christ and enter the body of Christ, these previous hierarchies of worth are rendered insignificant (Gal. 3:26–28; Col. 2:9–11). In Christ 'There is no longer Jew or Greek, there is no longer slave or free, there is no longer male and female; for you are all one in Christ Jesus' (Gal. 3:28). These differences are not erased, but they no longer matter, and they can neither divide nor stratify the new Christian community. . . . It enables – in fact requires – a Christian community not just to *include* both slaves and free people, men and women, but to *regard their differences in status as insignificant*, treating them no longer as markers of differential worth.[42]

4. Paul's remarkable symmetrical depiction of mutual authority over the bodies of husband and wife within the marriage relationships in 1 Corinthians 7:4. The spare translation of the Authorized Version captures well the symmetrical structure of Paul's grammar:

---

42. John M. G. Barclay, *Paul and the Subversive Power of Grace* (Cambridge: Grove Books Ltd, 2016), p. 17. See also his more detailed reflection in John M. G. Barclay, *Paul and the Gift* (Grand Rapids: Eerdmans, 2015), pp. 396–8. Thatcher also considers these questions briefly, but his exegesis is hampered by a hermeneutic of suspicion, and the pressing of Paul (against the evidence) into a 'one sex' model of humanity where the female is constantly subsumed into the male. Thatcher, *Redeeming Gender*, pp. 146–60.

The wife hath not power of her own body, but the husband:
    and likewise also
the husband hath not power of his own body, but the wife.

5. The complete absence of sex differentiation in the work of and gifts from the Spirit in 1 Corinthians 12. Barclay again comments lucidly:

> Did God give the Spirit on the basis of gender, and does the fruit of the Spirit grow better on a male tree? The idea is absurd because (unlike most philosophers of his day) Paul does not think that gender differentials have anything to do with the way that God distributes his gifts.[43]

There are some even more dramatic examples of indifference to sex identity in the book of Revelation. In visual representations of John's vision report of Jesus in Revelation 1, Jesus is universally depicted with male sex identity. But the actual picture is more mixed. The gold band is not wrapped around his *stethos*, chest, as it is in the source vision of the angel in Daniel 10 and the angels similarly girded in Revelation 15:6, but is around his *mastoi*, his female breasts. The best explanation for this is that Jesus polemically displaces the function of female goddesses, including Hekate, from whom he also steals the claims to 'hold the keys to death and Hades' and to be 'coming quickly'.[44]

The same applies to the depiction of the people of God; the 144,000 apparently male warriors in Revelation 7 are also the female virgins of Revelation 14. And the nuptial binary in the opening of Revelation 21 is quickly dissolved by describing the city itself as the holy of holies and the presence of God with his people.

In these different ways, at the very least, the New Testament is marginalizing the importance of sex difference as it has been previously construed.

Conclusion

Sex differentiation is not imagined to be absent in the resurrection, and indeed its absence would be unimaginable and implausible if the resurrection life is

---

43. Barclay, *Paul and the Subversive Power of Grace*, p. 22. See also Barclay, *Paul and the Gift*, pp. 423–42.

44. For a detailed exploration of this, looking at both exegetical issues in the cultural and theological context of Revelation, see Ian Paul, 'Jesus and Gender in Revelation', *Psephizo*, 1 December 2015, <http://bit.ly/1MSZY5e>.

indeed bodily – as it is vigorously claimed to be in all New Testament texts that explore the question. To be human and bodily means to be male or female, both in this age and in the age to come.

But sex differentiation is seen to have lost its primary significance, because of loss of interest in procreation, and therefore the loss of interest in both sexual intercourse and marriage. It is therefore not possible to dispense with sex difference in marriage without actually dispensing with marriage itself. The two are inextricably linked.

Robert Song's proposal, that because of the loss of interest in procreation in the age to come, we can envisage marriage-like sexual relationships which are non-procreative and therefore not necessarily other-sex relationships, fails in two directions. On the one hand, he fails to hold together sexual expression with the potential for procreation in the way we consistently find in Scripture, in which non-procreative sexual relations are characterized as (in some way) expressing the judgment of God. On the other hand, he imagines that there might be a form of marriage-like relationships which anticipate marriage in the age to come, when Jesus explicitly says that there will be no more marriage. The eschatological fulfilment of marriage is not non-procreative marriage, but the absence of marriage as an inter-human relationship in the light of the marriage supper of the lamb (Rev. 19:6–9), which is the union of God with his people. This absence of marriage (that is, singleness and virginity) is exemplified in the life of Jesus and Paul, and expounded in the theologies of the fathers.

Mike Higton's proposal, that we need to understand sex difference not simply by looking back to creation but by interpreting it through the lens of redemption in Jesus, is true to the extent that we need to rethink the significance of male and female in the light of the new covenant, as Paul consistently appears to. But this does not lead to a reconsideration of sex difference within marriage, since, in the eschatological fulfilment of our redemption in the final resurrection, the dissolving of sex differences is paralleled by the loss of the centrality of human marriage as both a pattern of human relating and the context for the essential task of procreation.

Yes, we will be 'sexed' in 'heaven' – but it will not have the significance that it does in the present age.

Appendix: a synopsis of the 'angels in heaven' pericope[45]

Mark 12:18–27	Matt. 22:23–33	Luke 20:27–38
[18]Then the Sadducees, who say there is no resurrection, came to him with a question. [19]'Teacher,' they said, 'Moses wrote for us that if a man's brother dies and leaves a wife but no children, the man must marry the widow and raise up offspring for his brother. [20]Now there were seven brothers. The first one married and died without leaving any children. [21]The second one married the widow, but he also died, leaving no child. It was the same with the third. [22]In fact, none of the seven left any children. Last of all, the woman died too. [23]At the resurrection whose wife will she be, since the seven were married to her?'	[23]That same day the Sadducees, who say there is no resurrection, came to him with a question. [24]'Teacher,' they said, 'Moses told us that if a man dies without having children, his brother must marry the widow and raise up offspring for him. [25]Now there were seven brothers among us. The first one married and died, and since he had no children, he left his wife to his brother. [26]The same thing happened to the second and third brother, right on down to the seventh. [27]Finally, the woman died. [28]Now then, at the resurrection, whose wife will she be of the seven, since all of them were married to her?'	[27]Some of the Sadducees, who say there is no resurrection, came to Jesus with a question. [28]'Teacher,' they said, 'Moses wrote for us that if a man's brother dies and leaves a wife but no children, the man must marry the widow and raise up offspring for his brother. [29]Now there were seven brothers. The first one married a woman and died childless. [30]The second [31]and then the third married her, and in the same way the seven died, leaving no children. [32]Finally, the woman died too. [33]Now then, at the resurrection whose wife will she be, since the seven were married to her?'
[24]Jesus replied, 'Are you not in error because you do not know the Scriptures or the power of God? [25]When the dead rise, they will neither marry nor be given in marriage; they will be like the angels in heaven.	[29]Jesus replied, 'You are in error because you do not know the Scriptures or the power of God. [30]At the resurrection people will neither marry nor be given in marriage; they will be like the angels in heaven.	[34]Jesus replied, 'The people of this age marry and are given in marriage. [35]But those who are considered worthy of taking part in the age to come and in the resurrection from the dead will neither marry nor be given in marriage, [36]and they can no longer die; for they are like the angels. They are God's children, since they are children of the resurrection.
[26]Now about the dead rising – have you not read in the Book of Moses, in the account of the burning bush, how God said to him, "I am the God of Abraham, the God of Isaac, and the God of Jacob"? [27]He is not the God of the dead, but of the living. You are badly mistaken!'	[31]But about the resurrection of the dead – have you not read what God said to you, [32]"I am the God of Abraham, the God of Isaac, and the God of Jacob"? He is not the God of the dead but of the living.' [33]When the crowds heard this, they were astonished at his teaching.	[37]But in the account of the burning bush, even Moses showed that the dead rise, for he calls the Lord "the God of Abraham, and the God of Isaac, and the God of Jacob". [38]He is not the God of the dead, but of the living, for to him all are alive.'

---

45. All translations NIV.

8. DEFERRING TO DAD'S DISCIPLINE: FAMILY LIFE IN HEBREWS 12

Nicholas Moore

Introduction[1]

In the middle of an argument that the audience should regard their current sufferings as the loving discipline of their heavenly Father, the author of Hebrews refers briefly to his and his audience's own experience of family life: 'We had human fathers as our discipliners, and we respected them [. . .] they disciplined us for a short time as seemed best to them' (Heb. 12:9–10).[2] This prompts us to ask what the audience's experience of family life was like, and what we may – or may not – infer about this from the text. It also, coming in a text written for oral delivery to a believing community, raises the pastoral question as to how this appeal to the common experience of paternal discipline might have been heard. And, for those committed to Scripture's relevance and authority for Christian living today, it raises the question of how it might be heard in our own contexts.

---

1. For P. J. T. M., who never knew his father's discipline, but rests secure in his heavenly Father's care.
2. Unless otherwise indicated all biblical translations in this chapter are the author's.

In the UK in 2015, 25% of households with children were lone-parent families;[3] in the parish I currently serve the figure is 40%.[4] The vast majority of these parents are women.[5] So it is not true that 'we all had human fathers'. It is also not necessarily true that 'we respected them' – the absent or abusive father is less likely to engender respect; and regardless of parental disposition, not all children respect their parents. Conversely, there are those fathers whose abuse or neglect does not stem their children's respect for them. The situation in the ancient world may not have been all that different: higher mortality rates and lower life expectancy, the impact of disease, war and divorce, would mean that lacking a father was not uncommon;[6] similarly, some children did not respect their parents, and some parents, perhaps especially fathers, were overly harsh with their children.[7] The point stands then as now, and the question to be addressed is not only what this generalized appeal to the audience's experience tells us about family life, but also how it works, pastorally and socially – or even, whether it works at all.

Two brief opening remarks are in order. First, Hebrews' ethical reflections are sparse in comparison to its extensive doctrinal exposition: as one commentator memorably puts it, 'the theological mountain goes into labour, and gives

---

3. An increase from 22% in 1996 (Office for National Statistics, *Statistical Bulletin: Families and Households: 2015*, section 5, <www.ons.gov.uk/ peoplepopulationandcommunity/birthsdeathsandmarriages/families/ bulletins/familiesandhouseholds/2015-11-05#lone-parents>, accessed 6 August 2016).

4. Stranton All Saints, Diocese of Durham (Church Urban Fund parish statistics, <www2.cuf.org.uk/parish/130264>, accessed 30 June 2016).

5. In 2015 women accounted for 90% of lone parents and men for 10%, a ratio which has changed little since 1996 (Office for National Statistics, *Families and Households: 2015*, section 5).

6. Paul Veyne estimates half of children in the Roman Empire had lost their father by the age of 20 ('La Famille et l'amour sous le Haut-Empire romain', *Annales: Économies, Sociétés, Civilisations* 33 (1978), pp. 35–63, at p. 36), while Beryl Rawson cites comparable estimates that by the age of 15 there was a 63% probability of one's father still being alive (*Children and Childhood in Roman Italy* (Oxford: Oxford University Press, 2003), pp. 226–7). Consider also the numerous OT references to the fatherless and widows, e.g. Exod. 22:22; Deut. 10:18; Job 29:12; Ps. 68:5; Isa. 1:17.

7. Cf. exhortations against harshness (e.g. Eph. 6:4). Suetonius, *Life of Augustus* 65, lists examples of Augustus' severe treatment of his children.

birth to a moral mouse!'[8] This both makes it harder to contextualize the reference to family life in Hebrews 12, and at the same time makes this reference all the more tantalizing for what it might tell us in what is otherwise, ethically speaking, a fairly thin document.[9] Second, beyond its well-known first three verses, the first half of Hebrews 12 has received relatively little attention in scholarship,[10] a lacuna which this chapter aims to help fill by drawing attention to family ethics and to the author's use of experience in his argument.

The first half of this chapter surveys portrayals of and expectations surrounding paternal discipline in other relevant ancient sources; these indicate that Hebrews' position is very much at home in the ancient world. A close reading of Hebrews 12 in the second half, however, reveals a careful reticence in the way human fathers are presented, which suggests great pastoral sensitivity on the author's part. At the same time, he unabashedly promotes God as the perfect Father whose discipline we can trust, whatever our experience of human discipline.

Paternal discipline in the ancient world

Ancient Near East and Old Testament

In ancient Mesopotamia the head of the household had ultimate authority over his family's affairs, and severe penalties or curses were prescribed if a child should dishonour his father.[11] Similarly, honour for both parents was a mainstay of the Mosaic law (Exod. 20:12; Lev. 18:7; 19:3; Deut. 5:16; 27:16), its infraction

---

8. 'Es kreißt der theologische Berg, und er gebiert eine moralische Maus!' Knut Backhaus, *Der sprechende Gott: Gesammelte Studien zum Hebräerbrief*, WUNT 240 (Tübingen: Mohr Siebeck, 2009), p. 215.

9. Note the teaching on marriage in 13:4.

10. For previous studies see Günther Bornkamm, 'Sohnschaft und Leiden: Hebräer 12,5–11', in *Geschichte und Glaube*, BET 53 (Munich: Kaiser, 1971), pp. 214–24; Peter Rhea Jones, 'A Superior Life: Hebrews 12:3–13:25', *RevExp* 82 (1985), pp. 391–405; N. Clayton Croy, *Endurance in Suffering: Hebrews 12:1–13 in Its Rhetorical, Religious and Philosophical Context*, SNTSMS 98 (Cambridge: Cambridge University Press, 1998); Matthew Thiessen, 'Hebrews 12.5–13, the Wilderness Period, and Israel's Discipline', *NTS* 55 (2009), pp. 366–79.

11. Victor H. Matthews, 'Marriage and Family in the Ancient Near East', in Ken M. Campbell (ed.), *Marriage and Family in the Biblical World* (Downers Grove: IVP, 2003), pp. 1–32, at pp. 1–3, 16.

sufficient ground for the death penalty (Exod. 21:15, 17; Lev. 20:9; Deut. 21:18–21).[12] Parents are responsible for educating and disciplining their children, as in Deuteronomy 6:7–9, 'Recite [these words] to your children and talk about them when you sit at home and when you journey on the road'.[13] This command is addressed to men (second person masculine singular verbs/suffixes), and the Old Testament as a whole suggests a patriarchal – or, better, patricentric – view of family life. The term 'patricentrism' reflects the fact that, while the father did have authority over his family, the primary interest of the Old Testament is in the restriction or right use of this authority, that is to say, on the father's responsibilities to his family more than his rights over them.[14]

Within wisdom literature parental instruction is a common theme. The opening chapters of Proverbs are cast as a father's address to his son (e.g. 2:1; 4:1, 10, 20; 7:1, 24), passing on instruction (Heb. *mûsār*, Gk *paideia*, 1:8). There is also mention of the mother's teaching (Heb. *tôrâ*, Gk *thesmos*, 1:8), and the hearer is addressed as the child of lady Wisdom (8:32). The noble wife of Proverbs 31 speaks wisdom to her children (31:26–28). Proverbs also frequently commends discipline to its readers, whether or not this is directly connected to a parental figure (e.g. 4:13; 19:18; 23:12; cf. Ps. 119:66). Proverbs clearly envisages physical discipline, with several references to using or not sparing the rod (13:24; 23:13–14; 29:17).

There are a few places in which God is directly or indirectly likened to a father.[15] Proverbs 3:11–12 (cited in Heb. 12) describes God's discipline as like a father's; Deuteronomy 8:5 also draws this comparison. In 2 Samuel 7:14 God promises to be a father to David's son, and states that he will reprove him (Heb. *yākaḥ*, Gk *elenchō*). In the Song of Moses (Deut. 32:6), God appeals to his status as Father and Creator to shame the people for their response to him. In Hosea 11:1–11, God is the father figure who nurtures his rebellious son Israel and refrains from imposing punishment. God's discipline is also described in contexts that do not directly evoke his fatherly role (e.g. Job 5:17; Jer. 2:30; 5:3).

---

12. Daniel I. Block, 'Marriage and Family in Ancient Israel', in Campbell, *Marriage and Family*, pp. 33–102, at pp. 92–3.

13. Cf. also Exod. 12:26–27; 13:14; Deut. 32:7.

14. On 'patricentrism' see Block, 'Marriage and Family in Ancient Israel', esp. pp. 40–44, 52–54, and 'The Patricentric Vision of Family Order in Deuteronomy', in this volume, pp. 12–29.

15. Cf. also Exod. 4:22; Ps. 68:5; Isa. 63:16; 64:8; Jer. 3:19; 31:9.

Other Jewish sources

Turning to later Jewish literature, in the book of Sirach, Wisdom disciplines her children (Sir. 4:17) and the reader should accept Wisdom's discipline (51:26); the one who loves his son will beat and discipline him (*mastix, paideuō*; 30:1–17); children are to be disciplined and made obedient (7:23). Philo also commends discipline: education is a rod supporting the actions of the virtuous (*Alleg. Interp.* 2.90). In line with the fifth commandment, children are expected to honour their parents (Sir. 3:2–16; Philo, *Decalogue* 165–66; *Spec. Laws* 2.224–36; Josephus, *Ant.* 4.260–64; *Ag. Ap.* 2.206).

Numerous sources describe God's discipline: he has mercy on those who accept his discipline, and chastises his people to test and admonish them, in order to avert punishment later (Tob. 13:4–5; Jdt. 8:27; Wis. 11:9–10; 12:20–22; Sir. 18:14; 23:1–2; 2 Macc. 6:12–17; 4 Ezra 14.34). God's discipline is explicitly connected with his fatherly role in a number of places. For Josephus God's discipline is like a parent's, for admonition not full retribution (*Ant.* 3.311). Philo states it is better for God to discipline us, like a tutor, than abandon us (*Worse* 145–46). Elsewhere he cites Proverbs 3:11–12 and, like Hebrews, notes that the proximity of the father–son relationship is evidenced by correction (*Prelim. Studies* 177; cf. *Creation* 156). In the *Psalms of Solomon*, the righteous do not despise God's discipline (3:4); he corrects them like a beloved son (13:9; 18:4). Similar sentiment is found among the Qumran documents: children are to honour their parents because God is like a father (4Q418 9.17–18); he disciplines Israel like a man chastises his son (4Q504 3.5–7).

Graeco-Roman sources

Under Roman law children were subject to the authority of their father (*patria potestas*) until his death, their release (*emancipatio*), or a transfer of responsibility to another *paterfamilias* (e.g. through marriage or adoption). It was thus not uncommon for adult Romans to be legally minors,[16] on top of the moral expectation that children owed their parents respect (*pietas in parentes*). The absolute authority of *patria potestas* included rights to make and break a child's marriage, hold and administer his property, and even put him to death, although convention tempered these, especially the last.[17] In practice, it seems that parental roles were roughly equivalent: both father and mother were responsible for providing

---

16. Veyne, 'La Famille', p. 35.

17. Suzanne Dixon, *The Roman Mother* (Norman and London: University of Oklahoma Press, 1988), pp. 26–9; Susan Treggiari, 'Marriage and Family in Roman Society', in Campbell, *Marriage and Family*, pp. 132–82, at pp. 134–41.

nurture, moral guidance and education,[18] and it was natural that both should love their children.[19] Some sources associate mothers with indulgence and nurture, and fathers with severity and discipline (e.g. Seneca, *De Prov.* 2.5). In the Greek-speaking world, the Spartans were notorious for their harsh discipline and state involvement in the upbringing of children – Seneca uses them as an example, stating that such harshness stems from love and not hate for their children (*De Prov.* 4.11–12) – but even this unique system did not override, but was rather founded upon, parental authority.[20] Plutarch offers a more measured regime, recommending nursing by the child's own mother, and the father's active involvement in his children's education – using encouragement over corporal punishment, and not placing too many demands on them (*Lib. ed.* 5, 7, 9–13). As among the Romans, parental affection was appropriate or even commended (Aristotle, *Eth. nic.* 8.12.2–3).

In Graeco-Roman literature, we also find the gods likened to fathers. Seneca describes God as having the mind of a father (*patrium*), accounting for his severe discipline (*De Prov.* 2.5–7); he is a glorious parent (*parens*) who raises his children strictly (*De Prov.* 1.5; cf. 4.11–12). Epictetus offers another perspective: in his *Dialogues* he describes Zeus as a good king and father (*basileōs, patros*, 1.6.40) who freely gives humans their faculties without constraining how they are used. Fluid boundaries between the gods and humans facilitated perceptions of gods as fathers; for example, Heracles as Zeus' semi-divine son accepts his father's orders (3.26.31).

Early Christian sources

Within the New Testament there are clear if brief instructions for relationships between children and parents. Children are to obey and honour their parents (Col. 3:20; Eph. 6:1–3), including by providing for them in later life (Mark 7:9–13; 1 Tim. 5:8). Fathers are not to provoke (*erethizō*, Col. 3:21) or anger (*parorgizō*, Eph. 6:4) their children. Instead they are to bring them up in the Lord's discipline and instruction (*paideia, nouthesia*, Eph. 6:4). More generally, Christians undergo discipline (administered by outsiders, 2 Cor. 6:9; the church, 1 Tim. 1:20; 2 Tim. 2:25; or by God, 1 Cor. 11:32; Titus 2:12; Rev. 3:19). Kinship

---

18. Dixon, *The Roman Mother*, pp. 111, 182.

19. Rawson, *Children and Childhood*, pp. 221–2, 236.

20. Nigel M. Kennell, 'Boys, Girls, Family, and the State at Sparta', in Judith Evans Grubbs, Tim G. Parkin and Roslynne Bell (eds.), *The Oxford Handbook of Childhood and Education in the Classical World* (Oxford: Oxford University Press, 2013), pp. 381–95, esp. pp. 391–2.

terminology is used within the church, whether of Paul as father to an individual (Phil. 2:22; Phlm. 10) or to a church (1 Cor. 4:15; 1 Thess. 2:11–12), of different ages and sexes within the church (1 Tim. 5:1, 4; 1 John 2:13–14), or of believers' adoption into God's family (Gal. 4:5–7).[21] In Galatians the law is described as a tutor (*paidagōgos*, 3:24–25), guardian and steward (*epitropos, oikonomos*, 4:2).

Clearly the major development in early Christian literature is the prominence given to God as father, a development which is not without precedent in the Old Testament or wider ancient world, as we have seen, but which far outstrips anything found there. This usage is most prominent in John's Gospel (109 occurrences), but is also found in the Synoptics (a total of sixty-three occurrences) – always on Jesus' lips, saving four exceptions in John – and in Paul's letters (e.g. 1 Thess. 1:1, 3). The Aramaic loan-word *Abba* (Gal. 4:6; Rom. 8:15) alongside the Gospel evidence strongly suggests that this usage is rooted in Jesus' earthly teaching.[22] Indeed, although its interpretation is contested, Ephesians 3:14–15 may imply not merely that God is a father but that human fatherhood is derived from and dependent on God's fatherhood.[23] Yet for all the prominence of the title 'father' for God in the New Testament, it is striking that it should be associated with God's discipline only in Hebrews 12.

Conclusion

Despite variations in emphasis and specific details and customs, a number of common themes emerge that hold true across much of the ancient world: (a) parents, and particularly fathers, hold the ultimate responsibility for disciplining their children; (b) as a corollary of this, it is expected that children will acknowledge and accept discipline from their parents; (c) more broadly, discipline is commended in and of itself, regardless of who administers it; (d) God or the gods are often said to exercise discipline towards people; (e) connected with this, it is sometimes explicitly stated that God or a god is or is like a father to human beings, at times in explanation of his discipline.

---

21. For Andreas Köstenberger kinship among believers holds priority within the NT, although biological family remains important: 'Marriage and Family in the New Testament', in Campbell, *Marriage and Family*, pp. 240–84, at pp. 268–9.

22. Larry W. Hurtado, 'God', in Joel B. Green, Scot McKnight and I. Howard Marshall (eds.), *Dictionary of Jesus and the Gospels* (Leicester: IVP, 1992), pp. 270–6, at pp. 271, 273–4.

23. Markus Barth discusses four interpretative options but declines to rule out or opt decisively for any of them, *Ephesians*, AB 34, 2 vols. (Garden City: Doubleday, 1974), 1:379–84.

Paternal discipline in Hebrews

The family of God in Hebrews
The application of kinship language to God, Jesus and Christians, which was seen to be widespread across the New Testament, is equally prominent in Hebrews.[24] Significantly, such language operates strictly christologically: it applies to Christ and only through him to believers. God is his Father (1:5). Jesus, the Son, shared humanity in every respect (2:14, 17) except that he was sinless (4:15). This establishes a sibling relationship between Jesus and human beings (2:11–12, 17; 3:1), qualifying him to deal with our predicament of slavery to the fear of death (2:15) through his atoning sacrifice (2:17), and enabling him to sympathize with his siblings in his ongoing ministry (2:18; 4:15; 7:25). Provided they persevere, believers are Jesus' brothers and sisters, part of his household (3:1, 6, 14). This entails a close relationship with God: believers are his children (2:13–14) and he is their father (2:11, Jesus and believers are 'all of one', *ex henos*; 12:7, 9); believers are 'the firstborn' (12:23), and as such God's heirs.

Hebrews is also concerned about genealogy, addressing Jesus' non-priestly descent from Judah (7:13–14), and proving the superiority of Melchizedek's priesthood over Aaron's by reference to Levi's descent from Abraham. For Hebrews, family clearly matters. Family patterns shape the way in which the people of God are understood, and are in turn reconstituted into the ultimate family, whose importance prevails even over physical descent.

The argument of Hebrews 12
We turn now to the argument of Hebrews 12:5–13, which I will trace in five sections.

Scriptural exhortation (12:5–6)
Hebrews 12:1–3 exhorts the audience to follow the example of the cloud of witnesses of chapter 11 and to look to Jesus, who provides both an example to follow and a guarantee that the race has been, and therefore can be, completed. Hebrews 12:4 is a transitional verse, moving from the preceding exhortations to comment that the audience has not yet shed blood in their struggle against sin. Verse 5 adds that they have forgotten the exhortation that addresses them

---

24. On family imagery in Hebrews see Amy L. B. Peeler, *You Are My Son: The Family of God in the Epistle to the Hebrews*, LNTS 486 (London: Bloomsbury, 2014).

as sons – characteristically, for Hebrews, framing an Old Testament quotation as direct speech – and goes on to cite Proverbs 3:11–12:[25]

> My son, do not regard lightly the Lord's discipline,
>   or grow weary when reproved by him;
> for it is the one he loves that the Lord disciplines,
>   and he chastises every son he accepts.

The citation in Hebrews is very close to the LXX, except that it reads '*my* son'
(*huie **mou***), like the MT.[26] The Hebrew text form of the MT is more conducive
to the author's argument – in the second half of verse 12 it reads 'like a father'
(*kě'āb*), making the identification of God as a father explicit. The Greek trans-
lators evidently read these consonants as the verb *ka'ab*, 'to cause pain', hence
the translation with *mastigoō*, to chastise or whip; this reduces the paternal and
intensifies the punitive nature of the discipline.[27] The fact that Hebrews does
not read 'like a father' suggests the author was not using a Hebrew text.

There is debate over whether the concept of discipline (*paideia*) is understood
in a formative or punitive manner, both in the wider Graeco-Roman and Jewish
literature,[28] and specifically in Hebrews 12. Space precludes exploration of this
question here, but it is clear that Hebrews does not develop the punitive aspect
of discipline that is explicitly present in the Greek version of Proverbs 3:11–12
that the author cites. The audience are not sinless, but here it is their encounter
with external hardship that is in view, and not trouble of their own making.[29]
Nevertheless, in the biblical tradition it is hard to force any absolute separation
between punishment and formation – rather, discipline incorporates aspects
of both.[30]

---

25. Peeler, *You Are My Son*, pp. 147–8, argues that God is the speaker.
26. This addition is natural (so Harold Attridge, *The Epistle to the Hebrews: A Commentary
    on the Epistle to the Hebrews*, Hermeneia (Philadelphia: Fortress, 1989), p. 361; Paul
    Ellingworth, *The Epistle to the Hebrews: A Commentary on the Greek Text*, NICGT
    (Grand Rapids: Eerdmans, 1993), p. 648), or arguably intensifies God's fatherly
    position (so Peeler, *You Are My Son*, pp. 149–51). It is lacking in Philo's quotation
    of the same verse (*Prelim. Studies* 177).
27. Philo, *Prelim. Studies* 177, also reads *mastigoi* in Prov. 3:12.
28. See the discussion of ancient sources in Croy, *Endurance in Suffering*, pp. 77–161.
29. So Croy, *Endurance in Suffering*, pp. 196–214; Peeler, *You Are My Son*, pp. 151–3. See
    Georg Bertram 'παιδεύω', *TDNT* 5 (1967), pp. 596–625, at p. 621, for the opposite view.
30. William L. Lane, *Hebrews*, WBC 47, 2 vols. (Dallas: Waco, 1991), 2:420.

First argument: discipline implies legitimacy (12:7–8)
Following the quotation, the author draws out its implications in verses 7–8, exhorting his hearers to persevere for the sake of discipline.[31] He backs this up by making more explicit the father–son relationship between God and believers: God is treating them as sons. He then adds a rhetorical question, 'for what son is there whom his father does not discipline?' This is an appeal to a generally recognized truth: sons undergo discipline from their fathers. This observation is well attested in the contemporary literature, as we have seen. Its negative corollary is then stated in verse 8: if they are without discipline, they are illegitimate and not sons. The parenthetical remark, 'in which all are sharers', is a reference to 'all sons', casting back to the general truth stated in verse 7. Yet the noun 'sharer' (*metochos*) is also one of the author's favoured terms for believers – they share in a heavenly calling (3:1), they are sharers in Christ (3:14) and in the Holy Spirit (6:4). Its use here subtly reinforces the overall argument that sharing in sonship entails sharing in discipline as well.[32]

At this point, it is worth pausing to address a question of translation: throughout 12:5–10 should we read 'fathers' and 'sons' or, as the NRSV has it, 'parents' and 'children'? It is not enough to point to the use of the term *patēr*, which in the plural can refer to both parents and indeed does in Hebrews 11:23, where it denotes Moses' parents – his father *and* mother. Equally the term can refer to ancestors more generally (as in 1:1; 3:9; 8:9; and probably 7:10 of Abraham). The term *huios* in the plural likewise does not automatically refer only to sons. However, I suggest that it is helpful to maintain the father–son terminology for several reasons: (a) Hebrews could have used a word for child such as *paidion* (2:13) or *teknon*; (b) *huios* and *patēr* in 12:7 occur in the singular, suggesting a point is being made not about a child and a parent, but specifically about a son and a father; (c) the contemporaneous evidence outlined above suggests that the association of fathers in particular with discipline was relatively commonplace; (d) the NRSV translation obscures the careful analogies and differences established between human fathers and the divine Father, as we shall explore further below, and between human sons and the divine Son, who underwent a similar process of discipline (5:7–9).[33]

---

31. Taking *hypomenete* as an imperative; Ellingworth reckons the expository context favours the indicative (*Hebrews*, p. 650).

32. Croy, *Endurance in Suffering*, p. 220.

33. Bornkamm, 'Sohnschaft und Leiden', p. 224.

To return to the verses in question: alongside Proverbs 3, one of the few places in the Old Testament where the theme of God's fatherly discipline occurs is Deuteronomy 8:5. Like Hebrews 12:7, this passage describes and justifies God's discipline of his people by appeal to the general truth that a father disciplines his son.[34] Not only does Hebrews draw on proverbial wisdom that fathers discipline their sons, it also draws on a biblical theme which connects this to God's discipline of his people.

Second argument: qal wahomer *based on experience (12:9–10)*
The author then turns to a further argument. This is like the previous one in that it relies on a relationship of similarity between God as father and human fathers. Yet it is also different in that it appeals more explicitly to the audience's experience, and employs a 'how much more' argument. This form of argumentation, known as *qal wahomer* or *synkrisis,*[35] is of huge importance for Hebrews as a whole.[36] The key point for our purposes is that there is a move from something that is known and accepted as good or true, to something that is less well known or accepted, or even completely unknown, and that is to a superlative degree better.

In verse 9 we move from the generalized question 'what son is there ... ?' to a concrete statement, 'we had human fathers'. As we have seen, the reciprocal paternal/filial duties of discipline and respect were expected in the ancient world. It is in the comparison drawn that things become interesting, as the first table on page 132 helps show.

Note in verse 9b the explicit marker of a *qal wahomer* argument, 'much more' (*poly mallon*). This presumes that the rightness of the basis of comparison, human fathers' discipline, is accepted. Next comes the verb, 'be subject' (*hypotagēsometha*), a strong word suggesting active submission and obedience whereas 'respect' (*entrepomai*) connotes an attitude of regard but no more. 'Father of

---

34. David M. Allen, *Deuteronomy and Exhortation in Hebrews: A Study in Narrative Re-presentation,* WUNT 2.238 (Tübingen: Mohr Siebeck, 2008), pp. 79–82.

35. On *synkrisis* and its importance for understanding Hebrews, see Michael W. Martin and Jason A. Whitlark, 'The Encomiastic Topics of Syncrisis as the Key to the Structure and Argument of Hebrews', *NTS* 57 (2011), pp. 415–39; 'Choosing What Is Advantageous: The Relationship between Epideictic and Deliberative Syncrisis in Hebrews', *NTS* 58 (2012), pp. 379–400.

36. *Qal wahomer* occurs in 9:14 ('how much more'); 12:9, 25 ('much more'). Cf. also 'how much worse', 10:29; and 'such a great salvation', 2:3.

v. 9a	v. 9b
furthermore	shall we not much more
we had fathers of our flesh[37]	to the father of spirits
as our discipliners[38]	
and we respected them;	be subject
	and live?

spirits',[39] denoting God, artfully reverses the designation 'fathers of flesh': not only does the Greek have an ABBA pattern (flesh–fathers–father–spirits), there is also a singular–plural–singular–plural pattern (*tous tēs sarkos pateras / tō patri tōn pneumatōn*). God's greater status is suggested by the fact that he is both singular and father *of spirits*, not simply of flesh. The most significant part of the statement, however, is the final two words. As can be seen from the table, there is no outcome stated for our respect of human fathers and their discipline, yet one *is* stated in regard to God, in emphatic final position: '*and live*'. This result echoes the promise attached to the fifth commandment, 'that your days may be long in the land' (Exod. 20:12; Deut. 5:16; Eph. 6:2–3), and the exhortation in Deuteronomy 30:19–20 to 'choose life'.

The comparison between human fathers and God continues in verse 10, implicitly carrying over the *qal waḥomer* argument and amplifying God's excellence:

v. 10a	v. 10b
they	but he
disciplined [us]	[disciplines us]
for a few days	
as seemed best to them	for good
	so that we might share his holiness

---

37. In Hebrews 'flesh' (*sarx*) is not pejorative, as in Paul's flesh–body (*sarx–sōma*) distinction, instead meaning simply 'earthly', 'bodily' or 'human' (see Heb. 2:14; 5:7; 9:13; 10:20). In 9:10 the reference is to 'regulations for the body' (NRSV), rather than something inherently sinful, as 'carnal ordinances' (AV) might suggest.

38. *Paideutēs* ('instructor', 'disciplinarian', 'teacher') often conveys the meaning of *paideia* under discussion here (cf. Hos. 5:2; *Pss. Sol.* 8:29); Attridge, *Hebrews*, p. 362.

39. An unusual expression, possibly used liturgically in traditional Jewish formulations, cf. Num. 16:22; 27:16; *1 Clement* 59.3; 64.1 (Attridge, *Hebrews*, pp. 362, 363 n.60). God is described as father in Hebrews only here and 1:5 (in a citation), in contrast to frequent references to Jesus as Son.

Human fathers discipline for a short time – presumably the period of their child's minority – and they do so 'at their discretion'[40] (*kata to dokoun autois*), as seems good or best to them. There is ambiguity as to whether this means for their children's benefit, so far as they could discern it, or whether it simply means as suited them, i.e. ultimately for their own benefit. The former is probably to be preferred, but in both cases it is humanly determined and not absolute. Moreover, the ambiguity here may be deliberate, encompassing both good and bad experiences of human fathers. By contrast, there is no corresponding statement regarding the duration of God's discipline; this and the omission of a verb (*paideuō* is clearly to be inferred) focuses all the attention on the two statements. God's discipline is 'for good' (*epi to sympheron*), absolutely and categorically: there is no question of misguided judgment of what the good is.[41] While the argument proceeds from the human exemplar to the divine father, it is probable that Hebrews views God's fatherhood as prior and human father-hood as derivative and dependent, as Christ's status as Son and the statement in 2:11 that we are all 'of one' (*ex henos*, 'all have one Father', NRSV) suggest.[42] Whatever one makes of this suggestion, God's fatherhood functions as a model for human fathers, whose goal should be the ultimate good of the children entrusted to their care. Finally, as in verse 9, no outcome of human discipline is mentioned, bringing out all the more emphatically the clear benefit of God's discipline: 'so that we might share his holiness'.[43]

In short, there is recognition of the givenness, the rightness of paternal discipline. Yet at the same time there is a marked reticence about the discipline of human fathers which suggests a degree of provisionality. Human fathers are not particularly commended;[44] the fact of their discipline is simply noted as a general empirical truth. The author refrains from giving any clear indication of good outcomes of human discipline. This is no doubt partly to allow the good outcomes of God's discipline to shine all the more brightly. But it also testifies to a realism and pastoral concern on the author's part. By avoiding holding up human fathers as a straightforwardly good example, he makes

---

40. Ellingworth, *Hebrews*, p. 654.

41. Croy, *Endurance in Suffering*, pp. 204–5, notes that this is practically a Stoic slogan.

42. Cf. Eph. 3:14–15, discussed above. This would cohere with Hebrews' view of the relation of heavenly to earthly realities elsewhere, especially the tabernacle's derivation from the heavenly pattern (Heb. 8:5).

43. Cf. *metalambanō* with *metochos/metechō* elsewhere, and note above.

44. Ellingworth goes so far as to suggest they are criticized (*Hebrews*, p. 652).

allowance for mixed or varied experiences of human parenthood among his audience; he implicitly acknowledges our flawed human nature, the sinful self, from which – as he stresses so strongly elsewhere – Christ's sacrifice cleanses our conscience. He is pastoral, realistic and sensitive to his audience's experience.

Supporting consideration: the fruit of discipline (12:11)

Verse 11 contrasts our experience of discipline with our fathers' perspective from the previous verse: while it is ongoing, discipline 'does not appear (*ou dokei*) pleasant but instead grievous'. The wordplay makes a subtle theological point: human discipline *seemed* good to our fathers, no discipline *seems* good to us, but God simply *does* what is for our best, and through it produces 'the peaceable fruit of righteousness'.

This is a common wisdom theme which appears in various guises. Diogenes Laertius records a comparable saying: '"The roots of education", [Aristotle] said, "are bitter, but the fruit is sweet"' (*Lives of Eminent Philosophers* 5.1.18). While the text postdates Hebrews by some 150 years the saying is certainly earlier. There are various thematic similarities but only two cognate terms – 'discipline' (*paideia*) and 'fruit' (*karpos*) – which are relatively common and not unnaturally associated, such that it would be hard to posit any influence, were it not for a further strong echo a few verses later. In verse 15 the author precedes his warning about Esau with a warning that the audience should not allow any 'root of bitterness' (*rhiza pikrias*) to spring up – language very close to that found in Diogenes' aphorism (*rhizas, pikras*). Furthermore, the character of Esau is prominent in tradition as a negative example of a son relating to his father and failing to be subject to his discipline.[45] This additional echo, then, suggests that it is not implausible to suppose the author had in mind a phrase like the one Diogenes attributes to Aristotle.

Conclusion: keep going in trials (12:12–13)

The argument concludes in verses 12–13, with language drawn from Isaiah 35:3, in a call to strengthen failing limbs and make straight paths. The first word, *dio*, is inferential and connects this exhortation to what precedes.[46] *Because* discipline is a sign of the community's legitimacy as God's sons, and *because* God's discipline, like the discipline of a human father but much more absolutely, tends towards our good, *therefore* keep going through this present hardship.

---

45. See Thiessen, 'Hebrews 12.5–13', pp. 376–8.

46. Lane, *Hebrews*, 2:426.

Other appeals to experience in Hebrews

It will be helpful, before concluding, to look elsewhere within Hebrews to see if a similar dynamic can be discerned – that is, use of empirical argumentation which nevertheless allows that such experience may not be uniform.

Hebrews refers to the audience's own experience, for example in 2:1–4 where the author mentions the gospel message they heard, its messengers, and the various accompanying wonders. But there are also general appeals to experience which hold true for any hearer, as for example in 2:5–10, where after citing Psalm 8 the author says 'as it is, we do not yet see everything in subjection to him' – that is, mankind – 'but we see Jesus'. This appeal to experience is a fundamental step in the argument, introducing Jesus as the pioneer for the rest of humanity. Arguably it allows that we might see different things in different degrees of subjection; the point is simply that we do not see *everything* in subjection.

The most relevant example for our purposes comes at the end of Hebrews 9: 'just as it is appointed for humans to die once, and after this the judgment, so Christ, having been offered once . . ., will appear a second time' (9:27–28). There is a subtle appeal to experience – we know that people die once, because that is what we observe. Moreover, this allows for exceptions: some have in fact died twice, namely those who have been miraculously raised and subsequently died a second time. The resurrection accounts found in the Old Testament and the Gospels, or others like them, were likely known to the audience. It is even possible, if speculative, that the miracles mentioned in 2:4 included resurrections.

Furthermore, Hebrews acknowledges the existence of such temporary resurrections. In 11:35, speaking of Old Testament saints, the author states: 'women received their dead by resurrection; others were tortured, not accepting release, so that they might obtain a better resurrection'. This recognizes both that some were raised from the dead, and that their resurrection was a 'lesser' one, so to speak, a resurrection to this earthly life once again, by contrast with the 'better', eternal one which awaits all the faithful. That is to say, Hebrews' author knows that some people die twice, and yet still states that 'all people die once'. The admission of exceptions to the general, observable rule does not nullify its validity. In the same way, the assertion that we have all experienced paternal discipline, and respected it, allows for exceptions: it is a general, empirical rule, but not necessarily an absolute or universal one. And like Hebrews 12, in Hebrews 9:27–28 this appeal to experience forms the basis for a comparison with Christ, patterning a divine truth on a temporal, observable one. Appeals to experience are part of the author's repertoire, deployed with great brevity but also to great effect at several points in the argument.

Conclusion: experience, discipline and perseverance

The foregoing study has implications for how we should regard Hebrews 12, and also for how Hebrews suggests we should regard ourselves. First, our understanding of Hebrews 12. This passage might be designated proverbial or aphoristic, drawing as it does on much common wisdom:[47] as we have seen, in both Jewish and Graeco-Roman traditions the father held ultimate responsibility for discipline, and respect was a child's right response. What is more, Hebrews not only directly quotes from Proverbs 3, but also echoes Deuteronomy 8:5 and an aphorism attributed to Aristotle. In addition the passage might be described as typological, if one accepts Matthew Thiessen's cogent argument that the construal of hardship as discipline in Hebrews 12:5–13 is patterned on the Israelites' endurance of discipline in the wilderness.[48] Yet neither of these descriptions does the passage full justice. This study suggests that the author's reference to paternal discipline is more than simply a stock reference to a generic cultural given. Instead, the audience's own family life is evoked, in a careful manner that allows for diverse experiences. Of course it is a false trichotomy to ask whether Hebrews 12 is proverbial *or* typological *or* empirical. Clearly all three have a part to play. Yet the explicit appeal to experience, alongside the explicit and implicit allusion to proverbial statements, and also alongside the entirely implicit evocation of the wilderness generation, should be given its due place and emphasis. The author's argumentation, like his gospel, is embedded in the everyday lives and experiences of his audience.

Second, and finally, our own self-understanding: for the author of Hebrews, the believer is among other things a member of God's family. He is keen to emphasize this, whatever our experience of our own human families may have been. As children of God, we are known and loved, redeemed, our consciences cleansed. But also, like any son, and supremely like *the* Son, Jesus, we must undergo discipline, training. In Hebrews 12, the author draws and builds on positive experiences of human fathers to suggest that God as a father is even more excellent. Yet he also reveals his pastoral sensitivity, acknowledging those whose fathers were absent, or who had negative experiences of their discipline, by exercising a careful and deliberate reticence. God, by contrast, knows absolutely what is best, unaffected by sin or fallible perspective, and is thus a positive model for all human fathers. Whatever the outcome of our experience or imperfect practice of human discipline, we can be sure that the outcome with

---

47. Attridge regards the whole passage as largely 'proverbial' (*Hebrews*, pp. 359–65).
48. Thiessen, 'Hebrews 12.5–13'.

our heavenly Father will be good, the ultimate good of sharing in his holiness. This knowledge changes the game, shifts our vision and perspective on whatever trials we currently face, and engenders the perseverance that the author so passionately desires.

9. EVIDENCE OF NON-HETEROSEXUAL INCLINATIONS IN FIRST-CENTURY JUDAISM

David Instone-Brewer

The early Jewish condemnation of homosexual activity is sometimes regarded as sufficient evidence that they condemned any deviation from heterosexual inclinations. However, a condemnation of anal sex within a hedonistic homosexual lifestyle does not necessarily condemn all homoerotic practices or committed and faithful homosexual relationships.

Of course these early authors may not have been aware that consistent and long-term homosexual inclinations or relationships existed or were possible. They may have had preconceptions about those who carried out non-heterosexual practices, as many do today. On the other hand, they may have recognized innate homosexual inclinations so that they regarded homosexual sex differently when it occurred within a committed relationship. A more likely possibility is that they condemned homosexual activity without condemning homosexual orientation.

To remove this uncertainty, we need to know precisely what they did condemn, and also whether they were aware that some individuals did have consistent homosexual inclinations. This chapter will therefore explore the specific aspects and extent of homosexuality that is being condemned. It will summarize the relatively well-explored statements in non-rabbinic texts before looking in more detail at a rabbinic tradition which may contain evidence that they were aware of consistent and innate homosexual inclinations.

Second Temple Jewish statements on homosexuality

Many statements about same-sex behaviour have survived from a variety of Jewish sources in the inter-testamental and other early Jewish literature. As usual with moral topics, there is very little in rabbinic sources (in Hebrew) that can be traced back to the first century, but fortunately one tradition has survived (see next section). To understand the import of this rabbinic tradition, we have to remind ourselves about the general stance of Judaism on homosexual practice (recorded in Greek, the language of the Jewish diaspora).[1]

In Alexandria, Philo was particularly scathing about Roman and Greek customs that threatened to infiltrate Jewish lifestyle. His audience was Jewish, so he had no need to disguise his disdain. When describing Sodom, he clearly had an eye on what he regarded as parallels in his own time.

> [L]ike cattle, they threw off from their necks the law of nature and applied themselves to . . . forbidden forms of intercourse. Not only in their mad lust for women did they violate the marriages of their neighbours, but also men mounted males without respect for the sex nature . . . Then, as little by little they accustomed those who were [by nature] men to submit to play the part of women, . . . did they emasculate their bodies.[2]

Philo clearly regards these men as hedonistic in both heterosexual and homosexual behaviour, without any innate homosexual orientation. However, he does say that they were gradually transformed and corrupted by their homosexual activity, so this may indicate that he recognized that some men did exhibit a consistent homosexual orientation and that he was presenting an explanation of how this might originate.

---

1. In view of their importance to the discussion, key terms are given in footnotes in their original language.
2. Abr. 1.135–136, Loeb. Yonge follows the Greek more closely: 'restive like cattle' who 'discard the laws of nature (φύσεως νόμον), pursuing . . . unlawful (ἐκθέσμους) connections (ὀχείας – from ὀχεία 'impregnation'); for not only did they go mad after women, and defile the marriage bed of others, but also those who were men (ἄνδρες) lusted after one another (ἄρρεσιν ἐπιβαίνοντες – 'male mounting'), doing unseemly things, and not regarding or respecting their common nature (φύσιν) . . . and so, by degrees, the men (ἄνδρας) became accustomed to be treated like women (θήλειαν – 'females') . . . as to effeminacy (μαλακότητι) and delicacy, became like women in their persons'.

Josephus was aware that he had a Roman patron and readers, though he also knew that most of them were disdainful of homosexual practices. So in the *Antiquities* he criticizes the Sodomites' lack of self-control and their disregard for rules of hospitality.

But the Sodomites, on seeing these young men of remarkably fair appearance whom Lot had taken under his roof, were bent only on violence and outrage to their youthful beauty. Lot adjured them to restrain their passions and not to proceed to dishonour his guests, but to respect their having lodged with him, offering in their stead, if his neighbours were so licentious, his own daughters to gratify their lust. But not even this would content them.[3]

However, in his apologetic work *Contra Apion*, he criticized homosexual practices in a more forthright manner.

199 What are our marriage laws? . . . Sodomy it abhors . . . (215) The penalty for most offences against the Law is death: for adultery, for violating an unmarried woman, for outrage upon a male, for consent of one so tempted to such abuse. The Law is no less inexorable for slaves. . . . (273) . . . the unnatural vice ('male intercourse').[4]

---

3. *Ant.* 1.200–201, Loeb. Whiston's translation follows the Greek in a more verbatim manner: 'Now, when the Sodomites saw the young men to be of beautiful countenances, and this to an extraordinary degree, and that they took up their lodgings with Lot, they resolved themselves to enjoy these beautiful boys by force and violence; (201) and when Lot exhorted them to sobriety (σωφρονεῖν – 'sound mind'), and not to offer anything immodest (αἰσχύνη – 'shameful') to the strangers, but to have regard to their lodging in his house; and promised, that if [their inclinations] could not be governed (ἀκρατῶς – 'were intoxicated'), he would expose his daughters to their lust instead of these strangers – neither thus were they made ashamed.' *The Works of Flavius Josephus*, tr. Whiston (1828).

4. C.Ap. 2.199–273. A more verbatim translation, with added square brackets to indicate the absence of any underlying Greek text: 'But then, what are our laws about marriage? . . . it abhors the mixture of a male (ἄρρενας) with a male (ἀρρένων); (215) Now the greatest part of offences with us are capital; as if anyone be guilty of adultery; if anyone force a virgin; if [anyone be so impudent as to attempt sodomy with] a male (ἄρρενι); or if, upon another's making an attempt upon him, he submits to be so used (παθεῖν ὁ πειρασθείς – 'he allows the attempt'). There is also a law for slaves of the like nature (ὁμοίως – 'similar'), that can never be avoided . . . (273) . . . that unnatural (παρὰ φύσιν) and impudent lust, which makes them lie with males (ἄρρενας μίξεως – 'male intercourse').' *Works of Flavius Josephus* (1828).

Josephus views the homosexual behaviour at Sodom as uncontrollably hedonistic and he regarded the men as heterosexuals because they might just as well have accepted Lot's daughters. When summarizing the laws, he makes such a close link between homosexual activity and heterosexual rape that they share the same verb: 'if anyone force a virgin or a male'. Just in case his readers regard this as referring only to homosexual rape, he adds that equal punishment applies to a man who 'allows the attempt'.[5] Surprisingly Josephus specifically adds that one may not even abuse a slave, which is certainly in the spirit of Jewish law, though no Roman reader was likely to agree with this restriction.

Aristeas summarizes Jewish law in a similar way but is more eager to show that most non-Jews are corrupt: 'The majority of other men defile themselves in their relationships, thereby committing a serious offense, and lands and whole cities take pride in it: they not only procure the males, they also defile mothers and daughters.'[6] Other early Jewish Greek literature is equally vehement against homosexual practices but it is generally less specific.

In Second Enoch the author is shown a cruel hell which is prepared for those guilty of all kinds of sins, but the first in the list is pederasty linked with Sodom: 'This place, Enoch, has been prepared for those who do not glorify God, who practice on the earth the sin which is against nature, which is child corruption in the anus in the manner of Sodom . . .'[7] The generation that was destroyed by the flood was characterized by adult homosexual partnerships:

God convicts the persons who are idol worshipers and sodomite fornicators and for this reason he brings down the flood upon them . . . but they began to worship vain gods, . . . and abominable fornications that is, friend with friend in the anus, and every other kind of wicked uncleanness which it is disgusting to report.[8]

---

5. Quotations respectively τις ἂν βιάσηται κόρην ἂν ἄρρενι and παθεῖν ὁ πειρασθείς.

6. Arist. 1.152 from James H. Charlesworth (ed.), *The Old Testament Pseudepigrapha*, 2 vols. (New York: Doubleday, 1983–5). The Greek text is followed in a more verbatim way in Robert Henry Charles (ed.), *The Apocrypha and Pseudepigrapha of the Old Testament in English: with Introductions and Critical and Explanatory Notes to the Several Books*, 2 vols. (Oxford: Clarendon Press, 1913). There it is translated: 'For most other men defile themselves by promiscuous (μολύνουσιν – 'impure') intercourse (ἐπιμισγόμενοι), thereby working great iniquity, and whole countries and cities pride themselves upon such vices. For they not only have intercourse with men but they defile their own mothers and even their daughters.'

7. Charlesworth, 2En. 10.4. Only MS P has 'in the anus'.

8. Charlesworth, 2En. 34.1–2. Only MS P has 'in the anus'.

Sibylline Oracles span a wide range of time and sometimes contain Christian redactions, but their consistent condemnation of homosexual activity has Jewish roots, even if it may be reinforced by Christian editing:

Do not practice homosexuality.[9]

[T]hey [Jews] do not engage in impious intercourse with male children.[10]

Neither have they [the righteous] disgraceful desire for another's spouse,
or for hateful and repulsive abuse of a male.[11]

With you [Rome] are found adulteries and illicit intercourse with boys.[12]

The Testaments of the Twelve also criticize homosexual behaviour at every opportunity.

[I]dolaters, adulterers, money lovers, arrogant, lawless, voluptuaries, pederasts,
those who practice bestiality.[13]

[Y]ou will be sexually promiscuous like the promiscuity of the Sodomites
and will perish, with few exceptions. You shall resume your actions with loose
women.[14]

Sodom, which did not recognize the Lord's angels and perished forever.[15]

They link this behaviour with hedonistic heterosexuality, both by association and by using the general term *porneia* (at T.Ben.9.1) to describe homosexual behaviour.

---

9. Charlesworth, Siby. 2.73. The Greek here (ἀρσενοκοιτεῖν) may indicate Christian influence because no use of this term is known outside the NT and its interpreters.

10. Charlesworth, Siby. 3.596: 'impious intercourse' translates ἀρσενικοὺς μίγνυνται, which may be influenced by the NT word ἀρσενοκοιτες.

11. Charlesworth, Siby. 4.34. The use of ἄρσενος ('male') is probably influenced by Lev. 20:13 (LXX).

12. Charlesworth, Siby. 5.166.

13. Charlesworth, T.Levi. 17.11.

14. Charlesworth, T.Ben. 9.1: 'pederasts' translates παιδοφθόροι.

15. Charlesworth, T.Ash. 7.1.

The most important testament in this regard is the Testament of Naphtali, because it uses very similar vocabulary and the same progression of reasoning as that found in Romans 1:24–27,[16] though that parallel is incidental to the subject of this chapter.

> The gentiles, because they wandered astray and forsook the Lord, have changed the order and have devoted themselves to stones and sticks, patterning themselves after wandering spirits. (4) But you, ... do not become like Sodom which departed from the order of nature (5) Likewise the Watchers departed from nature's order.[17]

Jubilees was popular at Qumran and probably in wider Judaism. Here too, homosexuality is associated with fornication and idolatry:

> And he told them the judgment of the giants and the judgments of the Sodomites just as they had been judged on account of their evil. And on account of their fornication and impurity and the corruption among themselves with fornication they died.[18]

> Just as the sons of Sodom were taken from the earth, so [too] all of those who worship idols shall be taken away.[19]

---

16. The phrase 'changed the order of their nature' used for both Sodom and the Watchers (ἐνήλλαξαν τάξιν φύσεως αὐτῶν, T.Naph. 3.3, 4) is mirrored in 'exchanged their natural function' (μετήλλαξαν τὴν φυσικὴν χρῆσιν – Rom. 1:26). In both accounts, this results from their pursuit of idolatry.

17. Charlesworth, T.Naph. 3.3–5. A more verbatim translation by Charlesworth better reflects the Greek 'changed their nature': 'The Gentiles went astray, and forsook the Lord, and changed (ἠλλοίωσαν from ἀλλοιόω) their order (τάξιν φύσεως αὐτῶν – 'order of their nature'), and obeyed sticks and stones, spirits of deceit. 4 But ye shall not be so, my children, recognizing in the firmament, in the earth, and in the sea, and in all created things, the Lord who made all things, that ye become not as Sodom, which changed (ἐνήλλαξε from ἐναλλάσσω) the order (τάξιν) of nature (τάξιν φύσεως αὐτῆς – 'order of their nature'). 5 In like manner the Watchers also changed (ἐνήλλαξαν) the order of their nature (τάξιν φύσεως αὐτῶν), whom the Lord cursed at the flood, on whose account He made the earth without inhabitants and fruitless.'

18. Charlesworth, Jub. 20.5.

19. Charlesworth, Jub. 22.22.

The Sentences of Pseudo-Phocylides appears to be a list of laws that the author felt were applicable in a universal way to Jews and Gentiles alike. These included:

> (188) Do not seek sexual union with irrational animals. (189) Do not outrage [your] wife by shameful ways of intercourse. (190) Do not transgress with unlawful sex the limits set by nature (191) For even animals are not pleased by intercourse of male with male. (192) And let women not imitate the sexual role of men.[20]

The common feature in all these sources is an utter contempt and condemnation for homosexual behaviour, which is specifically linked to other hedonistic behaviour in most instances.[21] The behaviour is sometimes defined, using terms such as 'in the anus', 'man-bedding', 'man mounting males', 'male with a male', 'intercourse with men', 'allowing the attempt' (i.e. allowing penetration), and pederasty.[22]

What were these Jews condemning?

These sources clearly condemn homosexual acts, though they referred primarily to the common Roman practice of sex with slaves, hired boys or young men. Most moral codes condemn any sexual behaviour that is harmful to others, which would include pederasty and forced homosexual or heterosexual sex.

---

20. Charlesworth, P.Phoc. 188–192. The Greek is translated in a more verbatim manner in Craig E. Evans *et al.*, *The Pseudepigrapha (English)* (OakTree Software, 2008), consulted in BibleWorks 10 where P.Phoc. 186–192 is: 'Nor lay your hand upon your wife when pregnant. (187) Nor cut a youth's male reproductive nature. (188) Nor to engage in sexual activity with unreasoning creatures. (189) Nor outrage [your] wife in shameless sexual activity. (190) Do not transgress (παραβῇς – 'overstep') with sex (εὐνὰς – 'bedding') that is of a nature (φύσεως) in wicked (ἄθεσμον – 'lawless') Cypris. (191) Not even animals are pleased with (συνεύαδον from συνανδάνω) sex involving male with male (ἄρσενες εὐναι – 'male bedding'). (192) Nor let women imitate the sexual activity (λέχος – 'marriage bed') of men (ἀνδρῶν).'

21. Abr. 1.135–136; *Ant.* 1.200–201; C.Ap. 2.199–273; Arist. 1.152; T.Levi. 17.11; T.Ben. 9.1; Jub. 20.5; P.Phoc. 188–192.

22. For the seven terms listed, see respectively: (a) MS P of 2En. 10.4; 34.2; (b) Siby. 2.73; P.Phoc. 188–192; (c) Abr. 1.135–136; (d) C.Ap. 2.199–273; (e) Arist. 1.152; Siby. 3.596; (f) C.Ap. 2.199–273; (g) Siby. 2.73; Siby. 3.596; Siby. 5.166; T.Levi. 17.11.

Roman law allowed forced sex with slaves, but even in Roman society this was looked down on.

Modern moral codes also condemn any sexual behaviour that is regarded as self-harming, and this can include treating another person as an object, even if he or she consented to this. This includes prostitution and possibly promiscuous behaviour based on casual pairings that do not include the forming of any personal relationship. In this regard, most morally-minded people would agree with these early Jewish condemnations of homosexual behaviour.

However, the unanswered question is whether ancient Jews condemned homosexual inclinations, and whether they allowed any consensual homosexual relationships. It is too easy to assume that the condemnation of one type of homosexual practice (such as hedonistic bi-sexuality) implicitly includes all related practices. Clearly we cannot expect each author to list every offence, so how can we infer what they are implicitly including?

In these sources, the behaviour named is normally the worst kinds of offences: bestiality, pederasty and homosexual hedonism that is often related to heterosexual hedonism. This leaves us asking whether they are implicitly including or excluding a condemnation of committed homosexual relationships?

This question, which is perhaps more important today than it was in the first century, cannot be answered with these texts, because there is no indication that any of these authors considered this option or even recognized that some individuals have an innate orientation. The only reference to a consistent homosexual inclination is found in Philo who theorized that men taking part in homosexual behaviour gradually became feminized (*malakos*, Abr.1. 135–136). However, in the rabbinic text that we will now consider, we find that first-century Jews were indeed aware that some individuals had an innate homosexual inclination, whether or not this was expressed in any homosexual activity.

Rabbinic traditions against pederasty, bestiality and homosexuality

Mishnah Kiddushin 4.13 contains a tradition that appears to assume innate homosexual tendencies in some men: 'Two unmarried men may not sleep together under the same cover.' This rule does not apply to married men, so it apparently makes a distinction between those who are likely to be heterosexual and those who may have homosexual inclinations because they have not yet shown themselves to be heterosexual. The remarkable implication is that this does not refer to hedonistic homosexual activity, because in that case it would prohibit married as well as unmarried men. It appears to recognize that there exists a class of men who are not interested in heterosexual sex, but may be tempted by taking part in homosexual activities.

This throws up all kinds of questions about the underlying assumptions. Why did the framers of this law think that unmarried men were more likely to take part in homosexual activities than married men? Singleness was certainly unusual among Jews,[23] and it was likely to be caused by refusing brides that had been chosen for them, so this may indicate they did not desire women. But did the rabbis not realize that those with homosexual inclinations might want to hide this fact by marrying? Perhaps they thought that someone with a homosexual orientation was incapable of heterosexual intercourse.[24]

Whatever the degree of their understanding, the interesting point is the assumption that underlies this ruling: that a person could have innate and consistent homosexual desires, whether or not they were acted upon.

Context of the tradition

The apparent plain meaning of this law is rejected by some modern and ancient Talmudic interpreters. We therefore have to explore its meaning in context, and then examine the ancient counter-interpretations. In orthodox Judaism the later sources such as Talmud are more important and authoritative than the earlier ones such as Mishnah. However, the purpose of this paper is to uncover the views prevalent as close as possible to the first century, for which the original meaning of the Mishnah is more important than its later interpretations.

The context of a passage in Mishnah is normally useful for confirming the subject matter and the meaning of vocabulary, at least as far as the framers of Mishnah were concerned when those passages were arranged in the order that we now have. The overall structure is very ancient, and certainly goes back to the first century CE, because all ancient collections of halakhic materials

---

23. The evidence for this is summarized well in Brian S. Rosner, *Paul, Scripture and Ethics* (Leiden: Brill, 1994), pp. 155–9. Boys were expected to be married at 12 (Lam.R. 1.2; cf. yQid. 1.7, 61a). These texts are relatively late, but there is nothing to suggest that this teaching had changed. The teaching about unmarried men (dealt with below) assumes that this was a rare condition.

24. Plutarch assumed that some men were 'unable or unwilling' to engage in heterosexual sex, in 'To Pollianus and Eurydice' 8 (in the middle of a discussion of effeminate men): 'Some men, either unable or unwilling to mount themselves into their saddles through infirmity or laziness, teach their horses to fall upon their knees, and in that posture to receive their riders.' *Plutarch's Morals*, ed. and tr. William W. Goodwin (Boston: Little, Brown, and Co., 1870).

(i.e. the Mishnah, Tosephta and Talmuds) follow the same overall plan. The material is divided into about sixty tractates, each dealing with separate subjects, and subdivided into chapters of sub-topics. Some traditions may not relate directly to the subject of the chapter they occur in, especially in Talmudic sources where comments on one subject may lead into others. However, the Mishnah and Tosephta follow these subject divisions fairly well, except for the ends of chapters where apparently random traditions sometimes accumulated.

Chapter 4 of Kiddushin concerns those who may not be betrothed or sleep together or even meet together without a chaperone. The first half deals with those who can marry an Israelite or a priest because they have a confirmed heritage, and also those who can marry a *mamzer*, i.e. someone who may have Gentile or illegitimate ancestry (4.1–11). This section is of interest to New Testament scholars because it is likely that Jesus' singleness was due to his status as an unofficial *mamzer*,[25] which meant that he could neither marry a pure Israelite nor an official *mamzer*. Another tradition in this chapter (m.Qid. 4.9) assumes that ending a betrothal required a divorce, which helps explain Joseph's intention (cf. Matt. 1:19). The second half of this chapter deals with whether a man can be alone with women (4.12), and whether an unmarried man can be alone with children or animals, or sleep under the same sheet as another man (4.12–14).

The last section (4.14) has been expanded by a tangential discussion concerning trades that require a man to meet with women, and debates about whether these and other trades are desirable. An interesting parallel with Jesus' teaching is included in this debate. When affirming that God will provide sufficient income whatever one's trade, they ask rhetorically: 'Have you ever seen a wild beast or a bird with a craft? Yet they are sustained without anxiety.' Although this saying is attributed to R. Simeon b. Eleazar who taught in the late second century CE, the parallels with Jesus' sayings (Matt. 6:26 // Luke 12:24) clearly suggest that either Simeon is reliant on Jesus, or (more likely) they are both reliant on a common theme. This illustrates the difficulty of dating rabbinic traditions. When a tradition is attributed to a particular rabbi during a debate, it indicates that this rabbi applied that tradition within this debate, and not necessarily that this rabbi was the origin of that tradition.

The immediate context of the ruling about unmarried men sleeping with

---

25. Chilton thinks that Jesus may have been considered an official *mamzer* in Galilee though not in Judea where the rules were slightly different (m.Ket. 1.5). See Bruce Chilton, 'Jésus, le mamzer (Mt 1.18)', *NTS* 47 (2001), pp. 222–7.

each other is a group of other rulings about unmarried men in Mishnah Kiddushin 4.13b–14a.[26] The differences in indentation are an indication of probable dating, as described below.

> An unmarried man must not be an elementary teacher
>> Nor may a woman be an elementary teacher
>> R. Eleazar [mid second century] said: one also who has no wife must not be an elementary teacher.
>> R. Judah [mid second century] said: an unmarried man must not tend cattle
> Nor may two unmarried men sleep together under the same cover
>> But the Sages permit it.

The unmarried man (*rawwoq*) may not be a teacher of elementary pupils (*sōpĕrîm*) – i.e. he must not teach writing, which was taught only to the youngest pupils. Also, he may not tend any 'cattle' (*bĕhēmah*) – a word used for domestic animals including sheep, goats and cows, though also sometimes of birds and wild animals. The word is feminine though it is used for both sexes. Also, two unmarried men may not sleep under a single cloak (*ṭallît*) – a wide piece of cloth that is doubled when worn, but can be spread out to cover two people sleeping closely together.

Development of the tradition
The indented layout of the tradition indicates a proposed history of its development. A greater indent indicates lines that are likely to have been added later. The earliest rulings are likely to be the ones forbidding unmarried men from teaching children and sleeping under the same cloak. The others all have indications of being reliant upon or responding to what preceded. The ruling about women teachers is out of place logically, but it is understandable as an expansion or wider application of the preceding ruling about men teachers. The response by R. Eleazar removes an inherent ambiguity concerning men whose marriage has ended due to death or divorce. There is no internal evidence that the ruling about tending cattle is a later addition, but the fact that the contributor is named may suggest this. On the other hand, R. Judah

---

26. Or 4.12-13 in some editions. לא ילמד רווק סופרים, ולא תלמד אישה סופרים רבי אלעזר
אומר, אף מי שאין עימו אישה, לא ילמד סופרים רבי יהודה אומר, לא ירעה רווק בהמה, ולא יישנו
שני רווקים בטלית אחת וחכמים מתירין

was known for preserving ancient traditions that might otherwise have been lost.[27]

The reference to 'the Sages' who rescind the ruling about sleeping under a single sheet indicates the outcome of a vote by scholars who later discussed this issue. The probable reasons for this revision are seen in the later discussions recorded in the Babylonian Talmud Kiddushin 82a:

> (Concerning the ruling about not teaching children):
>   What is the reason? Shall we say, on account of the children?
>   Surely it was taught: 'They said to R. Judah: Israel are not suspected
>   of either pederasty or bestiality'?
>   But an unmarried man [is forbidden] on account of the children's
>   mothers, and a woman on account of their fathers.
> R. Eleazar said: One also who has no wife.
>   The scholars propounded: [Does it mean,] one who has no wife at all,
>   or whose wife does not live with him?
>   Come and hear: Also one who has a wife but she does not live with
>   him may not be an elementary teacher.
> R. Judah said: an unmarried man must not tend etc.
>   It was taught: 'They said to R. Judah: Israel is suspected of neither
>   pederasty nor bestiality.'

This records debates on three rulings: not teaching children, the extension of this ruling to men who had been married, and not tending animals. The second one removes a further ambiguity: Eleazar had already clarified that 'unmarried' included previously married men, and now it is extended to any man whose wife is not living with him. This is presented as an unopposed decision ('Come and hear'). The two other issues are both answered using the same tradition: an assertion that no Israelite should be suspected of pederasty or bestiality. That tradition is not dated, but it is introduced as something that was spoken to (not by) R. Judah (i.e. in the mid second century), which indicates that he is passing on a tradition that he has learned.

---

27. For example, his ruling about the wording of a divorce certificate at m.Git. 9:3 is recorded nowhere else in rabbinic literature, but we now know that it was an independent ancient tradition because the same wording was used in a divorce certificate of 72 CE preserved at Masada. See Tal Ilan, 'Notes and Observations on a Newly Published Divorce Bill from the Judaean Desert', *HTR* 89 (1996), pp. 195–202.

The rule about unmarried men sleeping under the same sheet, which was rescinded by the Sages in Mishnah, is not discussed in Talmud presumably because it was regarded as overturned and irrelevant.

This chain of traditions therefore covers at least three generations. The middle one can be dated to the mid second century because it involved two named rabbis from that time. We will refer to the former and latter as first century and third century, though we must remain aware that these are very general dates.

These traditions condemn three activities that we have also found in Jewish Greek condemnations of Gentile sexuality. Most of the passages that contain detailed condemnations of homosexual behaviour also include references to pederasty and bestiality (2En. 10.4; T.Levi. 17.11; P.Phoc. 188–191). It appears that Jews not only linked these activities but may have assumed that the same people took part in all of them.

However, by the mid second century it was assumed that the rule against homosexual activity was no longer required in regulations written for Jews, and by the third century it was also unimaginable that bestiality or pederasty would be committed by an Israelite.

This created a problem for these later rabbis because they needed to explain why such rules had been required for Jews in the first place. If all children, animals and unmarried young men were safe among all Israelites, why were these restrictions placed on unmarried Israelite men?

With regard to tending cattle, they argued that what the rule really meant was that fathers should not encourage their unmarried sons to learn this trade. It was an undesirable trade like the others listed after these rules (m.Qid. 4.14), because it might cause you to work on a Sabbath. They were able to ignore the ruling about men sleeping close to each other because previous Sages had already rescinded this ruling, and because they were interested in religious rules, not in historical research.

It was more difficult to explain why unmarried men should not teach young children. There was nothing demeaning about this occupation, especially as it was associated with other higher and more honoured forms of education. Their solution was that this rule was made 'on account of the children's mothers'. That is, young children were brought by mothers who might not be accompanied by other adults. This meant that the unmarried men might be alone (other than the presence of their child who was not a legal witness) with mothers. These later rabbis concluded that this was the reason why single men should not teach young children, and that it had nothing to do with the potential temptation towards pederasty. They do not attempt to explain why the same situation would not be problematic for a married man.

The tradition in the first century

As a result of the above analysis, we can make some conclusions about the progressive growth of this tradition. In the first century, the text would have consisted of the three rulings:

> An unmarried man must not be an elementary teacher.
> An unmarried man must not tend cattle.
> Nor may two unmarried men sleep together under the
> same cover.

This inclusion of the second ruling at this time relies on the assumption that R. Judah was reminding the others of an ancient tradition that had been omitted at this point. Judah was certainly a repository of traditions. Most of his sayings consist of his own opinion about an issue being debated, as is the case with most rabbis. However, he occasionally inserted a neglected ruling at relevant points, which might otherwise have been lost. One way to recognize the difference is when Judah presents a complete ruling instead of adding his opinion to the ruling being discussed. For example, in this ruling, Judah could have said: 'Nor tend cattle', but instead he unnecessarily adds the start of the ruling 'An unmarried man must not . . .'. This stands out in stark contrast to the highly abbreviated nature of rabbinic comments, and makes him look verbose or even clumsy, unless he was interjecting a complete tradition that was not his own.

One of countless examples of R. Judah's normal rabbinic comments is at Mishnah Berakhot 4.1: 'The morning prayer [may be recited] until midday. R. Judah says, Until the fourth hour.' Examples where Judah preserves a complete tradition (as he does here) are much rarer. One example occurs in the list of blessings spoken on various occasions, where Judah adds 'He who sees the Great [Mediterranean] Sea says, "Blessed is he who made the Great Sea"'. If this was merely a contribution of his own, it would have been normal to summarize this by omitting 'He who sees', as done in the preceding items in the list after these words have occurred in the first one (m.Ber. 9.1–2). The fact that he cites the unabbreviated version suggests he is reciting an independent tradition that he had received in this form. Similarly in Mishnah Demai, after the ruling 'He who leases a field from a Gentile separates tithes and [then] gives to him [his rent]', R. Judah adds 'Also he who sharecrops his father's field for a Gentile separates tithes and [then] gives to him [his rent]' (m.Dem. 6.2). This addition is surprising because it unnecessarily repeats much of the preceding ruling. He could have been recorded as simply saying: 'Also he who sharecrops his father's field from a Gentile'. The fact that the ruling is transmitted in full implies that he is repeating something that he has received in this form.

Rabbinic assumptions about homosexuality

These three rulings are clearly related to the kinds of sins that other Jews recognized among Gentiles. Later rabbis assumed that no fellow Jew would ever commit such acts, so they reinterpreted these rules. However, this triad of rules, avoiding being alone with children, animals and single young men, is surely related to the same triad of deviant sexual behaviour that Jewish Greek literature condemned – pederasty, bestiality and homosexuality – and their alternative explanations are not convincing.

It may be worth asking why the ruling about two adult single males sleeping next to each other was the first to be regarded as unnecessary. Probably it was assumed that they would be a guard to each other. This is similar to an immediately preceding ruling, 'A man may not be alone with two women, but one woman may be alone with two men' (m.Qid. 4.12). Perhaps the best way to appreciate this is with the old joke about why you never take a Southern Baptist on a fishing trip: because he'll drink all your beer. Instead you should take two Southern Baptists because then neither of them will drink any beer. It was considered much more likely that someone would attempt deviant behaviour when it could not be legally reported by another man.

The assumptions behind these first-century rulings are that homosexual acts and the behaviour that they associated with this might occur even among Israelites. The type of rules that they created were not punishments for this behaviour or lists of evidence by which the crime might be proved, but preventative measures. It appears that they were hopeful, perhaps realistically, that these rules would stop these offences ever happening.

These rules also presume that the only persons likely to be tempted in this way were unmarried males. Whether or not this was accurate, the assumption behind this is remarkable. They assumed that these temptations occurred only to a small group of people who were not interested in heterosexual sex. In other words they regarded these people as having consistently non-heterosexual inclinations.

Also, there appears to be no interest in identifying these individuals in order to ostracize them from Jewish society. They merely wanted to make sure that they were not put into situations where they might be tempted to act on their inclinations. This implies that they would be happy to let them teach adults, or work on their farm crops, and even to share a bed with them. These were not homophobic rulings, but rules helping fellow Israelites who had this specific set of temptations, to live within the rules of Torah.

Conclusions from rabbinic and non-rabbinic attitudes

It would be easy to jump to the conclusion that rabbinic and non-rabbinic Judaism had very different attitudes, but that would be difficult to substantiate. Although rabbinic traditions are recorded in a very different way to Jewish Greek literature, we cannot therefore conclude that they represented completely divergent types of Jews. Jews such as Philo, Josephus, Aristeas and the sectarians who treasured books such as Jubilees and the Testaments were all seeking to obey the Torah. Minor differences in their interpretations concerning the calendar and purity laws created huge rifts between them, but there is no reason to believe that their attitude to homosexuality was affected by these distinctions.

The significant difference between Jewish Greek writings and rabbinic traditions was their subject matter and their readership. The Greek works were to be read by Gentiles and by Jews immersed in the Graeco-Roman culture. A strong condemnation of hedonistic homosexual behaviour was meant to both condemn the Gentiles and to remind Jews of their distinctive superiority. In contrast, the rabbinic traditions record academic and legal debates in schoolrooms and courtrooms. They faced up to the fact that some Jews might indeed fall into these same sins if they were not helped to avoid them.

These two sets of literature are not contradictory: they utterly condemned any acts of homosexual sex, bestiality or pederasty. They were also both written with the realization that a few Jews were tempted in these directions. However, they did not regard these sexual temptations or inclinations as sinful without the act, but regarded them like any other sinful inclinations that all humans have. So they dealt with this temptation in the same way as the general inclination to break Torah commands: they built a fence. That is, they created additional rules to help prevent individuals from stepping over a line that might lead to breaking a divine commandment.

From this evidence, we have to conclude that first-century Jews did regard some individuals as having innate non-heterosexual inclinations. That is, they would be tempted by homosexual and related behaviour if the opportunity arose. They did not seek to identify these individuals in order to isolate them or punish them, but instead they tried to help them avoid temptation. At the same time, they utterly condemned homosexual acts, which they saw Gentiles committing, even when they didn't have the excuse of this inclination. They emphasized the point that they lacked this mitigating inclination by accusing these same individuals of heterosexual immorality.

Although the evidence from rabbinic traditions is extremely thin, it is consistent with what we know from elsewhere, albeit representing the situation from a different angle. It is possible that much of the population was unaware of the insight that these rabbis had, but these rules had to be public in order for them to be effective, so this approach was not a secret. This suggests the rabbis' non-condemnatory attitude towards these individuals must have been widely recognized.

We conclude that the loud condemnation of pederasty, bestiality and homosexual hedonism was not a sign of homophobia. Rabbinic rules in the first century assumed that even Jewish young men had inclinations in those directions, and were designed to help them avoid such temptations. There is no evidence that these individuals were ostracized or treated differently in any other regard.

© David Instone-Brewer, 2017

10. MARRIAGE IN EARLY, CHRISTIAN AND AFRICAN PERSPECTIVES

Onesimus Ngundu

In Africa, a Shona proverb says *Aiva madziva ave mazambuko*, 'Pools once uncross-able have now become crossing points'. For marriage, a significant change came when the British Parliament passed the Civil Partnership Act in 2004 and the Marriage (Same Sex Couples) Act in 2013. This was a departure from the previously universal understanding and practice of marriage. Parliament, which has had jurisdiction over marriage in Britain since the seventeenth century, had previously defined it as 'the voluntary union for life of one man and one woman, to the exclusion of all others'. This new legislation has now divided churches and society.

Long before either church or state gained jurisdiction over marriage, it was the responsibility of parents to regulate their children's marriages. When Protestant theologians rejected the Catholic sacramental theology of marriage, they turned to the state to regulate Christian marriage. But should marriage ever have been solemnized by either church or state? This chapter will highlight key aspects of both civil and church marriage traditions, the problems they have posed in Africa, and a creative way forward.

Early perspectives

Jesus and Judaism

Jesus affirms to the Pharisees that marriage occurs between a man and a woman (Matt. 19:3–9; Mark 10:2–12). He recalls how at creation God made humankind 'male and female' (citing Gen. 1:27; cf. 5:2) and the outcome: 'For this reason, a man shall leave his father and mother and be joined to his wife, and the two shall become one flesh' (Matt. 19:5; citing Gen. 2:24).[1] Jesus clearly attributes the words of the Genesis author to God himself, noting that the one man and one woman relationship was designed by God as the marriage structure for humankind. Jesus also affirms that marriage is a binding commitment or covenant: 'Therefore what God has joined together, let no one separate' (Matt. 19:6).[2] A marriage was public in that the man would clearly leave his parents. Various Old Testament marriage accounts provide evidence of its formal recognition, with careful preparation (Gen. 24) and celebration (Gen. 29; Judg. 14:10–12). Finally, marriage was completed by sexual consummation with the goal of producing offspring (Gen. 1 – 2). In summary, a valid marriage should be characterized by life commitment, public celebration and sexual consummation.[3] How has this blueprint for marriage fared over the centuries in different cultures?

In Jesus' time, a valid marriage contract had two parts, betrothal and wedding, with up to a year between them. Both ceremonies took place in homes, never in the synagogue or temple. The couple became legally bound in marriage at their betrothal ceremony (cf. Mary as Joseph's 'wife', Matt. 1:18), but didn't live together as husband and wife until their marriage ceremony.[4] In Semitic cultures generally, after betrothal and presentation of the *mohar* or bride price by the groom to the bride's father, 'the woman would henceforth be referred to as the wife and the man as the husband'.[5] So the customary mutual declaration of betrothal (cf. Gen. 24:49–55; Deut. 20:7; Judg. 14:7–10) was in fact a serious commitment to a valid marriage relationship.

There is no evidence that Jews viewed their customary marriage as a universal pattern of marriage to be imposed on converts. Whatever arguments are proposed for church marriage ceremonies, they cannot legitimately claim Judaism as their authority, because 'matrimony, being a private affair of the parties and of their respective families, required no public ceremony, religious

---

1. All biblical translations in this chapter are from the NRSV.

2. William Heth and Gordon Wenham, *Jesus and Divorce* (Carlisle: Paternoster, 1997), pp. 1–3.

3. Andrew Cornes, *Divorce and Remarriage: Biblical Principles and Pastoral Practice* (London: Hodder & Stoughton, 1993), p. 41.

4. Marcus Braybrooke, *How to Understand Judaism* (London: SCM, 1995), p. 34.

5. Ephraim Neufeld, *Ancient Hebrew Marriage Laws* (New York: Longmans, Green and Co, 1944), p. 43.

or otherwise, for its legalisation'.[6] The institution of marriage was never a matter for the priesthood.

The Old Testament narrators present God as involved in such non-religious social marriage ceremonies and celebrations: God provides a wife for Adam; he leads Abraham's servant to a wife for Isaac; he directs Ruth to Boaz, etc. Similarly, Jesus socialized with people at the marriage celebration of Cana.[7] Throughout the medieval period Jewish betrothal and marriage ceremonies continued to take place at the home of the bride's parents, with witnesses and a banquet. Wedding days became a meaningful occasion for young couples, their parents and the entire community. A later combining of betrothal and marriage ceremonies meant that the wedding days specified in the Talmud were no longer of consequence. Instead, the general custom was to celebrate weddings on Fridays, just before the Sabbath, when people were free to join in the festivities.[8]

If Jesus had been asked about polygamy as he was about divorce, he may well have made a similar appeal to God's original purpose of marriage. Just as divorce was known among Israelites from Moses' time onwards, so polygamy is an issue in some modern societies, notably in sub-Saharan Africa. In his dialogue with the Pharisees, Jesus refused to justify divorce because it violated the principles of marriage as originally designed by God. In the same way, any attempt to justify or defend polygamy, either on the basis of its common practice or as a reaction to the ruthless treatment of converted African polygamists by many European missionaries, falls short of biblical principles of marriage. According to Jesus, any wife taken in addition to a man's first wife constitutes adultery (Matt. 5:32).

If Jesus had been asked about same-sex marriages as he was about divorce, he may well have made a similar appeal to God's original design of marriage as between a man and a woman. Just as divorce was known among Israelites, so same-sex marriages have become a burning issue in Western societies. Just as Jesus refused to justify divorce since it violated principles of marriage as originally designed by God, so he would not approve of same-sex marriage today.

---

6. Neufeld, *Ancient Hebrew Marriage Laws*, p. 149.

7. Schillebeeckx has accused other Catholic scholars of wrongly using Jesus' presence at a wedding feast to imply that he thus inaugurated a universal spiritualization of the marriage ceremony itself. Edward Schillebeeckx, *Marriage: Human Reality and Saving Mystery* (London: Sheed and Ward, 1965), p. 109.

8. Abraham Bloch, *The Biblical and Historical Background of Jewish Customs and Ceremonies* (New York: Ktav, 1980), pp. 29f.

Rome

In traditional Roman society, *matrimonium* meant that a man married a woman to be a mother of their legitimate children as free-born Romans. Betrothal, solemnly conducted by the respective fathers, was the first step and served as important evidence of the intention to marry. There should not be any cohabitation or sexual relations before marriage, as noted in the common saying, 'The bed of a virgin is approachable only through marriage'.[9]

On the wedding day the girl's father would hand her to her husband in the presence of formal witnesses. The groom would give his bride either a ring or some gold.[10] The ring had symbolized to the Egyptians the conferral of possessions, but to the Romans it became a symbol of the cycle of life, and was worn on the third finger of the left hand. The bride would then be led in procession to her new home, while guests made suggestive jokes. On arrival, the bride would be initiated into her groom's family religion by repeating ritual prayers to the god of her new home. In this sense, solemnizing a marriage was also a religious act. The marriage celebration or wedding banquet would follow, including a sacred cake.

Pre-Christian Britain

Among the Celtic people of Britain, the main method by which a man would establish an indisputable claim to the sole possession of a woman as his wife was by capturing her. Marriage by capture continued at least until the reign of Ethelbert, King of Kent (552–616), who outlawed it as an act of theft. Marriage by purchase eventually replaced it. In theory, the bride price was compensation for the economic loss to a family at the marriage of their daughter. But it became so expensive that 'many a poor fellow was unable to marry at all'.[11] Marriage by elopement was one way to avoid it. In practice, girls were viewed as the property of their fathers. The Saxon legislators, many of whose marriage practices were later adopted by the church, eventually declared marriage by purchase illegal.

The later common law of marriage can be traced back to the Norman Conquest, and the British adoption of Roman customary marriage law has been

---

9. Joseph McCabe, *The Influence of the Church on Marriage and Divorce* (London: Watts, 1916), p. 8; Angeliki E. Laiou (ed.), *Consent and Coercion to Sex and Marriage in Ancient and Medieval Societies* (Washington DC: Dumbarton Oaks Research Library and Collection, 1993), p. 117.

10. McCabe, *Influence of the Church*, p. 9.

11. George E. Howard, *A History of Matrimonial Institutions Chiefly in England and the United States* (Chicago: University of Chicago Press, 1904), vol. 1, p. 189.

described as 'one of the greatest seizures of social power in history'.[12] As elsewhere, the traditions of indigenous and invading tribes became intertwined in both law and practice.

Christian perspectives

The early church
As far as we know, early Christians followed traditional marriage practice. An important second-century document certainly suggests this:

> For Christians are not distinguished from the rest of mankind either in locality or in speech or in customs. For they dwell not somewhere in cities of their own, neither do they use some different language, nor practise an extraordinary kind of life. They follow the native customs in dress and food and the other arrangements of life. They marry like all other men and they beget children; but they do not cast away their offspring.[13]

Christian leaders like Tertullian and John Chrysostom did not fault customary marriages as the way to enter into legitimate marriage,[14] though they encouraged Christians to replace vulgar language with psalms and hymns. Tertullian first used the phrase 'Christian marriage' in reference to two baptized Christians, male and female, sharing the same faith, jointly participating in the eucharist, practising Christian charity, and praying together at home.[15]

Priestly marriage blessing is first attested in the late fourth-century papacy of Damasus I.[16] This domestic liturgy prayed for offspring for the new couple, and was therefore offered in the bedroom. But the validity of marriage was still wholly vested in the customary ceremony, not in a priestly blessing.[17] Clerical participation and benedictions were not necessary to make marriages of Christians

---

12. John McMurtry, 'Monogamy', *The Monist Journal* (1972), p. 592.

13. Joseph B. Lightfoot, 'The Epistle to Diognetus', in John R. Harmer (ed.), *The Apostolic Fathers* (London: Macmillan, 1891), pp. 503–11. The epistle's writer and recipient are both unknown; estimates of dating range from early to late second century, with the latter now preferred.

14. Stanley L. Greenslade, *Early Latin Theology* (London: SCM, 1956), p. 102.

15. Schillebeeckx, *Marriage*, p. 254.

16. Ibid., p. 250.

17. George H. Joyce, *Christian Marriage: An Historical and Doctrinal Study*, 2nd edn (London: Steed and Ward, 1948), p. 90; Schillebeeckx, *Marriage*, p. 251.

valid and legitimate. In sixth-century Byzantium the Justinian Codex stipulated that both parties needed to consent to marriage, and also introduced the marriage certificate, a major improvement in the legal position of married women.[18]

The Middle Ages

With the fall of the Western Roman Empire and the gradually waning influence of Roman culture, the medieval church eventually 'claimed an unprecedented jurisdiction – power to proclaim and enforce law'.[19] As John Witte comments:

> In the Middle Ages, the church was not merely a voluntary association of like-minded believers gathered for worship. Its canon law was not simply an internal code of spiritual discipline to guide the faithful. The church was the one universal sovereign of the West that governed all of Christendom. The canon law was the one universal law of the West that was common to jurisdictions and peoples throughout Europe. The great nation-states of Western Europe were not yet born. The Catholic Church with its canon law held pre-eminent authority.[20]

Through its popes and canon law the medieval church began to make pronouncements on marriage.[21] After William the Conqueror became the first Norman king of England in 1066, he declared that canon law and common law should not be dispensed in the same courts.[22] This separation gave rise to the process by which the church and its clergy made marriage their own special province, and thus raised the question of whether marriage was a spiritual or a social matter.[23]

---

18. Laiou, *Consent and Coercion*, p. 113; Andrew Borkowski, *Textbook on Roman Law* (London: Blackstone Press, 1994), p. 122.

19. Harold J. Berman, *Law and Revolution: The Formation of the Western Legal Tradition* (Cambridge, MA: Harvard University Press, 1983), p. 221.

20. John Witte, *From Sacrament to Contract: Marriage, Religion, and Law in the Western Tradition* (Louisville: Westminster John Knox, 1997), p. 30.

21. Francis G. Morrisey, *The Canon Law: A Practical Guide to the Code of Canon Law* (London: G. Chapman, 1995), p. 1. The Greek word *kanon* originally meant a rod for measuring or rectifying the crooked; the term 'canon' was later adopted to mean a rule of belief or conduct decreed by the Catholic Church.

22. Jack Goody, *The Development of Marriage and the Family in Europe* (Cambridge: Cambridge University Press, 1983), p. 150.

23. Medieval marriage is examined anthropologically by Goody, *Development of Marriage*, and theologically by James A. Brundage, *Law, Sex, and Christian Society in Medieval*

Since then, theologians, historians, lawyers and politicians have tried to explain marriage as one or the other. Eventually in the early nineteenth century Lord Stowell laid down that it was both: 'Marriage is not merely either a civil or a religious contract, and is not to be considered as originally and simply one or the other.'[24] But whether social or spiritual, marriage has always been recognized as a binding relationship between a man and a woman.

For centuries, popes gave judgment on practical marital questions arising from Christian mission.[25] It took centuries to determine at what point a man and a woman should be considered married. In 866 Pope Nicholas I told a delegation from Bulgaria that it was at the time of mutual consent. However, in 1140 the father of canon law Pope Gratian spoke of a marriage contract in two stages, initiated at consent and ratified in sexual intercourse. This two-stage view was soon challenged by Peter Lombard, who argued that consent alone made marriage.[26] Pope Alexander III then resolved this by decreeing that consent was all that mattered.[27] The striking thing about Alexander's rules is what they did *not* require: whether consent of anyone else (parents or feudal lords) or ceremony or witnesses.[28] This resulted in problems with clandestine

---

Europe (Chicago: University of Chicago Press 1987); idem, *Sex, Law and Marriage in the Middle Ages* (Aldershot: Variorum, 1993); idem, *Medieval Canon Law* (London: Longman, 1995).

24. James T. Hammick, *The Marriage Law of England* (London: Shaw, 1873), p. 2.

25. For instance: For how long after childbirth should couples abstain from intercourse? What were the permissible degrees of kinship? What can be done if a wife is permanently prevented by illness from sexual relations? Is intercourse permissible on a Sunday? Cf. Richard Fletcher, *The Conversion of Europe: From Paganism to Christianity 371–1386* (London: HarperCollins, 1997), pp. 279–84.

26. *Magistri Petri Lombardi Sententiae in IV libris distinctae* (Grottaferrata: Editiones Collegii S. Bonaventurae ad Claras Aquas, 1971–81).

27. Richard H. Helmholz, *The Oxford History of the Laws of England, Vol. 1, The Canon Law and Ecclesiastical Jurisdiction from 597 to the 1640s* (Oxford: Oxford University Press, 2004), p. 524.

28. Charles Donahue, 'The Dating of Alexander the Third's Marriage Decretals', *Zeitschrift der Savigny-Stiftung für Rechtsgeschichte: Kanonistische Abteilung* 99 (1982), pp. 69–124; idem, 'The Canon Law on the Formation of Marriage and Social Practice in the Later Middle Ages', *Journal of Family History* (Summer 1983), pp. 144f.; Helmholz, *The Laws of England*, p. 524.

or secret marriages.[29] However, if one party later denied that the marriage had taken place, the other party would have to prove it, and church courts generally required two witnesses to prove any proposition.[30]

Alexander's rules were more than a synthesis of previous views on marriage. They represented a vision of what marriage ought to be, far from the reality of the time. The church did not encourage customary or clandestine marriages, but it left the door open for them. In Britain it would take the Act for the Better Preventing of Clandestine Marriage of 1753 to outlaw secret marriages.

In response to the Manichean tendencies of the Cathar and Albigensian heresies, which condemned all marriage unions as fundamentally evil,[31] the Synod of Veron in 1184 officially affirmed that marriage was a sacrament like baptism, the eucharist and penance.[32] Augustine had used the term sacrament in describing marriage as a three-corner structure of procreation, faithfulness and sacrament.[33] But he was simply expressing marriage's sanctity and indissolubility.[34] He did not use *sacramentum* to indicate a means of grace, as Aquinas would later argue.

Peter Lombard listed marriage as a sacrament along with baptism, confirmation, eucharist and unction, effectively saying that marriage was a holy

---

29. Secret marriages outside the control of families, the church and the public resulted in much local legislation in thirteenth- and fourteenth-century England, as outlined in the First Statutes of Salisbury, pp. 83–4.

30. Charles Donahue, 'Proof by Witnesses in the Church Courts of Medieval England', in Morris Arnold, *On the Laws and Customs of England* (Chapel Hill: University of Carolina Press, 1981), pp. 127–58.

31. Karl Rahner (ed.), *Sacramentum Mundi: An Encyclopaedia of Theology* (London: Burns & Oates, 1968), p. 394.

32. Schillebeeckx, *Marriage*, p. 357.

33. Augustine, *De Bono Conjugali*, I. vii (6), xiii (15), xv (17), xviii (21); *Patrologia Latina*, XI, 378, 384–5, 387; 'Against Julian', in Roy J. Defarrari (ed.), *The Fathers of the Church*, vol. 35 (Catholic University of America Press: New York, 1957); 'On Marriage and Concupiscence' and 'A Treatise on the Grace of Christ, and on Original Sin', in Philip Schaff (ed.), *A Select Library of the Nicene and Post-Nicene Fathers*, vol. 5 (Grand Rapids: Eerdmans, 1956).

34. Similarly, baptism remained valid even if the officiating priest later left office. Augustine, 'On the Good Marriage', in Philip Schaff (ed.), *A Select Library of the Nicene and Post-Nicene Fathers of the Christian Church*, vol. 3 (Grand Rapids: Eerdmans, 1969).

institution. However, it was not meritorious for salvation.[35] Thomas Aquinas and St Bonaventure argued for the sacramental nature of marriage.[36] To emphasize marriage as a sacrament, Aquinas appealed to the Vulgate's use of *sacramentum* to translate the Greek *musterion* (Eph. 5:32: 'this is a great *mystery*') and to various patristic texts.[37]

For Aquinas, the sacraments (baptism, confirmation, eucharist, penance, extreme unction, holy orders and matrimony) are the spiritual and intelligible means by which humans are sanctified.[38] Hence 'matrimony [is] a holy thing in which the secular power hath no authority'.[39] Only the church, as the custodian of spiritual things, should oversee it. This sacramental character of marriage was enshrined in the Council of Florence in 1439: 'The sacrament of matrimony contains grace and communicates grace to those who receive it worthily.'[40]

The Reformation

The Protestant rejection of the sacramental nature of marriage created a legal vacuum which made developing a new court system a matter of urgency.[41] The Reformers produced many ideas which contributed eventually to the development of civil marriage in the Western world.[42] Although Reformation theologians spoke with one voice against the Catholic doctrine of marriage,[43] they did not themselves have a uniform understanding of marriage.[44]

Martin Luther and his colleagues Philip Melanchthon and Martin Bucer taught that marriage was a social estate of the earthly kingdom of creation, not

---

35. *Epitome Theologae Christianae*, 28; *Patrologia Latina*, 178, col. 1738.
36. Thomas Aquinas, *The Summa Theologica of Thomas Aquinas*, Part III (London: Burns, Oates and Washbourne, 1914). Bonaventure, *Breviloquium* (London: Herder, 1947), pp. 210–14.
37. The word sacrament is sometimes narrowly defined as the outward and visible sign of an inward and spiritual grace. It can also refer more broadly to images like the tree of life and brazen serpent. In the Vulgate and early Fathers, it also more loosely includes any mystery of faith. Cf. Oscar D. Watkins, *Holy Matrimony: A Treatise on The Divine Laws of Marriage* (London: Rivington, Percival, 1895), pp. 137–42.
38. Aquinas, *Summa Theologica*, III, art. 81–83.
39. Hammick, *Marriage Law of England*, p. 3.
40. Rahner, *Sacramentum Mundi*, p. 394.
41. Eric J. Carlson, *Marriage and the English Reformation* (Oxford: Blackwell, 1994), p. 6.
42. Witte, *From Sacrament to Contract*, p. 42.
43. Carlson, *Marriage and the English Reformation*, p. 72.
44. Witte, *From Sacrament to Contract*, p. 5.

a sacred estate of the heavenly kingdom of redemption.[45] As part of the earthly kingdom, marriage was subject to the state, not the church. To Luther, marriage was still subject to God's law, but this law was now to be administered by civil magistrates who were God's vice-regents in the earthly kingdom.[46] Although divinely ordained, marriage was directed primarily to human ends, to 'the fulfilling of uses in the lives of the individual and of society'.[47] According to Luther, marriage restricted prostitution, promiscuity and other public sexual sins. In the Lutheran tradition, church officials were expected to counsel magistrates about God's law on marriage and to cooperate with civil authorities in publicizing and disciplining marriages.[48] As the priesthood of believers, Christians in general were also required to counsel those who contemplated marriage and to admonish those who sought annulment or divorce.[49] The church, however, no longer had legal authority over marriage.

John Calvin, the legally trained French Reformer, developed a covenantal model of marriage, which confirmed many of the Lutheran theological and legal reforms but cast them in a new framework.[50] Calvin taught that marriage was not a sacramental institution of the church, but a covenantal association of the entire community. A variety of parties participated: the groom and the bride made their vows before God, rendering marriage a tripartite agreement; the couple's parents, as God's lieutenants, gave their consent; two witnesses served as God's priests to their peers; the minister, holding God's spiritual power of the Word, blessed the couple and admonished them in their spiritual duties; and the civil magistrate, holding God's temporal power, registered the marriage and protected the couple in their person and property.[51] The state's marriage courts had to learn and administer 'a new marriage law, based on Scriptural texts'.[52] All these parties were essential to the legitimacy of the

---

45. J. Wayne Baker, *Heinrich Bullinger and the Covenant: The Other Reformed Tradition* (Athens, OH: Ohio University Press, 1980), p. 2; James M. Estes, *Christian Magistrate and State Church* (Buffalo: University of Toronto Press, 1982).

46. Henry Wace (tr.), *Luther's Primary Works* (London: Hodder & Stoughton, 1904), pp. 377f.

47. Ibid., p. 387.

48. Witte, *From Sacrament to Contract*, p. 6.

49. Wace, *Luther's Primary Works*, pp. 389–90.

50. Witte, *From Sacrament to Contract*, p. 5.

51. John Calvin, *Institutes of the Christian Religion* (London: SCM, 1961), 4.19.34–37; 4.20.1–8.

52. Thomas A. Lacey, *Marriage in Church and State*, rev. edn (London: SPCK, 1947), p. 148.

marriage, for each represented a different dimension of God's involvement in the marriage covenant. To omit any of them was, in effect, to omit God. The Calvinist view of marriage was first embraced in Scotland,[53] and would later underpin marriage law in most of the states of the American Union and the British colonies.

Post-Reformation societies

In response to decades of Protestant dissent and a host of political incursions into the church's jurisdiction,[54] the Roman Catholic Council of Trent endorsed the declaration of the Council of Florence. It 'expressly defined against the Protestants that marriage is a sacrament', affirming instead that 'the church can and must regulate it according to the mind of the church and the role of marriage in the church'.[55] Translated into multiple languages and widely disseminated, the Council of Trent's marriage decree provided a common and familiar guide not only for the private life of Catholic believers but also for the marriage law of Catholic countries and later their colonies.[56]

England's breach with Rome in the sixteenth century resulted in the monarch becoming the head of both church and state, so the church's law and jurisdiction now rested on the state's sanction. However, marriage under English common law remained valid. Under James I, the Canterbury convocation made several canons concerning the government of church, clergy and marriage.[57] Then with Oliver Cromwell's insistence on the authority of Parliament rather than monarchy, marriage laws were for the first time made by Parliament. The Civil Marriage Act of 1653 decreed that the Registrar would publish the couple's intent to marry, on three successive Sundays in church or chapel, or on three market days in the market; the Registrar would then issue an enabling certificate, which the couple would present to a Justice of the Peace;[58] the latter would marry them with a simple exchange of vows, pronouncing them husband and wife. Their marriage was 'good and effective in law; and no other marriage whatsoever within the Commonwealth after

---

53. Ibid., p. 152.
54. Witte, *From Sacrament to Contract*, p. 37.
55. Rahner, *Sacramentum Mundi*, pp. 394, 395. See also Henry J. Schroeder, *The Canons and Decrees of the Council of Trent* (Rockford: TAN Books, 1978).
56. Brundage, *Law, Sex and Christian Society*, pp. 572–4, 608–17.
57. Hammick, *The Marriage Law of England*, p. 8.
58. Minors would also provide proof of parental consent; Richard B. Outhwaite, *Clandestine Marriage in England* (London: Hambledon Press, 1995), p. 12.

29 September, 1653' was to be considered valid according to the laws of England.[59]

The Civil Marriage Act brought two related changes. Judicial authority over marriage was for the first time vested in the state rather than in church tribunals. Similarly, authority to make specific marriages was conferred to local Justices of the Peace rather than parents or church.[60] This was a watershed: henceforth civil authorities on both sides of the Atlantic regulated marriage.

However, proponents of church marriage took advantage of the clause, 'Couples are permitted to use the accustomed religious rites if they preferred',[61] which appeared in the 1656 edition when the Act was actually confirmed by Parliament. This meant that a civil marriage could also be contracted at church.[62] Nonconformists later fought a hard campaign to have marriage ceremonies celebrated in their own chapels.[63] This led to a crucial statutory change, the Civil Marriage Act of 1836, which allowed Nonconformists and Roman Catholics to marry in their own places of worship by use of a Registrar's certificate or licence. Also, those who wanted an entirely secular marriage could legalize their unions in a Registrar's office using prescribed formulae.[64]

In spite of the 1653 Civil Marriage Act, clandestine or customary marriages remained prevalent in Britain, especially in the countryside, until Hardwicke's Act for the Better Preventing of Clandestine Marriage of 1753 effectively outlawed them.[65] This explains why European authorities and mission organizations later regarded all African customary marriages as illegitimate. Only marriages conducted at the magistrates' court or in registered churches could be deemed valid in the eyes of the state and mission churches. But this policy has resulted in social and moral dilemmas for many Christian African couples.

---

59. Thomas Lathbury, *A History of the Book of Common Prayer and Other Books of Authority* (Oxford: J. H. and J. Parker, 1858), p. 310.

60. Outhwaite, *Clandestine Marriage in England*, p. 12.

61. Edward J. Wood, *The Wedding Day in All Ages and Countries* (London: R. Bentley, 1869), p. 279.

62. Joyce, *Christian Marriage*, p. 115.

63. Stephen Parker, *Informal Marriage, Cohabitation and the Law, 1750–1989* (London: Macmillan, 1990), pp. 48–74; Outhwaite, *Clandestine Marriage in England*, pp. 145–67.

64. Ibid., p. 165.

65. Hammick, *The Marriage Law of England*, p. 12.

African perspectives

Traditional practice

The recognition of kinship relations and the assumptions made about them, as well as the nature and implications of marriage, are essentially the same in all Bantu-speaking societies in Southern Africa.[66] Customary law is regarded by Africans, including Christians, as the necessary method of establishing a valid marriage.[67] In a regular approach to African marriage,[68] there are at least three distinguishable stages: first, courtship and proposal, with exchange of marriage commitment-tokens; then marriage negotiations, with *lobolo* transactions; and finally handing the bride over to the groom's family, with marriage celebrations.[69]

In the first stage, if after courtship the girl accepts the boy's marriage proposal, they exchange marriage commitment-tokens (similar to a Western ring), with his paternal aunt as a key witness. Later the aunt informs her brother of his son's desire to start a family. If the father agrees to this, he sends a go-between to the girl's family, generally a male friend in good standing with both families.

The second stage consists of the *lobolo* marriage negotiations. *Lobolo* is a man's payment in cattle, money or other forms to a woman's father or legal guardian in order to marry her.[70] In principle, a customary marriage is only validly contracted 'when the *lobolo* transaction between the members of the *lobolo*-giving family and the *lobolo*-receiving family is entered into or completed'.[71] *Lobolo* is the buttress of the whole gift-system of African marriage, and pervades

---

66. Solomon Mutswairo, *Introduction to Shona Culture* (Harare: Juta Zimbabwe, 1996), p. 40.

67. M. F. C. Bourdillon, *The Shona Peoples* (Gweru: Mambo Press, 1998), p. 45.

68. Traditionally there is a clear distinction in concept and vernacular language between a regular marriage, which follows customary law, and irregular unions, which do not.

69. Johan F. Holleman, *Shona Customary Law* (Manchester: Manchester University Press, 1969 (1952)), pp. 98f.

70. M. Chinyenze, 'A Critique of Chigwedere's book *Lobola – The Pros and Cons*, in Relation to the Emancipation of Women in Zimbabwe', *The Zimbabwe Law Review*, 2 vols., 1983–4, p. 229.

71. G. L. Chavhunduka, *Social Change in a Shona Ward* (Salisbury: University of Rhodesia, 1970), p. 5; Eugene Cotran, *The Law of Marriage and Divorce* (London, Sweet & Maxwell, 1968), p. 73.

every area of personal law.[72] The *lobolo* transfer has been frequently misunderstood, especially by Europeans who see it as the sale and purchase of women. But this fails to consider African culture. Others respond that 'there is no man in African society who buys a wife; there is no woman who is part of the property of her husband';[73] and that *lobolo* transaction has a deeper significance than just the acquiring of cattle and other material things.[74] More fully, '*lobolo* is not a purchase of the wife', but a practical way of showing that the husband accepts responsibility for his wife, and that from marriage till death he will protect and care for her.[75] Moreover, if a woman moves in with a man without *lobolo* transactions, she cannot be addressed as daughter-in-law by the man's relatives, and is considered a loose woman or a mistress who can move out at any time to another man.[76] Even African women's rights groups don't oppose the *lobolo* transaction system, but instead argue against its modern commercialization.[77]

The final stage is the handing over of the bride, including marriage celebration. Traditionally this is seen as official permission for the bridegroom to receive his bride into his sleeping room for their first intercourse.[78] The *lobolo* transaction thus legitimizes a husband–wife relationship for the procreation of legitimate offspring.[79]

Christian tensions

European Christian missionaries imposed their own marriage traditions in African society, insisting that a church marriage ceremony was a necessary consequence of genuine conversion. But it is questionable whether church and civil

---

72. Joan May, *Changing People, Changing Laws* (Gweru: Mambo Press, 1987), p. 41.

73. Aeneas Chigwedere, *Lobola – The Pros and Cons* (Harare: Books of Africa, 1982), p. 4.

74. Isaac Schapera (ed.), *Western Civilisation and the Natives of South Africa: Studies in Culture Contact* (London: Routledge, 1967 (1934)), p. 8.

75. Friedrich W. T. Posselt, *Fact and Fiction: A Short Account of the Natives of Southern Rhodesia* (Bulawayo: Rhodesia Printing Press, 1935), p. 64.

76. May, *Changing People, Changing Laws*, p. 41.

77. 'The Report on the Rights of Women in Zimbabwe', Harare, 14th to 17th November 1984, p. 10.

78. Herbert Aschwanden, *Symbols of Life: An Analysis of the Consciousness of the Karanga* (Gweru: Mambo Press, 1982), p. 178.

79. Albert E. Jennings, *Bogadi: A Study of the Marriage Laws and Customs of the Bechuana Tribes of South Africa* (Tiger Kloof, South Africa: London Missionary Society, 1933), p. 21.

marriage laws passed in Europe in different historical, social and ecclesiastical contexts could justifiably be extended to African Christians, for whom they were definitely not designed. Nothing officially prevented traditional African marriages from coexisting with a civil contract or church service. But the main problem was that, when a marriage was celebrated in a Christian or civil service, the principles of traditional marriage were deemed no longer to apply.[80]

Failure to recognize African traditional marriage practice has resulted in social and moral dilemmas for Christian couples. A new couple is expected by family members to consummate their relationship after customary marriage, but if a Christian couple did so before their church wedding they faced public discipline in mission-established churches. Even today, mission churches expect couples to refrain from sex during the long interval between customary and church ceremonies, and many churches expect the bride to wear white signifying virginity. So Christian couples face a dilemma: on the one hand they believe they are already married, so sexual intercourse is acceptable; on the other, under the influence of church teaching which forbids sex before a church wedding, they feel guilty for apparently breaking God's law.

In spite of recent overwhelming urbanization, resembling the urban growth of Europe more than a century earlier,[81] Africans remain generally traditional in their approach to contracting marriage. Even today, civil or church marriage is usually considered an incidental addition to a regular traditional marriage:[82] registration at the magistrates' court or solemnization in church merely satisfies civil or ecclesiastical law.[83] If Africans continue to consider customary marriage as the only culturally acceptable way to establish valid and legitimate lifelong husband–wife relationships, then the church needs somehow to recognize customary marriages as valid, legitimate and legally binding unions.

Creative compromise

The Churches' Research on Marriage in Africa (CROMIA) strongly recommended that the church should participate in celebration of the customary marriage of Christian couples within the community, instead of insisting on a

---

80. Holleman, *Shona Customary Law*, p. 146.

81. P. Stopforth, 'Survey of Highfield African Townships', *Occasional Paper 6* (Salisbury: University of Rhodesia, 1971), p. 18.

82. Bourdillon, *Shona Peoples*, p. 45.

83. G. E. P. Broderick, 'Betrothal Ceremony among the *WaZeruru* of the Salisbury District', *Native Affairs Department Annual* (1945), p. 49.

church wedding.[84] Marriage banns should be read in church for three consecutive Sundays before the *lobolo* transactions begin. The church minister should be a government-registered marriage officer, and should meet with the couple and their family to explain his role in the ceremony in order for the marriage to be recognized by the state. On the day of the customary marriage contract, the pastor and church leaders should accompany the groom and his relatives to the bride's home where the *lobolo* transactions will take place. The pastor should participate in the ceremony both by presenting the biblical view of Christian marriage and by signing the marriage certificate. The couple and their families should then proceed with the traditional cultural rituals and the consummation of their marriage.

When the couple later return to their local church, the minister should introduce them as husband and wife ('Mr and Mrs'). If the couple want another celebration weeks or even months after their customary marriage, as is often the case, it must be clearly a marriage reception and not a marriage ceremony. The couple may decide to wear wedding attire at this reception – nearly all women respondents to the marriage questionnaire wanted to wear a white wedding gown.[85] But the pastor must make a clear distinction between a marriage ceremony and a marriage reception.

This approach to African Christian marriage has several advantages. First, while maintaining customary marriage as the essence of valid and legitimate marriage in African society, it takes seriously the significance of both divine blessing and state law. Second, the date on the marriage certificate is the date of their customary marriage, and the names of witnesses are those of the couple's family and their pastor. Third, the church need not discipline couples who consummate their marriage after the customary ceremonies but before a church wedding. And fourth, it places less economic pressure on the couple than the European system of expensive church weddings and celebrations.[86] Whatever the arguments for church weddings, symbols and rituals, they cannot legitimately claim the Bible as their source, since marriage there is essentially a

---

84. Benezeri Kisembo, Laurenti Magesa and Aylward Shorter (eds.), *African Christian Marriage*, 2nd edn (Nairobi: Paulines Publications Africa, 1988 (1977)), p. 53. CROMIA was a five-year programme of research into the sociology and theology of marriage, with special reference to East, Central and Southern Africa.

85. Onesimus Ngundu, *Mission Churches and African Customary Marriage* (Saarbrücken: LAP Lambert Academic Publishing, 2010), ch. 7.

86. Titus Kivunzi (ed.), *A Biblical Approach to Marriage and Family in Africa* (Machakos: Scott Theological College, 1994), p. 110.

matter between two families which needs no formal religious recognition to be valid in God's sight.

Conclusion

The most radical change in the history of marriage in Britain occurred in 2013, when Parliament redefined marriage by legalizing same-sex marriages. Biblically this appears to be a blatant violation of what God, the creator and designer of marriage, intended. Historically, early Christians apparently followed local marriage customs; the medieval Catholic Church sacramentalized marriage and exercised authority over it; Protestant churches rejected this theology and vested the state with its oversight. European missionaries in Africa largely overlooked customary marriage and insisted that the church and state must legitimize marriage. This usurped traditional parental responsibility over their children's marriages, and led to social and moral dilemmas for Christian couples. However, there is now a creative compromise, consisting of an African customary marriage ceremony with Christian elements, followed later by a church marriage reception. This brings together the strengths of both African and European traditions.

© Onesimus Ngundu, 2017

11. HUMAN SEXUALITY AND CHRISTIAN ANTHROPOLOGY

A. T. B. McGowan

Introduction

This chapter addresses the question of how our theological anthropology impacts upon our understanding of human sexuality, with particular reference to same-sex relations. The argument presented is that the biblical teaching concerning the fall of humanity into sin, including the effects of that sin on the mind (the noetic effects of sin) has a bearing on any Christian view of same-sex relations and also has a bearing on the nature of the debate and dialogue which takes place on these issues. Other chapters discuss exegetical, ethical and philosophical issues, but, based on the Tyndale Christian Doctrine Lecture for 2016, this chapter approaches the subject from the standpoint of Christian dogmatics.[1]

In 2015 I was a commissioner to the General Assembly of the Church of Scotland. Amid the theatre of the opening ceremonies, with the welcome to

---

1. It is not my intention to consider here the biblical arguments against same-sex relationships. I have already engaged in that exercise as part of the Theological Commission of the Church of Scotland. The three of us on that Commission who were evangelicals wrote a section of the final report, laying out those arguments: *The Church of Scotland Theological Commission on Same-Sex Relationships and the Ministry* (Edinburgh: APS Group (Scotland) Ltd., 2013), Section 7, 1/85–1/118.

the Lord High Commissioner (the Queen's representative) and the election of a new Moderator, we engaged in worship. The reading from Scripture was from Romans 12 and included the words, 'Do not conform any longer to the pattern of this world, but be transformed by the renewing of your mind'.[2] When the Assembly later moved into its first business session, it approved an Overture permitting congregations to choose as their minister someone in a same-sex marriage. This had been approved at the previous General Assembly, had been supported by a majority of presbyteries in the ensuing year and now became part of the law of the Church of Scotland, the Overture becoming an Act of the General Assembly.

I was struck by the contrast between the words of Scripture read at the beginning of the Assembly and one of the first actions taken by the Assembly. It seemed to me that the command of the Apostle Paul, 'Do not be conformed to the world', had been ignored and the Assembly had done just that. As I reflected on this, being grieved at the decision my church had taken, I reflected further on the alternative approach outlined by Paul. We are not to be 'conformed to the world', rather we are to be 'transformed by the renewal of our minds'. It had already been my intention to focus in this chapter on issues concerning Christian anthropology, not least the effects of sin on the mind, and this helped to anchor my thoughts.

As part of my preparation for this chapter, I had taken to reading during the evenings at the General Assembly a short book called *Holiness* by Professor John Webster. My increasing appreciation of the book was tragically heightened when, on the Wednesday of the Assembly, I learned that John had died very suddenly. Given that it is not possible in a chapter of this length to explain in full one's theological perspective, I would like to take four themes from the first chapter of that book as a summary of the presuppositions for what follows.

The nature of Christian dogmatics
Christian dogmatics is a work of holy reason which is 'complementary but strictly subordinate to the exegetical task'[3] and exists to serve the church. Such theology is not, like much modern theology, either 'conversationalist or

---

2. All biblical translations in this chapter are taken from the Holy Bible, New International Version. Copyright © 1973, 1978, 1984 by International Bible Society. Used by permission of Hodder & Stoughton, a division of Hodder Headline Ltd. All rights reserved. 'NIV' is a trademark of International Bible Society. UK trademark number 1448790.

3. John Webster, *Holiness* (Grand Rapids: Eerdmans, 2003), p. 3.

comparative' in approach.[4] Rather, it is focused on a specific and limited range of texts, the biblical canon.[5] In other words, 'Dogmatics is that delightful activity in which the church praises God by ordering its thinking towards the gospel of Christ'.[6]

The nature of reason

In opposition to modernity, Christian dogmatics insists that reason is not a natural nor a transcendent faculty or competency, which lies outside the reconciling and redeeming act of God. Like all other sectors of the human condition, it needs to be redeemed. Webster goes on to say: 'If what Paul calls the renewal of the mind (Romans 12.2) is to be visible anywhere, it has to be in Christian theology, in which holy reason is summoned to address the great matter of God and of all things in God.'[7]

The nature of revelation

Christian theology is impossible apart from revelation, which is the 'self-presentation of the holy Trinity'.[8] Revelation determines both the context and the content of Christian theology. Two quotations from Webster sum this up. First, 'revelation is the self-giving presence of the holy God which overthrows opposition to God, and, in reconciling, brings us into the light of the knowledge of God'. Second, 'Christian theology is enclosed by, and does its work within, the sphere of the revelatory presence of the holy God'.[9] Revelation, then, is not simply the communication of truths but the self-presentation of the holy God.[10]

The nature of Scripture

This 'revelatory presence of God is *set forth in Holy Scripture*'.[11] The text of Scripture has come to us as men spoke 'from God', being carried along by the Holy Spirit (2 Pet. 1:21). This means that Scripture carries the authority of God. Scripture's authority is not conferred by the church or by theology, rather 'it is the servant of the living voice of God as truth that enables the Church to live

---

4. Ibid., p. 4.
5. Ibid., p. 5.
6. Ibid., p. 8.
7. Ibid., p. 12.
8. Ibid., p. 13.
9. Ibid., p. 14.
10. Ibid., p. 13.
11. Ibid., p. 17, italics original.

from and in the truth'.[12] The sufficiency of Scripture is also important because there 'holy reason finds its limit'.[13] As Webster says, 'Scripture is sufficient for its end, which is the publication of the saving knowledge of God'.[14]

With that introduction and writing from that perspective, I want to ask what bearing our theological anthropology has on our theology of same-sex relations. My underlying conviction here is that there is an increasing tendency to do theology *de novo*, paying little attention to the dogmatic tradition and the fundamental doctrines of the Christian faith as agreed from the third and fourth centuries onwards and as refined and clarified during the Reformation and post-Reformation periods. By contrast, I believe that we must take seriously the dogmatic tradition of the church and depart from it only after careful and considered thought. What then does our dogmatic tradition have to say about the human condition, not least in respect of human sexuality? Or, to put it another way, what bearing does our theological anthropology have on the current debates on same-sex relations? It is my contention that there are three areas in which our biblical and theological anthropology impacts upon our discussion of same-sex relations, namely, in respect of the body, the mind and the spirit.

The body

Some time ago, I had a dream. I was driving a car down a corridor inside a hotel. I realized that I was about to come to a corner and that there was no way the car would be able to turn through 90 degrees into another corridor. I have no idea what a psychiatrist would make of that dream but happily I woke up. I had been living briefly in a strangely disordered world where cars drove inside buildings instead of outside. When I woke up I was back to normality.

You will remember that in *Alice in Wonderland* by Lewis Carroll, Alice falls down a rabbit hole and finds herself in a strange fantasy world where nothing is quite as it should be. There is a rabbit and a large Cheshire cat who wear clothes and talk, and there is a mouse who gives a lecture on William the Conqueror! There is also a caterpillar who gives advice and frogs who work as footmen in the grand house where the Duchess lives. The story creates a complete parallel world where everything is disordered. The story was actually

---

12. Ibid., p. 20.
13. Ibid.
14. Ibid.

written under the pseudonym of Lewis Carroll by the Rev. Charles Lutwidge Dodgson, a mathematician at Christ Church, Oxford. It is strange to think that a mathematician who lived in such an ordered, structured, logical world could write such a wonderful fantasy tale and paint a picture of a completely disordered world. When I woke up from my dream I left the strange disordered world in which I had briefly been living and came back to the normal world. When you stop reading *Alice in Wonderland*, you leave that peculiar world, with all its distortion of reality, and return to normal.

The question we have to ask, of course, is 'What is normal?' Is the world that we experience every day 'normal', such that everything else is distorted and disordered? We sometimes take it for granted that what we experience every day is 'normal' and when we have dreams or read fantasy books we assume that those disordered worlds in which we find ourselves are 'not normal'. I want to argue that our world is not normal. It is disordered and distorted and confused. How can it be normal for children to be dying of hunger a few hours by plane from very rich countries? How can it be normal for men and women to cheat and lie and steal and use violence against one another? How can it be normal for relationships to break down so easily and for families to be so easily fractured and destroyed? How can it be normal for governments to stockpile weapons, so that they can destroy other human beings? How can it be normal for international traders and bankers to play roulette with the financial markets and risk the savings and livelihoods of millions of ordinary people? How can our world be considered normal when those who kick a football for a living are paid millions of pounds, while nurses are paid very small salaries? What does normality mean when so-called celebrities act out their pathetic, disordered lives in full view of the media? The fact is that human beings have been deceived into thinking that all of this is normal. In other words, we have been fooled! The truth is that our world is just as distorted, disordered and confused as Alice's wonderland.

If we want to know why the world is so disordered, we must turn to Genesis 1 – 3. The first three chapters of the book of Genesis are critical for everything which follows in the Scriptures. In those chapters we are told that God created all things and that all things were 'good'. Our first parents lived in harmony with God, with the creation and with one another. There was no human sin, although the appearance of the serpent, which John later tells us was Satan (Rev. 12:9), indicates that disobedience and sin had entered the universe, even when it had not yet affected human beings. Then in Genesis 3 we have a description of the fall, when our first parents chose to disobey God and instead to follow the advice of the serpent. They disobeyed God's express command by eating the fruit of the tree of the knowledge of good and evil and, as a result, they fell into sin and were banished from the garden; every human being since then (except Christ) has been affected. It is clear that the impact of this fall was enormous, even cataclysmic. From this point on, human beings were sinners, separated from God by that sin and in need of forgiveness by God and reconciliation to God.

You know the story well, but I want to highlight something about the fall which is relevant for understanding why our world is so disordered and why people are unable to recognize that it is so disordered, namely, the problem of self-centredness. As I have argued elsewhere, I follow Cornelius Van Til and John Murray in believing that, in a certain sense, the fall took place before they took the forbidden fruit![15] It took place when our first parents decided that they would listen to Satan, listen to God and then make a decision. In other words, the basis of their sin was to put themselves rather than God at the centre of the universe. Herman Bavinck, speaking of the 'knowledge of good and evil' as described in Genesis 3, put it like this:

> The nature of the knowledge of good and evil in view here is characterized by the fact that humans would be like God as a result of it (Gen. 3:5, 22). By violating the command of God and eating of the tree, they would make themselves like God in the sense that they would position themselves outside and above the law and, like God, determine and judge for themselves what good and evil was.[16]

It is vital that we see the point at issue in this matter. Sin is to be self-centred rather than God-centred. Human beings were created and designed to live in a God-centred way and, apart from that relationship, human beings are not what they should be. Fallen human beings, of course, neither understand nor accept this analysis of their condition. As Calvin wrote: 'For, since blind self-love is innate in all mortals, they are most freely persuaded that nothing inheres in themselves that deserves to be considered hateful.'[17]

At the beginning of the Reformation, Martin Luther followed Augustine in teaching a doctrine of original sin. Melanchthon, the first Protestant theologian of the Reformation, whom Luther called 'the greatest theologian that ever lived',

---

15. A. T. B. McGowan, *Adam, Christ and Covenant: Exploring Headship Theology* (London: Apollos, 2016), p. 176.

16. Herman Bavinck, *Reformed Dogmatics* (Grand Rapids: Baker, 2006), 3:33.

17. John Calvin, *Institutes of the Christian Religion*, ed. F. L. Battles, vols. XX and XXI in the *Library of Christian Classics* series, ed. J. T. McNeill (Philadelphia: The Westminster Press, 1977), 2.1.2, p. 243.

spelled out this doctrine. He emphasized the sin of our first parents and the results of that sin for their posterity. He believed that they possessed the Holy Spirit before the fall and so wrote that they

> fell under God's wrath and punishment; and they lost the Holy Spirit and the wonderful virtues which they enjoyed previously, both for themselves and for all mankind, who were to have a beginning in them, and were naturally to come from them. They stood in the place of future mankind. To them the gifts were given; the same would have devolved on their successors if they had remained steadfast in obedience. But when they fell, they lost the gifts for themselves and for all mankind who were naturally to be born of them.[18]

The key elements of the later catechetical and confessional teaching on sin are already here in summary form.

Calvin spoke of sin as an infection and wrote, 'Therefore all of us, who have descended from impure seed, are born infected with the contagion of sin. In fact, before we saw the light of this life we were soiled and spotted in God's sight'.[19] Adam was responsible for this 'because he infected all his posterity with that corruption into which he had fallen'.[20] In Reformation and post-Reformation theology, the language of 'depravity' began to be used to describe the human condition. Calvin himself spoke of how 'in the person of the first man we have fallen from our original condition'[21] and went on to describe the new state of humanity as 'the universal condition of human depravity'.[22] This language was used in the subsequent catechisms and confessions of the period. Later Calvinist theologians began to use the language of 'total depravity', but this has to be understood carefully. As Berkouwer rightly shows, it is too simplistic to regard the Reformed position as 'holding a view of *total* corruption which threatened man's being man'.[23] In other words, we must resist any suggestion that, since the fall, human beings have ceased to be truly human or have ceased to bear the image of God. Most Reformed theologians have insisted

---

18. Philip Melanchthon, *Loci Communes 1555*, tr. and ed. Clyde L. Manschreck (Grand Rapids: Baker, 1982), p. 73.
19. Calvin, *Institutes*, 2.1.5, p. 248.
20. Ibid., 2.1.6, p. 249.
21. Ibid., 2.1.1, p. 242.
22. Ibid., 2.3.4, p. 293.
23. G. C. Berkouwer, *Man: The Image of God*, Studies in Dogmatics (Grand Rapids: Eerdmans, 1962), p. 124.

that the 'remnants' of the image remain. Calvin does speak of the image of God in human beings as having been 'obliterated'[24] but, even while speaking about the depravity of human beings, he recognized that depraved sinners could yet do good things, due to the grace of God.[25] Kuyper and Bavinck would later develop and expound this doctrine of what came to be called 'common grace'.[26]

In the popular media, when someone is described as being 'totally depraved', it is normally in reference to a particularly evil person: a serial killer, a child rapist or someone who is judged to have committed crimes against humanity. The theological use of the phrase 'total depravity' refers to the fact that the 'totality' of the human person has been affected by sin. Those who use this language of 'total depravity' do not mean that human beings are as bad as they could be, but rather that the totality of their being has been impacted by sin. In other words, it is not simply the will which has been damaged by sin but also the body, the mind, the emotions, the character, the personality and so on.

All human beings, then, are damaged in every part of their being by the fallenness which resulted from Adam's sin. Even among those who accept this general principle, of course, the key biblical teaching has been interpreted in a variety of ways, not least in respect of the matter of the transmission of sin. Tertullian and Augustine viewed the transmission of sin in realist terms, believing that all humanity was seminally present in Adam. Thereafter, the contagion of sin passed from generation to generation by propagation. The Scottish Presbyterian tradition from which I come interprets the nature and transmission of sin in terms of imputation, involving a covenant of works made with Adam, a covenant of grace made with Christ and sometimes also a covenant of redemption between the Father and the Son. In my book *Adam, Christ and Covenant: Exploring Headship Theology*, published recently, I look in more detail at the headship of Adam and the headship of Christ as described in 1 Corinthians 15 and Romans 5 and offer a way of understanding the nature and transmission of sin which maintains the principle of imputation but which does not require an underlying covenantal structure. These differences aside, however, all of the early Reformed theologians were agreed that sin is universal, that it can be traced back to Adam's sin and fall and that it affects every aspect of our humanity.

What then can we say about human sexuality, given our fallenness? If the argument concerning the fall, sin and human depravity is sound, then we must

---

24. Calvin, *Institutes*, 2.1.5, p. 246.
25. Ibid., 2.3.3–4, pp. 292–294.
26. Herman Bavinck's inaugural lecture at Kampen was on this subject and Abraham Kuyper wrote three volumes on common grace.

argue that our sexuality, along with every other aspect of our humanity, has been damaged by sin. In a fallen world, rather than the perfect world God originally created, we can expect that there will be some people who are born with physical deformity, or mental incapacity, or diseases which limit lifespan. There will also be human beings who are psychopathic, whose natural inclinations lead them to violence and murder. There will be those whose genetic make-up, character and personality mean that they find it very difficult to fit into society, not least those with severe Asperger's syndrome. In the same way, the sexuality of each one of us has been damaged by our inherited fallenness, in different ways and in different measures. For some of us that will mean that they experience same-sex attraction, some will experience gender confusion, others will be sexually attracted to children, yet others will only be sexually satisfied with multiple partners and so on.

It has always been the conviction of the Christian church in all its branches, based upon Holy Scripture, that sexual relationships outside of that between husband and wife are contrary to God's intention. This is not just the view of a few ultra-conservative theologians but has been the historic conviction of the church for two thousand years and remains the moral conviction of the vast majority of the world's Christians today. It is also a view shared with the other Abrahamic faiths.

A common argument used by some who experience same-sex attraction is that 'this is the way God made me', with the implication that their sexuality is God-given and therefore endorsed by God, with the further implication that it should be practised and celebrated. The response to this argument is that each of us is a product of a fallen world and each of us is damaged in some way by sin. We are not all damaged in the same way but certainly we are all damaged. Therefore, far from regarding same-sex attraction as a God-given gift, the Christian church has always regarded it as one form of the multiple human aberrations caused by the fall.

In Scripture we are taught that sexual relations are to be between one man and one woman. Any other expression of sexuality is described as sinful and even perverted.[27] We should not underestimate the pain and suffering of those whose sexual attractions do not fit into this biblical norm of one man and one woman. The pain is perhaps even more pronounced for Christians who

---

27. See the report referenced in note 1. There are also numerous other works of scholarship which bear this out, e.g. (to reference only two) Richard B. Hays, *The Moral Vision of the New Testament* (San Francisco: Harper, 1996), ch. 16; and Robert A. J. Gagnon, *The Bible and Homosexual Practice* (Nashville: Abingdon Press, 2001).

experience same-sex attraction and yet, at the same time, accept the teaching of Scripture. I have a friend, a biblical scholar, who experiences same-sex attraction but who, because he holds to the orthodox interpretation of the teaching of Scripture, has maintained a celibate life. This is a difficult and painful choice, especially when his choice of a celibate life has not been accompanied by the 'gift' of celibacy. This is a matter which, in the church, needs to be approached with a deep pastoral sensitivity.

The mind

Following the dogmatic tradition, the argument of this chapter is that sin affects every aspect of our humanity. For example, in describing the fall, the Westminster Confession of Faith puts it like this: 'By this sin they fell from their original righteousness, and communion with God, and so became dead in sin, and wholly defiled in all the faculties and parts of soul and body.'[28]

This most certainly includes the mind. In describing the condition of the Colossian Christians before they were reconciled to God by Christ through the cross, Paul says in Colossians 1:21, 'Once you were alienated from God and were enemies in your minds because of your evil behaviour'. This is most significant. They were not simply enemies of God in their actions but in their minds. Paul expresses this noetic effect of sin very powerfully in Romans 8:5–7:

> Those who live according to the sinful nature have their minds set on what that nature desires; but those who live in accordance with the Spirit have their minds set on what the Spirit desires. The mind of sinful man is death, but the mind controlled by the Spirit is life and peace; the sinful mind is hostile to God. It does not submit to God's law, nor can it do so.

The unbeliever, then, has a 'mindset' which is opposed to God and unbelievers are enemies of God in their *minds*. How has this situation arisen? In 2 Corinthians 4:4, Paul says that it has come about because of the fall and the work of the devil: 'The god of this age has blinded the minds of unbelievers, so that they cannot see the light of the gospel of the glory of Christ, who is the image of God.'

These passages of Scripture convey powerfully that the damage done by sin has affected the human mind. Our minds, when we are unbelievers, have been

---

28. *Westminster Confession of Faith*, ch. 6, section 2.

blinded by an enemy so that they are simply unable to comprehend the truth about Christ. We might say that the minds of unbelievers have been programmed, by the noetic effects of the fall and by the deliberate action of the devil, such that they are unable to understand spiritual truths or see things properly from a God-centred perspective. Only when minds are opened by God can people understand and believe. We see that in the case of the disciples to whom Jesus appeared after his resurrection. As we read in Luke 24:45: 'Then he opened their minds so they could understand the Scriptures.'

On 11 May 1997, the reigning world chess champion, Garry Kasparov, was beaten by a computer called 'Deep Blue', designed by software engineers at IBM. Kasparov went on to win the six-game match, but the fact that a machine had beaten the world champion in one of those games made news and made history. Deep Blue did not 'think', it merely calculated the best move in each situation by considering the numerous scenarios arising out of each possible move, to a depth of around two hundred million alternatives! Its moves were determined by the programme written by the computer designers. A good deal of chess computer programming consists of 'book moves', such as standard opening sequences. It has sometimes been said that the way to beat a chess computer is to make a move which is not a standard 'book move', in the hope that the computer will not know how best to respond. It is certainly true that simply learning screeds of openings will not ultimately be beneficial unless one knows *why* these are the best moves in any particular opening.

We are not computers (and I do not want to compare the software engineers at IBM with the devil!), but the fact is that the thinking of human beings has also to some extent been 'programmed'. That is to say, it has been predetermined by a number of factors. First, by our genetics, our upbringing and the social environment in which we grew up; second (at least for those of us in the northern hemisphere), by Western civilization as formed by the Enlightenment; and third, by more recent factors such as scientism, relativism, pluralism and the equality and diversity agendas. Supremely, however, our thinking has been pre-determined and 'programmed' by the fall, by sin and by the work of the devil.

In order to spell out the noetic effects of sin and see the connection with human sexuality, we must turn to Romans 1:18–25. As I have argued elsewhere, Paul here says some quite striking things:

He says that every human being possesses true knowledge of God and that this knowledge is of such clarity that human beings have absolutely no excuse if they deny that they know God. Indeed, he goes so far as to argue that human beings deliberately suppress this knowledge and this truth, because of the innate sinfulness of all fallen creatures. The result of this, he says, is that human beings have exchanged truth for lies and their thinking has become futile. To put it bluntly, they are fools.[29]

We as human beings are people whose minds and hearts are distorted by sin. Those we speak to about Christ know the truth about God but deliberately suppress it. They are not objective, clear-minded people who simply need to hear the best argument. Paul knew that when he went to Corinth. He did not go with 'wise and persuasive words' (1 Cor. 2:4) because he knew that this would leave them at the mercy of a more articulate, more persuasive speaker with a better argument. Rather, he depended upon the Holy Spirit to use his faltering, nervous words to change lives.

How then does this aspect of our theological anthropology impact on the issues of same-sex relations? There are perhaps two ways. First, unbelievers cannot accept the biblical arguments about human sexuality because their minds are blinded, such that they cannot see and understand spiritual truths. They often reject a Christian analysis out of hand because our views are based on the revelation of a God in whom they do not believe. The Christian response to such people has often demonstrated a lack of coherence in our Christian dogmatics. In our anthropology, we might say that human beings by nature are spiritually dead and spiritually blind but then, in our evangelism and apologetics, treat those same human beings as if they were sensible, rational, objective human beings, with no axe to grind, who are able to weigh up the teaching of Scripture, including the teaching on sexuality, and come to right conclusions. We must recognize the true condition of unbelievers and their need for a transforming work of the Holy Spirit, before they will understand and accept biblical teaching.

Second, there is a danger that we give too much credence to the intellectual arguments of those who oppose a biblical view of homosexual acts. A desire to be regarded as intellectuals and as part of the academy has sometimes led evangelical theologians to compromise on our theological anthropology and to underplay the biblical teaching that unbelievers simply are not equipped to understand spiritual truths. In other words, we sometimes make the mistake of assuming that we are debating on a level playing field with atheists and agnostics, providing rational arguments to persuade rational people to accept truth. In fact, we are working with entirely different epistemologies. Van Til argued that the fundamental error of evidentialism was to submit the biblical teaching about God to the assessment of unbelievers, as if they had the right and the capacity to determine truth. He writes, 'In the last analysis we shall have to choose

---

29. A. T. B. McGowan, *The Divine Spiration of Scripture* (Nottingham: Apollos, 2008), p. 44.

between two theories of knowledge. According to one theory, God is the final court of appeal; according to the other theory man is the final court of appeal'.[30] We might say that the dialogue between the believer and the unbeliever does not consist in a disagreement over the facts but rather in a radical difference in epistemology. As Van Til goes on to say, 'Sin will reveal itself in the field of knowledge in the fact that man makes himself the ultimate court of appeal in the matter of all interpretation. He will refuse to recognize God's authority'.[31] Only through regeneration will the mind of the unbeliever come to the place where the reality of God is recognized to be that which 'ultimately controls a truly Christian methodology'.[32]

The spirit

Fallen human beings are not only damaged in body and mind by the effects of the fall and of sin, there is also spiritual damage. In Ephesians 2:1–5, Paul describes the spiritual condition of unbelievers and then contrasts this with the condition of those who are in Christ:

> As for you, you were dead in your transgressions and sins, in which you used to live when you followed the ways of this world and of the ruler of the kingdom of the air, the spirit who is now at work in those who are disobedient. All of us also lived among them at one time, gratifying the cravings of our sinful nature and following its desires and thoughts. Like the rest, we were by nature objects of wrath. But because of his great love for us, God, who is rich in mercy, made us alive with Christ even when we were dead in transgressions – it is by grace you have been saved.

Unbelievers are spiritually dead until God makes us alive with Christ. In other words, spiritual death is the 'natural' condition of human beings, due to the fall. In its chapter on 'Original Sin', the Scots Confession of 1560 puts it like this: 'Everlasting death has had, and shall have, power and dominion over all who have not been, or are not, or shall not be reborn from above.'[33] The Second Helvetic Confession, which was adopted by the Church of Scotland in 1566,

---

30. Cornelius Van Til, *The Defense of the Faith* (Philadelphia: Presbyterian and Reformed, 1976), p. 34.

31. Ibid., p. 35.

32. Ibid., p. 100.

33. *The Scots Confession*, 1560, ch. 3.

spells out what is meant by death in this context: 'By death we understand not only bodily death, which all of us must once suffer on account of sins, but also eternal punishment due to our sins and corruptions.'[34] One of the texts Bullinger used to support this statement was Romans 5:12: 'Sin entered the world through one man, and death through sin, and in this way death came to all men, because all sinned.'

Spiritual life is not a natural but rather a supernatural condition, the gift of God which comes through faith in Jesus Christ. There is a great deal of talk about various forms of 'spirituality' today, but the New Testament knows of only two spiritual conditions: those who are spiritually dead and those who are spiritually alive. This spiritual life comes to us when God, by his Holy Spirit, moves to regenerate us, unite us with Christ and renew our natures.

This stark contrast between believer and unbeliever, between those who are spiritually dead and those who are spiritually alive, is taken further by Paul in 1 Corinthians 2. There he argues that all spiritual understanding comes from the Holy Spirit and that it is impossible to have any real knowledge of God or of spiritual things except through the work of the Holy Spirit. We see this particularly in verses 12–14:

> We have not received the spirit of the world but the Spirit who is from God, that we may understand what God has freely given us. This is what we speak, not in words taught us by human wisdom but in words taught by the Spirit, expressing spiritual truths in spiritual words. The man without the Spirit does not accept the things that come from the Spirit of God, for they are foolishness to him, and he cannot understand them, because they are spiritually discerned.

Notice, it is not simply that the unbeliever *does not* understand the things of the spirit, rather he *cannot* understand them. The believer, however, is able to understand because of the work of the Holy Spirit producing in the believer 'the mind of Christ' (1 Cor. 2:16).

This transformation from spiritual death to spiritual life, from spiritual darkness to spiritual light, is described in various ways in Scripture. In John 3, Jesus tells Nicodemus that new birth is necessary in order to see the kingdom of God. In John 5:24 he says: 'I tell you the truth, whoever hears my word and believes him who sent me has eternal life and will not be condemned; he has crossed over from death to life.' Paul, in 2 Corinthians 5:17, wrote that if anyone was 'in Christ' that person was a 'new creation'.

---

34. *The Second Helvetic Confession*, ch. 8.

The key to the movement from spiritual death to spiritual life is the work of the Holy Spirit. We see this in John 7:37–39:

> On the last and greatest day of the Feast, Jesus stood and said in a loud voice, 'If anyone is thirsty, let him come to me and drink. Whoever believes in me, as the Scripture has said, streams of living water will flow from within him.' By this he meant the Spirit, whom those who believed in him were later to receive. Up to that time the Spirit had not been given, since Jesus had not yet been glorified.

One of the results of the fall is that the natural condition of human beings is spiritual death. This situation is transformed when, by the work of the Holy Spirit, people are brought from death to life and are united spiritually with Christ.

Given the spiritual effects of the fall, how does this impact on issues of human sexuality? To answer this question, we must turn to 1 Corinthians 6:9–11:

> Do you not know that the wicked will not inherit the kingdom of God? Do not be deceived: Neither the sexually immoral nor idolaters nor adulterers nor male prostitutes nor homosexual offenders nor thieves nor the greedy nor drunkards nor slanderers nor swindlers will inherit the kingdom of God. And that is what some of you were. But you were washed, you were sanctified, you were justified in the name of the Lord Jesus Christ and by the Spirit of our God.

Here is a letter to Christians. Paul describes what they were like before they came to Christ and then speaks of the transforming power which they experienced in their lives. They had been spiritually dead and were now spiritually alive. This transformation affected them in various ways. One of these concerns human sexuality. Some of them were sexually immoral, some were adulterers, some of them were male prostitutes and some of them were engaged in same-sex sexual activity. The emphasis here is on the words, 'That is what some of you *were*'. They were no longer living in that immoral way. They had been changed. What brought about that change? It was the work of the Holy Spirit who effected regeneration ('you were washed'), justification and sanctification.

Does that mean that the homosexual offenders no longer felt same-sex attraction? I would doubt it. It did mean that, in obedience to the teaching of Scripture, they brought their lives into accord with the biblical teaching on human sexuality. We cannot assume that those who are made alive spiritually in Christ will not suffer temptation, same-sex attraction and so on. What we can expect is that, by the power of God's Holy Spirit, behaviour will change, however difficult and painful that might sometimes be.

Conclusion

In conclusion, we return to the passage from Romans 12, read at the General Assembly of the Church of Scotland. When we become Christians, our minds, as well as our wills, are renewed and reoriented. We are then called to rethink everything. This is the meaning of Romans 12:1–2: 'Do not conform any longer to the pattern of this world, but be transformed by the renewing of your mind.' We must think in a new way, see the world in a new way, rethink everything out of a centre in God. Thereafter the task is to bring our minds, our flesh, our emotions and every other aspect of our humanity into obedience and submission before God, on a daily basis.

We live in a disordered world because fallen men and women live self-centred rather than God-centred lives. We fail to see our true condition and do not understand how disordered the world is, because our minds have been blinded by Satan. When we put our faith in Christ, we begin to see things clearly. We then recognize that our world is not normal but distorted and disordered. We then see that the only solution to the problems of our world is for men and women to turn to Christ, that they might be renewed in body, mind and spirit. Then they can join with other believers to rethink everything out of a centre in God, with a view to the reformation, renewal and reconstruction of every aspect of life, taking every thought captive to make it obedient to Christ (2 Cor. 10:5).

12. 'ONE MAN AND ONE WOMAN': THE CHRISTIAN DOCTRINE OF MARRIAGE

Oliver O'Donovan

It is widely believed and stated that there is no such doctrine as the doctrine of marriage, or, if there is, it is an unfortunate mistake which has to be recovered from. That there should be Christian doctrine about the being of God and the history of salvation needs no argument; for the claim that there can be Christian doctrine on moral topics, on the other hand, an argument is often demanded. Yet the argument is readily forthcoming: moral doctrine springs necessarily from the doctrine of creation, which is, only partly but nevertheless essentially, a doctrine of the good of what God has made and the way in which that good is given to humankind as a blessing on human life. And while a moral theologian may leave the doctrine of the Trinity to the systematic theologians, at least in its finer points, he or she has some responsibility for the doctrine of marriage. I summarize what the church has taught, simply for documentary convenience, in words from the Church of England's Canon B30: 'According to our Lord's teaching . . . marriage is in its nature a union permanent and lifelong, for better for worse, till death them do part, of one man with one woman, to the exclusion of all others on either side . . .'[1]

Before we come to this, however, a word to clarify what is meant by 'doctrine'. Two different New Testament concepts are referred to by this one

---

1. *Canons of the Church of England*, 7th edn. (London: Church House Publishing, 2012), p. 51.

word.[2] The Pastoral Epistles speak of 'the deposit' (*parathēkē*), meaning the essential content of the apostolic message entrusted to the ministry of successor generations, which we are told is to be 'guarded' (2 Tim. 1:12), as God himself undertakes to guard it, ensuring against our forgetting or misunderstanding it over the passage of time. There is also a noun with a more active sense, *didachē*, which refers to the church's ongoing exercise of its teaching ministry. A permanent and unchanging testimony to the saving work of God in Christ, on the one hand, and on the other a continuing exposition and communication of it to the intelligence of successive generations: the word 'doctrine' speaks of both these aspects, unchanging and changing. We could no more think of *changing* the *parathēkē* than we could think of changing God himself; but the living task given to Christian teachers in every generation is bound to take on the changing shape of the questions and anxieties that each age throws up.

About the changeable and the unchangeable elements in Christian doctrine there are a couple of misunderstandings that commonly arise:

(a) Unchanging doctrine is not to be swallowed up in institutional continuities. In English-speaking theology the recognition that doctrine changes is associated especially with the nineteenth-century theologian John Henry Newman, who first popularized the term 'development'.[3] The idea of development that he advanced was not that of simply changing with the times. Development, he thought, could be either 'true' or 'false', and authentic development was the prerogative of the catholic mind – which is to say, it could not arise from a wilful determination to go one's own way and think one's own thoughts, but had to be in continuity with the living tradition of the universal church. There would always be a dynamic relation between the way the gospel *had* been proclaimed in the past and the ways in which proclamation was *now* to be shaped, so that the challenges of the past were never lost sight of, but recalled and appreciated in each generation. Development was by learning, not by forgetting or repudi-ating. As the book of Ecclesiasticus (ben Sirach) declares, 'When a man of understanding hears a wise saying, he will praise it and add to it; when a reveller hears it, he dislikes it and casts it behind his back' (Sir. 21:15). In this there is a great measure of truth, but Newman's temptation was to identify the unchanging criteria of truth with an unchanging institution, rather than with the written witness of the apostolic documents. He was too sanguine, we must think, about the faithfulness of the institutional church, and therefore too suspicious of movements of reform and renewal. We have to be alert to the possibility, of

---

2. Unless otherwise indicated biblical translations in this chapter are from the RSV.
3. *An Essay on the Development of Christian Doctrine* (1845).

which the Reformation was an instance, of doctrine being renewed out of Scripture in a way that takes the church by surprise.

(b) The line between the changeable and the unchangeable in doctrine does not divide between one and another set of topics, as though we could declare in advance that teaching on certain matters (say, on morality) lay in our power to change as much as we saw fit, while teaching on other matters (the being of God or the history of salvation) was, as it were, reserved business. When doctrine develops authentically, it is not because somebody thought it would be a good idea to develop it; it is because the church has been instructed by the Holy Spirit how to expound and defend the deposit faithfully in a new phase of its missionary experience. It develops out of a critical attention to phenomena, which engages the whole church and not only the leadership, the ordained ministry or the theologians. The theologians may articulate, bishops may define, but they can do so authentically only when the church has faithfully discerned under the authority of Scripture. To say this is simply to say that the church is not exempt from the ordinary conditions of intellectual life, which are (in Hegel's famous words) that the owl of Minerva flies at dusk after the daytime of experience. Doctrinal development is not a *scheduled* flight, to suit the traveller's convenience. It is the whole difference between doctrine and ideology that ideology *prescribes* experience, whereas doctrine *reflects* on it. The test of good doctrinal development is its capacity to be integrated into the wider understanding of the whole, and to shed new light where light has already fallen, so that the faithful know themselves possessed of a richer, clearer and more coherent understanding of their lives before God, more equipped in thought to meet the challenges of their contemporaries. When the faithful are at odds, struggling to understand and unable to agree, development of doctrine has not happened.

There may be currents and fashions in Christian thought; the opinions of one generation of Christian teachers may not be the opinions of the next, and not everything that is believed and taught within the church, not everything that is seriously thought within the church, is church doctrine. The Greek theologians like to speak of *theologoumena*, which are legitimate conclusions of theological reasoning not to be classed as *dogmata*. There does not have to be a Christian doctrine about everything; philosophical assumptions, theological explorations, even exegetical interpretations are all subject to change and development without entailing change of doctrine as such. Christian doctrine is a crystallization of the teaching of the church made when it appears that clear boundaries need to be formally marked. In faithfulness to the apostolic deposit of faith the church finds itself from time to time required to highlight certain definitive steps of Christian thought, ruling out some possibilities, pointing to others. These boundaries are drawn as and only as they are needed – which is why we do not find ancient formulae stating that marriage is between one man and one woman, for it was wholly unnecessary at that time to state what appeared to be obvious. Once drawn, these boundaries serve to liberate Christian thought by preventing it going round in circles, lost in fruitless speculation upon old mistakes.

It was from very early days that the church needed to draw a boundary around the work of God as *maker of heaven and earth*, that is to say, of *all that is*. In certain periods, out of misplaced jealousy for redemption, Christians have succumbed to a temptation to disregard the doctrine of creation and not to think coherently about the form and design of the world we live in, its beauty and form as the communication of God's goodwill toward the work of his hands. This error arose first among the gnosticizing thinkers of the second century; it occurred again in Protestant theology both in the Reformation period and the twentieth century. But we must be able to conceive of what God has made as a whole, a coherent universe, and of God as the giver of order and beauty in the totality of things: 'God saw everything that he had made, and behold, it was very good' (Gen. 1:31) – 'it was', not 'they were', we notice, for all the things there are make one coherent work of God. Creation is the root of our moral criteriology, as we learn to see God's work with God's eyes as 'very good', i.e. as *complete and finished*, not in the sense that God is now inactive, but that his ongoing activity preserves and redeems what he has perfectly accomplished. Only on those terms can we speak of God's own goodness as faithfulness to his creation, and of the goodness of our own active lives, as they are given us, as faithfulness to his work.

And so at key points Christian doctrine has had to venture beyond the general assertion of creation to warn us against mistrusting certain specific goods that God has made for us, warning us against those who would 'forbid marriage and enjoin abstinence from foods which God created to be received with thanksgiving by those who believe and know the truth' (1 Tim. 4:3). On the other hand, doctrine reminds us to discern the working of God not only as the maker of the world and its time, but as its redeemer, and it must sometimes frame warnings against mistaking the created goods that God has made for the ultimate goals of history. 'The kingdom of God is not food and drink but righteousness and peace and joy in the Holy Spirit' (Rom. 14:17). 'In the resurrection they neither marry nor are given in marriage, but are like angels in heaven' (Matt. 22:30). A well-balanced doctrine of marriage has warnings to give on both those sides: marriage is a created good, a first thing but not a last.

But before we come to the doctrine of marriage, however, there is a prior step: the doctrine of human nature. To speak of our existence as *human* is to speak of ourselves as *a kind of worldly* being. It is to recognize not only that we find ourselves *existing*, 'thrown' in the world, as Heidegger put it, but that we find ourselves possessing a form which is 'given'. Human nature looks in two directions at once: to meet instinctual animal needs, on the one hand, and to exercise freedom and faithfulness that goes with speech and covenant-making, on the other. In both directions it is a primary characteristic of our nature that we are social; but society is vastly enhanced as it is taken beyond the level of bare need-satisfaction to free mutual engagements. A conference centre contains a space for human beings to meet and talk in, but it also contains some beds for human beings to sleep in. When we glance at ourselves in the mirror we see the light of intelligence in our eyes, but we also see the material con-struction of a kind of mammal: skin, bone, sinew, limbs, etc. We have to situate our human existence in terms of what we have in common with the non-human nature around us as well as in terms of what makes us special. And we have to be clear that *both* aspects of our human nature are the good gift of the Creator. From the first breath of Adam, self-transcendence – the sacred narrative calls it 'dominion' (Gen. 1:26) – is given to the human creature as well as a material constitution, and both are engaged in the social capacity to love one another. Love means helping another to realize the twofold form of existence that God has given. Those who believe that love means feeding the hungry and clothing the naked have remembered something important. So have those who believe that love means regarding promises as binding, telling the truth, sustaining partnerships, suffering for one another's sake. Love is concrete; one must love this person or that, and this person or that is always both a material and a spiritual being.

We enjoy cultivating a certain amount of dizzy transcendence about the human situation in the vast cosmic order; but a recognition of our immanence is at least as important. You may, perhaps, be familiar with the famous prayer about God's creation of 'interstellar space, galaxies, suns, the planets in their courses, and this fragile earth, our island home'. But 'this fragile earth' is not only 'our island home', it is ourselves, for we, too, are fragile earth. A doctrine of humanity has to warn against overlooking the material conditions of human existence, which begin from our specific designation in the world of living creatures as *social mammals*. Everything about our physical constitution, everything about our social organization, is predicated on the mammalian structure of our species. Of course, that is not all that being human is, but it is an inseparable part of it. This means that we have a distinct form of embodiment, the dimorphic sexual differentiation that serves mammalian reproduction, and a distinct form of *co*-embodiment, the social forms of neighbourhood in which we look to one another to perform differentiated tasks and roles. These bodily and social forms in which we are cast have an immense fruitfulness for us, going far beyond the immediate ends of reproduction and child-rearing. The pair-bond is raised beyond a reproductive partnership to form deep and lifelong friendship; our social organization allows not only safety for our young, but the enriching and complexification of cultural communications – art, science, technique and worship. And at each point the basic biological conditions are the foundation for the extensive intellectual and moral superstructure that confers on us the freedoms we enjoy as individual members of our species. Without the foundation, we could not have the superstructure. One and the other, they are both the good gifts of God. That is what we have to hold on to if we are to see the redemption of the human race as the vindication of the work of a good Creator. In the terms of patristic theology, this is what is at stake between Christianity and Manichaeism.

And here we have a framework within which to set (and none too soon) the distinct character of *marriage* as a gift of creation. It is a social institution, uniquely serving both the natural needs of the species as a whole and the spiritual freedom that forms the core possibility in individual existence. Precisely that is what differentiates it from other types of friendship. They, too, serve freedom; they, too, serve individual expansion of mind and personality; they do it through social engagement. But friendships grow and fade in immediacy together with the challenges of the moment, and the pattern of friendships we have in old age rarely looks as it did in youth. They cannot unify the exercise of freedom through the successive experiences of youth, maturity and age. Marriage, on the other hand, with its specific structure of rules and permissions, is a social provision for beings who know themselves called by God to live consistently through a lifetime of unknown length, those for whom their old age is a question for them in their youth, and their youth a question for them in their old age. It is a distinctive way of binding natural structure together with reflective freedom, and makes its own, quite irreplaceable, testimony to the goodness of the Creator's gift.

A Western doctrine which, with variations, had ecumenical currency from Augustine until well into the twentieth century, speaks of the 'three goods' or 'three ends' of marriage: *proles, fides, sacramentum* – the good of children, the good of faithfulness and the good of embodying meaning, a physical, moral and spiritual good all at once. To appreciate the strength of this formulation one has to appreciate that it is intended as an *ascending* list, from the material to the moral and spiritual goods, and in it Augustine was consciously improving on a tradition that said that the only good of marriage in the Christian era was the begetting of children. Marriage was also a structure through which God would enable us to overcome our natural instability and practise faithfulness to one another; furthermore, in the permanence of the relationship it built between the couple, it offered us a way of comprehending the love of Christ for his church.[4] It is a concurrence of different goods fit for both natural and existential demands, and that is what marks marriage as a gift of the Creator, which we could never simply have invented. We can analyse the different strands that comprise the complex good of marriage: the fascination with the other, the satisfaction of sexual desire, the companionship and cooperation, the courage to venture upon parenthood, the reinforcement of memory in old age, and so on. We can imagine these strands separately from one another, and speculate on, even experiment with, putting them together differently. But such speculations and experiments do not constitute real and viable alternatives for human nature. To imagine other possibilities is not to make a success of them, and when people say 'Why should it not be thus and so . . . ?' they are still living in the sphere of the imagination. Marriage preserves this complex of goods concretely, reinforcing each good by holding it together with the others, and in this way it is more than the sum of its parts.

Within this context we can understand the stipulation 'one man and one woman'. It means, in the first place, an exclusive and permanent partnership of *two individuals*, allowing the life of each to develop as a unified moral enterprise, from youth to old age. Older people often ask, Can I be the same person, morally, that I was when young? Can I be true to the ideals I had then, or am I, after all, a completely different person? There are different levels on which this question can be addressed. A final answer must rest with baptism, which unifies our lives eschatologically within the kingdom of heaven. But there is also a natural ground for believing in the possibility of self-consistency, and that is marriage, which keeps us the same as we relate primarily to the one partner. In the second place, it means a partnership *between the sexes*. What this means and makes possible in terms of temperamental adaptability and mutual faithfulness is something that most of us have intuitions of rather than clearly formed ideas. It is famously difficult to theorize ways in which men and women typically differ from one another and complement one another, and almost any broad generalization can be stopped in its tracks quite easily by counter-examples. One reason this is so, of course, is that masculinity and femininity are not fixed quantities, but forms of development, so that a young man is different from an old man, a young woman from an old woman. Yet for the most part people persist in supposing that this complementarity is perfectly real, however difficult to decipher and pin down its elements may be. One reason is that it is such a common experience to find our own emotional reactions difficult to understand

---

4. For this logic see especially *De Bono Coniugali* 3.3, and for the doctrine in its developed form *De Nuptiis et Concupiscentia* 17.19.

without seeing them as part of a pattern that belongs to our sex. But let us suppose, for the sake of argument, the most sceptical view of masculinity and femininity, let us write it all off as a cultural construct and accept that to get along in an intimate day-to-day manner it only needs two 'persons'. There is still one thing that must be said about the partnership of man and woman: the one who keeps us company from youth to age is the one with whom we share our procreative role as a member of the human race, a role that can otherwise split dangerously apart from our conscious moral projects and become an anarchic and anti-social force. With that person's help, as with no other help, it is unified with the remainder of our moral goals in the form of family affection. The often-despised expansion of the second good as 'a remedy for sin' has its force at this point. Through the stabilizing effect of marriage the fragmenting and self-contradictory tensions within our practical and emotional impulses are brought into harmony, offering us the prospect of stable personal maturity. And that, we must note, is a *moral* contribution of marriage to the life of the human race, not merely a useful procreative service.

The hardest of the three goods for the church to formulate satisfactorily has been the third. It arises from the observation of St Paul at Ephesians 5:32 that speaks of marriage as an analogy to the love of Christ for the church. Despite an embarrassed tradition of Protestant exegesis that has struggled to avoid the point, the apostle seems quite clearly to apply the term *mystērion* to the institution of marriage, and since *mystērion* is uniformly the Greek equivalent for the Latin *sacramentum*, we may go so far as to say (provocatively, of course!) that marriage is the only ritual that is ever described as a 'sacrament' in Holy Scripture, though of course that leaves open the question of what 'sacrament'/'mysterion' means. When Augustine used the word for the third good of marriage, it was very loosely defined, and applied to any ritual performance of Old or New Covenant that symbolically represented the gospel. The marriage of Christians, undertaking to love one another with the permanent fidelity of Christ's love for his church, set forth the gospel, even though marriage itself was an institution of creation, not of the gospel. The Reformers, as we know, had difficulty with this. They had to confront the doctrine, originating with Peter Lombard in the twelfth century and elaborated in the scholastic age, which counted seven sacraments corresponding to seven thresholds of human life, each analysed as a means of saving grace. This monstrous dogmatic construction was rightly rejected, throwing into higher relief the two 'sacraments of the gospel' actually ordained by Christ, baptism and eucharist. (Should the Reformers also have noticed that Christ commanded his apostles to lay hands upon the sick? At any rate, they did not do so!) They therefore separated the third good from its sacramental language, leaving it as the English Prayer Book has it, somewhat denuded, as the 'mutual comfort and help which the one shall have of the other . . .' Elsewhere, they tried to put back something of what had been lost to the third good in speaking of marriage as 'instituted of God in the time of man's innocency, signifying unto us the mystical union that is betwixt Christ and his church' – Cranmer's words are almost wholly drawn from Augustine.[5]

What is at stake here? We can summarize it in two questions. First, is marriage, understood in the way Christian doctrine has understood it as a lifelong union of one man with one woman, an aspect of 'natural law'? If 'natural law' means universal consensus, apparently not. There have, as is often commented, been many cultural variations on marriage. Yet, to the extent that universal consensus is important for natural law, there is one feature of marriage that has as good a claim to be universal as anything in this world, and that is that marriage must be between two persons of the opposite sex. Cultures differ in many things to do with sex, but not in that. As it stands, that is simply a factual observation; but it is a striking one, if we believe that marriage has any connection at all with created order. It tells us at least that the idea of a marriage between two people of the same sex is a major conceptual innovation, which cannot breezily be assumed as one more variant among the plurality of traditions. That said, the weight of the concept of natural law does not rest on sheer consensus. It rests on the discovery of what allows humanity to flourish, individually and socially. Distortions and corruptions beset every aspect of creaturely life, and though we have no reason to think that our sexual life is more corrupted and distorted by sin than other aspects of our human way of being (as an academic, I tend to be more impressed by our universal incapacity to tell the truth!), it is a sphere of life typically beset by paralysing fears and desires, which very easily become culturally oppressive. (We may recall the horrible traditional Chinese practice of maiming women's feet in order to enhance their sexual attractiveness.) The important point to be said about the *naturalness* of any form of marriage is that it protects the humanity of the couple against exploitation, and helps them to realize themselves as constructive social beings. On that score any innovation is speculative, and the result cannot be safely predicted. Will it prove liberating? Will it deliver us back into bondage? It is for Christian deliberation to make discernments here, not for Christian doctrine. But Christian doctrine can frame that discernment for us with warnings and encouragements not to ignore important aspects of the created gift as we have received it, but to appreciate the role of that gift in God's purposes for creation and redemption of the world.

---

5. 'Solemnization of Matrimony', in the Book of Common Prayer (1549).

But still the church has 'solemnized' marriage, incorporating it into the life of faith within the sacramental community of believers. And so the second question is this: can Christian marriage constitute a distinct form of Christian life and service? It is popular to say that Protestants do not believe in 'Christian marriage' but in 'the marriage of Christians', but that, I think, is an oversimplification. Can we follow Cranmer's, and Augustine's, interpretation of the wedding at Cana in Galilee in John 2, namely, that Christ 'adorned and beautified' the estate of marriage 'with his presence and first miracle that he wrought'? The unmarried Lord makes himself present to the married state, blessing it, not simply as a meal is blessed when we recognize it as the Creator's gift, but as the disciples were, when they were sent forth to witness to the ends of the earth, and promised Jesus' abiding presence. Here, in marriage, there is a witness borne to Christ himself, a witness that consists in the constructive unity of opposites and not only in the cooperation of the like-minded. I have been struck, when studying the thought of those who embrace the idea of same-sex marriage, that the epistle to the Ephesians and the Gospel of John disappear without trace from the account of marriage they give. But that is true of very much Protestant thinking as a whole.

So much, then, for what the Christian church has taught about marriage as a way of life. But, of course, it has also taught, and very decisively, that there is an alternative way of life to marriage. For the disciples of an unmarried Jesus, baptized into the drawing-near of the kingdom of God, procreation was no longer urgent, and it was no longer necessary to be married to find a coherent moral direction for their lives. Viewed eschatologically, the unattached state was clearly superior, though that did not mean that it was right for everybody. At certain points in the history of Christian thought, in the fourth century, the twelfth and perhaps again, as the Reformers thought, in the fifteenth and early sixteenth, this eschatological possibility was so strongly emphasized as to drown out the support of Christian marriage to which the tradition was committed, while in some modern periods the opposite imbalance has sometimes prevailed. But taken all in all, the doctrine of the church has seen these two patterns of life as alternative vocations: either a married state in procreative partnership, or a state of single discipleship without family and procreative responsibilities. All else has been classed as 'fornication'. That was the church's doctrine, not immediately biblical theology, but convincingly derived from biblical theology, and it ought not on any account to be lightly dismissed.

Our present discontents, however, have faced us with the question whether the either–or is final, or whether we can imagine forms of relationship that are not quite marriage or quite singleness, but resemble one or the other of them. I articulate that question simply because it is asked of us, and when a question is persistently asked, it must be responsibly answered, not pushed aside. It is, of course, in the highest degree frustrating to be asked questions that perhaps ought not to be asked. Sometimes the very discussion of a question seems to give away too much, and sometimes it seems to promise an answer which is then not given. Our contemporary habits of thought, dominated as they are by the crude sloganizing of political debates, do not teach us very well what it is simply to acknowledge a question as a question, a confession of a need of insight, a prayer for illumination.

An approach to the question will naturally look for analogies, and here we observe certain very familiar types of marriage that differ from the normal form by failing to present all the three goods of marriage together. There is the marriage of widows, on the one hand (which has sometimes been described as 'polygamy'!), and the marriage of elderly couples, with no procreative expectations, on the other. (*De facto* childless marriages are not to be included here; childless couples share the will to be parents, if children should be given them.) These two anomalous cases have sometimes in the past been controversial among Christians, which is to say that those who had no doubt about the good of Christian marriage could still be in doubt about them. From a formal point of view there are two ways we may describe them. One is to insist that they are marriages, in the strict sense, and to qualify the understanding of marriage sufficiently to accommodate them. The other is to view them as analogous forms, which correspond to the norms of marriage in most ways, but not in everything. If we build our understanding of marriage upon them, we take restrictive views, in the first case, of the lifelong vow, which is taken to mean 'for as long as *we both* shall live', not 'for as long as *I* shall live', and in the second case, of procreation among the goods of marriage, which is to be mentioned only when it is possible to include it in the particular couple's goals. Removed from the horizon of death, removed from the horizon of children, the constitutive goods of marriage thus seem to be reduced from three to two, or perhaps to one. But if we approach the question of same-sex unions armed only with a doctrine of one good of marriage, the good commonly called 'relationship', their status as marriages is difficult to argue against. And that is, I believe, the journey that liberal thought has taken on the matter, forgetting the first and second goods, the goods of nature and time, and treating marriage simply as special friendship expanded by sexual union, leaving us without any way of conceiving why same-sex partnerships would be other than marriages.

There is, however, the alternative approach, which is to agree that the two cases are not-quite marriage, but marriage-like possibilities that have opened up by extension in response to pastoral needs. This approach then requires us to ask whether other forms of pastoral accommodation can be imagined, other relations with a marriage-like status. In recent decades churches have in fact adopted such forms in unusual or unprecedented situations. The provision made by the African churches for polygamous households was one such example. More striking, because on the face of it more dramatically in tension with the words of Christ, was the provision made by many churches in the second half of the twentieth century for the marriage of divorced persons with a previous partner living. A good pastoral accommodation is designed to meet a quite specific need; if well designed, it will witness in its own way to the normative form from which it derives. As an adoptive family, where the genetic connection between parent and child is lacking, does not undermine the natural family as a form, but affirms it by modelling itself as closely as possible upon it, so the provisions for the marriage of the divorced aimed to affirm Jesus' teaching on the lifelong character of marriage, while still helping those whose marriages had failed to live in conjugal holiness. We need not decide upon their success in achieving that. The important point is simply this: those churches that first proposed and experimented with forms of prayer to accompany the beginning of a same-sex union – the Swedish church was to the forefront in the 1970s – initially understood themselves as engaged in a pastoral accommodation of this kind. Whether well or badly advised, successfully or unsuccessfully designed, the experiment began as an attempt to deal with a practical problem as pastoral accommodations had done in the past. For reasons we need not go into, this carefully-judged self-understanding has now been swept away, and there is a universe of difference between that and the proposals some churches now entertain. The Scottish Episcopal Church intends simply to remove from its canons the statement of the Christian doctrine of marriage – as though to prove ben Sirach right about 'the reveller' who 'casts it behind his back' (Sir. 21:15).

The point of this discussion, let me repeat, is not to advocate such a pastoral accommodation, which is not for a theologian to do. It is merely to point out that such an approach could allow for continuity with the doctrine of the church, as others do not. A pastoral accommodation has an experimental character; it seeks ways of ministering the gospel to particular needs, and waits upon the Holy Spirit for signs following – evident holiness, faithfulness, fruitfulness in the life of discipleship. A church may have good and sufficient pastoral reasons for engaging in an experiment, which fall far short of grounds for modifying its teaching. Of the future we know only this: we shall be led by the Holy Spirit into new understandings and new practices. When we have been led, we shall appreciate and practise those understandings together, in conscious obedience to Scripture and in the unity of a common mind. But until that happens, we cannot pretend to have been led. No one can programme the Holy Spirit to suit his or her convenience, which is the lesson taught by Simon the magician of

Samaria, who, as Peter said, thought he could possess the gift of God (Acts 8:20).The deep offence of what the Scottish Episcopal Church has done lies in its determination to conceal the tentative character of its action by rewriting the teaching of the church, as though Christian doctrine were nothing but church law under its control, an assumption made quite explicit by the theological paper produced to justify it.[6] In response to any pastoral experiment involving a marriage-like ceremony with same-sex couples, we can only reply: So long as you clearly uphold the doctrine of the universal church, you are free in conscience to act experimentally as you believe the Spirit prompts you; and so is the wider church free to watch, form a careful judgment of the Holy Spirit's leading, and draw appropriate conclusions. But if you demand guarantees in advance that you will be proved right, you are a false prophet!

© Oliver O'Donovan, 2017

---

6. 'A paper laying out the theology of marriage as currently articulated through the Canons and Liturgy of the Scottish Episcopal Church, and exploring whether there is a case for change based on scripture, tradition and reason.' The URL <http://www.scotland.anglican.org/wp-content/uploads/2015/05/General-Synod-2015-Agenda-and-Papers.pdf> continues, as of summer 2016, to give access to the pdf, on which the paper occupies pp. 56–92. For detailed criticism see my article, 'The Wreck of Catholic Identity', <https://www.fulcrum-anglican.org.uk/articles/the-wreck-of-catholic-identity-marriage-canon-revision-in-the-scottish-episcopal-church/>.

13. COVENANT PARTNERSHIPS AS A THIRD CALLING? A DIALOGUE WITH ROBERT SONG'S *COVENANT AND CALLING: TOWARDS A THEOLOGY OF SAME-SEX RELATIONSHIPS*

Andrew Goddard

Robert Song's book, *Covenant and Calling: Towards a Theology of Same-Sex Relationships*, is undoubtedly one of the best and most significant accounts of an alternative to the traditional Christian ethic in relation to sex and marriage.[1] It offers a creative and original contribution which is solidly theological and focused on respectful engagement with Scripture and tradition. It explicitly rejects common paths which are liberal in method, any appeals to contemporary culture and the downplaying of the importance of bodily difference (xi–xvii). Its tone is measured, lucidly setting out its reasoning in dialogue with Scripture and tradition and with foreseen criticisms of its proposed way forward.

Despite its subtitle, which sums up its undoubted ultimate goal, its primary focus is not in relation to same-sex relationships. Instead it presents a wider proposal for non-procreative covenant partnerships as a framework within which same-sex relationships can be affirmed. This chapter therefore focuses on that wider argument with only minimal reference to same-sex relationships. This is for two reasons. First, Song's wider reconfiguration of the traditional

---

1. Robert Song, *Covenant and Calling: Towards a Theology of Same-Sex Relationships* (London: SCM, 2014). All page references in the text are to this book. In preparing this chapter I am grateful to Robert Song for a number of conversations with him about his argument and for comments on an earlier draft.

ethic is important in its own right. Second, it provides the foundation on which his case for same-sex unions rests. If, as I believe, that wider argument faces major problems, then his case for same-sex relationships is undermined.

Song's central argument is that alongside the two callings recognized in Christian tradition – marriage and celibacy – we should recognize a third, covenant partnership. These are non-procreative covenantal relationships which may be sexual and either same-sex or opposite-sex. He acknowledges the novelty of his proposal: 'Throughout Christian history there has been an assumption that there are at most two callings, to marriage or to celibacy, in accordance with the New Testament pattern which never envisages any possibility of a third' (23). This means he needs strong arguments showing his case is nevertheless consonant with Scripture and rectifying a flaw in the tradition, or is able to be accommodated as a development in continuity with, rather than destructive of, tradition.

In what follows I explore the four major elements in his case for covenant partnerships, adding only a brief comment on his further argument that they can be same-sex. I am raising questions which I see as hurdles that need to be cleared if the calling of covenant partnerships in general and same-sex unions within them is to be convincing.

1. By teaching that marriage is now not the only vocation, as there is the calling to celibacy, the church has recognized what Song expresses as 'the significance of the advent of Christ for sexuality. Sex BC is not the same as sex AD' (x). How persuasive is Song in arguing that this development also provides the basis for a further third calling of 'eschatologically grounded covenant partnerships that are not procreative in nature' (59)?

2. Song then argues that covenant partnerships are 'like marriages . . . marked by three goods' (28). How should we evaluate his account of these and the theological rationale for them he offers based on the impact of Christ on the goods of marriage?

3. Does Song establish a strong case for his central claim that 'the fundamental distinction within committed relationships is not whether they are heterosexual or homosexual, but whether they are procreative or non-procreative in orientation' (38)?

4. What are we to make of his claim that covenant partnerships can be sexual partnerships because 'sex may have . . . a different and separable meaning from procreativity' (59)?

Finally, after a brief comment on the further challenges in relation to same-sex unions, I explore whether, if his case for covenant partnerships is accepted despite my concerns, it is better understood not as a third calling but as a reframing of the calling of marriage.

Celibacy plus covenant partnerships as callings post-Christ?

Song's opening chapter offers a clear, concise statement of the classic Christian understanding of the place of marriage within salvation history and how Christ's coming opened up the second calling of celibacy. Song claims that 'certain other kinds of relationships are also made possible which were theologically speaking never possible before' (23). But is New Testament teaching able to be extended in this way?

Song's primary textual basis is the discussion of resurrection and marriage in Luke 20:27–38 (and parallels in Matt. 22:23–33 and Mark 12:18–27). This records a challenge to Jesus by resurrection-denying Sadducees on the basis of Deuteronomy 25:5–10 requiring Levirate marriage. They create a scenario in which a woman consecutively marries seven brothers who each die when she is childless, leading to the question of whose wife she will be at the resurrection. Jesus responds, according to Luke,

> The people of this age marry and are given in marriage. But those who are considered worthy of taking part in the age to come and in the resurrection from the dead will neither marry nor be given in marriage, and they can no longer die; for they are like the angels. They are God's children, since they are children of the resurrection. (20:34–36)[2]

Song's argument is that the assumption here is 'that marriage is instituted to deal with the problem that people die' (15). So – 'Where there is resurrection, there is no death; where there is no death, there is no need for birth; where there is no birth, there is no need for marriage' (15). In the eschatological fulfilment of creation the nexus of marriage and procreation therefore becomes redundant. This opens up a new calling of celibacy as a witness to that future beyond marriage and children. But can it also open up another new calling – to non-procreative covenant partnerships?

Four aspects of this passage, set alongside other New Testament passages which directly relate to marriage and celibacy, cast doubt on Song's argument that the New Testament provides a firm biblical and theological foundation for his third calling.

---

2. Unless otherwise indicated all biblical translations in this chapter are from the NIV.

First, Song's argument stresses the saying, 'for they can no longer die', which is unique to Luke. By highlighting the presumed assumptions and logic behind it, he appears to develop a reductionist rationale for marriage as instituted to deal with the problem that people die. This is in tension with the rest of Scripture, including Jesus' appeal to Genesis 1 and 2, prior to death's entrance in Genesis 3. While Levirate marriages – the focus of this debate – are simply about procreation in the face of death, it is at best misleading to draw conclusions from this about marriage generally.

Second, all three Synoptic Gospels give the reason why there is no 'being given in marriage' in the age to come as that we will then be like or equal to angels. A commonly held explanation of this is that it refers to the angels not marrying and to the lack of angelic sexual activity. Loader writes that 'the vision reflects a value system which sees no place for sexuality in the resurrected life'.[3] Song seems to recognize this later when he writes, 'The whole eschatological and ascetic thrust of the NT is towards a vision of the resurrection life which, against the majority Jewish teaching of the time, is not a repristination of marriage and family life but *a life beyond marriage, sex and family altogether*' (74, italics added). This explains why the church understood Christ's teaching – and the breaking in of the eschaton – to open up the path of celibate singleness. It creates problems, however, for a *sexual* relationship which is similarly grounded eschatologically.

This problem is increased by the commendation of celibacy in Matthew 19:12 in terms of 'becoming a eunuch'. Loader again comments that 'in the future kingdom, the life to come, sexual relations will cease; accordingly some are called to live like that already now'.[4] A life beyond sex is also evident in 1 Corinthians 7: if the unmarried and widows 'cannot control themselves, they should marry, for it is better to marry than to burn with passion' (7:9). The two ways of life are thus clear: either celibacy which involves no sex or, if that is not possible, marriage. There is no way of extending either of these texts into a third calling of committed sexual relationships.

Third, the problem is actually even deeper than whether or not covenant partnerships can be sexual. Song is arguing for a new pattern of 'committed relationship' alongside marriage. The basis in all three Synoptic Gospels for an alternative way of life to marriage opening up is that it bears witness to the resurrection life where we will be 'like the angels'. One assumes that Song does not believe that there will be covenant partnerships in the eschaton and that

3. William Loader, *The New Testament on Sexuality* (Grand Rapids: Eerdmans, 2012), p. 435.
4. Ibid., p. 444.

those in covenant partnerships are more 'like the angels' than those who are married. If covenant partnerships, like marriage, have no place in the 'age to come' then it is hard to see how Luke 20 can be extended to support covenant partnerships as an eschatologically grounded calling.

The wider New Testament again supports this. Jesus' language of 'eunuchs' likely alludes to the total devotion to the king required of eunuchs while Song notes that in 1 Corinthians 7 'the point of remaining unmarried is to enable followers of Christ to devote themselves to the works of the Lord with their loyalties undivided' (18). But this rationale would entail not only remaining unmarried but also remaining free of a covenant partnership. Far from being a possible new third calling, covenant partnerships in this respect fail in exactly the same way as marriage fails.

Finally, celibacy is also opened up as a new calling by being embodied in Jesus' own life. Any third calling can appeal neither to creation nor to Israel's history nor to Christ's example nor to the teaching and practice of the apostolic church. It rests on a particular understanding of the nature of eschatological life to offer a novel proposal as to a new calling that might take shape in history. Rather strangely, the only text which provides any textual basis for that shape is a passage where, on Song's understanding, we do not in fact have seven marriages but rather seven covenant partnerships.

To sum up, Song rightly challenges us to consider the impact of Christ's coming for our understanding of sex and marriage. His account is, however, highly selective, with its concentration on Luke 20, the non-procreative character of the eschaton, and the claim that marriage is transcended by the resurrection because it is there to deal with the problem of death. Once the fuller New Testament picture of the relationship between marriage, celibacy and the eschaton is considered, it is clear that although covenant partnerships could be understood as witnessing to eschatological life as beyond procreation, it is very hard to extend the logic of biblical texts which justify celibacy as a new calling, to justify this further new calling. These texts are indeed eschatologically based and perhaps partly related to the overcoming of death and the end of any obligation to procreate. But this is not their only, or even their primary, rationale for celibacy. At no point in the New Testament is celibacy explicitly encouraged or expounded as a new calling *because procreation has been transcended and no longer has the place it had in God's purposes*. Once the other, more explicit, eschatological rationales for a new calling alongside marriage are understood, these cannot be extended to a covenant partnership. Like marriage there is no evidence such a partnership, particularly if sexual, prefigures a pattern of human relationships present in the eschaton and, like marriage, covenant partnerships entail commitments restricting people's freedom to serve Christ and his kingdom.

Although Song's theological *rationale* for covenant partnerships is related to the theological rationale for celibacy – the eschaton – their theological *shape* is much more related to the theological shape of marriage. Here again, there are a number of questions.

The goods of marriage and of covenant partnership: What difference does Christ make?

The eschatological basis of covenant partnerships marks them out in terms of what they are not: they are not procreative. What marks them out positively and what is the theological basis for this account?

Song proposes three characteristics for covenant partnerships in order to give them a moral shape and to explain the obligations people undertake and commitments they make on entering into them. He does so by reference to the three traditional goods of marriage, but replacing procreation with 'fruitfulness' to speak of faithfulness, permanence and fruitfulness. How he constructs this vision is not totally clear but appears to have the following steps.

The goods of marriage and Christ

The three traditional goods of marriage are distinguished theologically in the light of the coming of Christ. In particular, 'Of the three goods of marriage, procreation has become redundant, theologically speaking, for those who are in Christ' (27). Song contrasts the goods in terms of their 'final intelligibility': procreation is 'a good of creation that gains its final intelligibility from its being a participation by created beings, in a manner appropriate to created beings, in the original gift of creation itself' (27). In relation to Christ, he claims that 'just as creation has now been fulfilled in Christ, so the purpose of procreation has now been fulfilled' (27–8). In contrast, faithfulness and permanence 'are goods that gain their final intelligibility from their witnessing to the future relationship between humankind and God' (28). They witness 'to the future relationship between humankind and God that has been made real in Christ and will be revealed in its fullness in the eschaton' (28). So, 'while the three goods are inseparable as goods of creation, the coming of Christ reveals their different logics and divergent trajectories' (28).

The undergirding theology here – particularly the proposed interrelationship between creation, Christ (especially his incarnation) and new creation in relation to the three goods – is left unexplored. In fact a good case can be made that all three goods are creation goods fulfilled in Christ and that all three also have eschatological significance.

Faithfulness and permanence are made real and intelligible from God's work in creation (often understood in terms of a covenant) and in his covenants, beginning with Noah. Given that covenant partnerships 'gain their ultimate intelligibility from being a witness to God's covenant love to human beings' (28), it is therefore not clear why we needed to await Christ's coming for this calling to have a place. Is it also not better to speak of faithfulness and permanence gaining their final intelligibility from their witnessing to Christ rather than from 'their witnessing to the future relationship between humankind and God'? And if so, have they not also, in an important sense, been fulfilled in Christ? Indeed it could be argued that it is precisely because of this fulfilment of *all* the goods of marriage in Christ that the second calling of life beyond marriage in celibacy opens up in human history post-Christ: that which marriage pointed to has now been fulfilled in Christ, who is in a sense the *telos* of marriage. But if so, then surely that which covenant partnerships supposedly point to has also been fulfilled in Christ. Why then do they suddenly appear post-fulfilment?

In relation to the good of procreation, Song seems to go beyond the claim based on Luke 20 that procreation itself has no place in the new creation, to claim that procreation has no eschatological significance. It appears to be theologically fully intelligible within creation and without reference to the new creation and so 'has become redundant, theologically speaking, for those who are in Christ' (27). However, at its simplest, the only way in which there are humans to share in 'the future relationship between humankind and God' (and 'those who are in Christ') is because of procreation. Procreation continues to be the created means to this eschatological goal. This created good finds its fulfilment not in the conception of a new human creature, but in the 'great multitude that no one could count, from every nation, tribe, people and language, standing before the throne and before the Lamb' (Rev. 7:9) where the final intelligibility of procreation is clear as humans 'glorify God and enjoy him for ever'.

In summary, Song's argument seems to require a sharp contrast between one good – rooted in creation and fulfilled in Christ and now theologically redundant as lacking any eschatological significance – and two goods which, although described as goods of creation and 'made real' in Christ, remain and bear witness to a future fulfilment. It is far from clear he has given sufficient theological rationale for such polarization.

Faithfulness and permanence in covenant partnerships

Song's next step is to make the twin goods of faithfulness and permanence jointly essential to covenant partnership. Limits of space prevent a full exploration of this but a number of questions are raised:

- Why are these required features?
- Do they arise from created human nature or solely the pattern of God's covenant-making?
- What response would be given to someone (for example, a bisexual person wishing to have a covenant partnership with a same-sex and an opposite-sex partner) who argues for a union embodying only one or neither good?
- If sex requires these goods, covenant partnerships need not be sexual so why need they be permanent and faithful?

Fruitfulness as a third good

Finally, Song adds the good of fruitfulness which seems to be the post-Christ transformation of procreation. Its substantive content remains vague ('restricted only by the limits of the imagination' (29)) as does the way in which it distinguishes covenant partnership from other fruitful callings, including marriage. Its establishment as a *third* good and its broadening of biological fruitfulness however ensures that covenant partnerships remain 'like marriages' (28) apart from being non-procreative. Having raised questions about whether covenant partnerships can be a third calling opened up alongside celibacy but shaped by reference to marriage, we now turn to explore this crucial distinction and whether it can bear the weight placed on it by Song's account.

Procreation and non-procreation: The fundamental distinction?

In arguing for covenant partnerships and their distinction from marriage, Song is clear that 'the fundamental distinction within committed relationships is . . . whether they are procreative or non-procreative in orientation' (38). We will return to definitional questions later, but by procreation Song appears to mean something like 'the creation of a new human life in which the couple are the biological parents'. This section examines this distinction in the light of Scripture, then tradition and then reason.

The witness of Scripture

It is indisputable that procreation is central in the Old Testament. The issue is the change brought about by the coming of Christ. Luke 20 refers, by implication, to the ending of procreation in the age to come, but not in the present age post-Christ. Song argues that 'there is almost nothing in the New Testament which actively encourages having children, nor is procreation ever given as a reason for Christians to seek marriage', and that 'the case for actively *having* children, as opposed to welcoming or giving instruction to those children that already exist, is very hard to make from the pages of the New Testament' (19). He here diminishes, almost eliminates, procreation within the New Testament. There are three weaknesses with this.

First, Song is presenting an argument from silence to claim biblical support for his strong claim that having children 'has become redundant, theologically speaking, for those who are in Christ' (27). Is it not, however, possible that child-bearing is such a God-given, created human desire, spoken of so highly in the Old Testament, and producing the blessing and good (as Song accepts) of children, that it is not surprising that our snapshot of apostolic teaching in the New Testament canon does not have to reiterate such a theological vision? We have here an interesting paradox. Song is arguing that, although Scripture is totally silent about it, we should recognize a theologically based non-procreative calling. He is doing so in part on the basis that, despite Scripture as a whole speaking very highly of procreation, the New Testament's silence means that procreation is theologically redundant in Christ.

Second, the New Testament is not as silent as Song presents it. He admits only one 'possible counter-example' (19): that women 'will be saved through childbearing' (1 Tim. 2:15). But three chapters later Paul writes, 'I counsel younger widows to marry, to have children, to manage their homes and to give the enemy no opportunity for slander' (1 Tim. 5:14). The verb appears only here in the New Testament but *teknogonein* quite clearly means to bear children. Paul is, in other words, calling on young widows not only to marry but specifically to procreate. Song's silence about this text is telling.

Third, in his discussion of Romans 1, Song offers a remarkably conservative reading where non-procreation is a key factor in Paul's critique. This must mean that non-procreation was not viewed as positively by Paul as Song wishes us to view it.

In summary, not only is it the case that the New Testament 'never envisages' (23) a third non-procreative calling, but also that the theological key to unlocking such a calling in Song's argument – the New Testament's claimed lack of interest in procreation and indifference to non-procreation in history post-Christ – is not as strong as he claims.

The witness of tradition

Turning to Christian tradition, three further problems with highlighting this procreative versus non-procreative distinction can be noted.

First, the patterns of relationship Song wishes to distinguish as a third distinct calling are well known to the tradition and in their heterosexual form are simply marriages. As Song acknowledges (35), Augustine was in no doubt that marriage was permanent even in the face of infertility. Reformation churches, more tolerant of divorce, did at times allow the ending of marriage due to infertility but this was not the only view. In the Middle Ages sterility did not constitute an impediment to marriage and modern Roman Catholic Canon Law is equally clear that 'sterility neither forbids nor invalidates marriage' (Canon 1084, §3). Even more difficult for his case is the recognition, even celebration, of spiritual or Josephite marriages where the married couple refrained from sex, and the related, but distinct, matter of the consensus from around the twelfth and thirteenth centuries that consent even without consummation made a marriage. At no point in the tradition was it held that a marriage required children in order to be a genuine marriage and that therefore marriages which were childless – even deliberately so – were not marriages but something else. A strong argument therefore needs to be made as to why all these judgments are wrong and we must instead recognize a new calling.

Second, Christian tradition does, however, reject *deliberately* childless marriages where, in Song's words, 'the couple enter upon marriage with the express under-standing between themselves that they will not have children *as a result of their sexual relationship*' (29–30, italics added). Song is sympathetic to this traditional rejection in his own understanding of marriage but proposes covenant partner-ships as a third divine calling. But the tradition did not only deny such a pattern of life the designation of 'marriage', it viewed it as wrong. In contrast, Song's acceptance of deliberately childless but sexual unions means he has given much more space than he wishes to a voluntarist, in danger of becoming consumerist, approach to children and hence to 'the preferred idioms and conceptualisations of contemporary secular culture' (xiii).

Third, the tradition has not focused on biological procreation. Its concern has not been the union of gametes, but children – their birth and formation. So the 1662 Anglican Book of Common Prayer (following earlier liturgies) is clear that marriage 'was ordained for the procreation of children, to be brought up in the fear and nurture of the Lord, and to the praise of his holy Name' and canon B30 of the Church of England similarly refers to marriage as 'for the procreation and nurture of children'. Roman Catholic Canon Law opens its section on marriage with the definition of 'the matrimonial covenant' as one 'ordered by its nature to the good of the spouses and the procreation *and education* of offspring' (Canon 1055, emphasis added). In contrast, Song's focus on marriage in terms of procreation is understood simply as 'a participation by created beings, in a manner appropriate to created beings, in the original gift of creation itself' (27). This is necessary because he sees the bringing up of children as part of the fruitfulness for covenant partnerships and perhaps also from his focus on Luke 20 and the argument that creating new life is eschatologically not necessary. Such a definition is, however, reductionist and risks distorting the tradition's much larger and more dynamic conception of the procreative good of marriage.

The witness of reason

Finally, it needs to be considered whether focusing the distinction on procreation narrowly defined is reasonable. Procreation contrasts with the other goods in that it is not in the gift of the people who marry, either as individuals or as a couple. It is a creative work of God in and through the parents' actions. In entering marriage there are therefore promises to forsake all others and to commit to one's spouse until death but no promise to procreate. The questions here relate to Song's definition of procreation and language of being 'non-procreative in orientation' (38).

It makes most sense to understand procreation as a good accomplished by conception but this makes the distinction between the two callings a strange one which is, in many cases, impossible to discern, certainly publicly, and perhaps even for the couple themselves. According to this differentiation, a couple who are childless through miscarriage or abortion are married while a couple who have never conceived are not married. Even without reproductive technologies, Song's proposal creates odd situations. Any couple 'marrying' without having already conceived are in an unclear situation as to their calling within Song's account. Whatever their subjective 'orientation' towards possible future children (positive, neutral or negative), their 'procreative' or 'non-procreative' outcome is unknown. This can make distinguishing the two callings very difficult in reality. Song appears to hold that – as long as they are male and female and not too old to bear children – a committed couple should be viewed as married unless and until they either declare they are deliberately childless or find they are contingently childless. If Song's distinction is to be made between two callings on the basis of whether a partnership is procreative or not then perhaps the better solution would be that proposed by Nigel Biggar:

> Perhaps we should have a two-tier system, with committed relationships, whether hetero- or homo-sexual, beginning with the status of 'amicable union' and only graduating to 'marriage', when they become parental. That would be the most rational arrangement. And the fact that it's rational doesn't make it unchristian. On the contrary, it's rational precisely because it would rescue the Christian affirmation of the goodness of procreation from waters that have become muddied by modern technological developments. You heard it here first!

To my knowledge, no one else has proposed this, and I'm not about to start campaigning for it.[5]

To sum up, Song is clear that it is important that 'if we are to introduce the category of covenant partnership at all, the fundamental distinction it connotes is . . . between procreative and non-procreative relationships' (37). This section has, through appeal to Scripture, tradition and reason, raised a number of problems with defining a third calling on this basis. A key issue raised by some of these problems and by some earlier discussion is the relationship between sex and procreation to which we now turn.

Sexual covenant partnerships?

The distinctive character of covenant partnerships may be that they are non-procreative, but what makes them particularly controversial is that they may be sexual relationships. The key change Song is arguing for is the opening up of a pattern of non-procreative *sexual* relationship, a divine calling which intentionally seeks to prevent conception from every act of sexual intercourse or restricts sexual expression to inherently non-procreative forms of sexual behaviour. What follows explores Song's case for this in relation to two areas: his use of the arguments about contraception and whether a case can be made that sex has changed in this way before and after Christ.

Sex, contraception and procreation

In relation to the first, Song argues that marriage is unavoidably linked to procreation but that sex need not be (54). It need not be, he says, because it is not the case that 'every time a married couple has sex, they must be open to the possibility of having children . . . Sex . . . would always have to have that procreative possibility' (54–55). That judgment is what has made contraception acceptable and Song claims that it must also remove any objection to non-procreative covenant partnerships being sexual. But is that so?

One problem here is that when thinking about the purpose of sex and its link to procreation Song uses the phrase, 'every time a married couple has sex'. He therefore focuses on each separate sexual act rather than the series of acts in the context of the sexual relationship. Yet he is later quite clear that, quoting

---

5. Nigel Biggar, 'Gay Marriage: What's All the Fuss About?', Sermon preached 25th March 2012.

O'Donovan, 'Marriage should not be conceptualised in a way that reduces it to a series of one-night stands' (58) and so 'procreativity is properly predicated of marriage as a whole, not of particular occasions of sexual intimacy' (58). Here then he is not focused on 'every time' but on 'marriage as a whole' and so contraception may be legitimate.

It is also noteworthy that he says 'marriage as a whole' not 'a sexual relationship as a whole'. In the traditional Christian understanding, however, marriage and legitimate sexual relationship are coterminous. Therefore, to reword the quotation above, Christian teaching holds that 'procreativity is properly predicated of a sexual relationship as a whole, not of particular occasions of sexual intimacy'. This is a view which is incompatible with his argument for sexual, non-procreative covenant partnerships but allows for the legitimate use of contraception within a sexual relationship.

It is therefore not the case that once one accepts contraception it follows that sexual but purposefully non-procreative relationships are also acceptable. Song seems to think that this does follow on the grounds that 'if one concedes that contraception is justifiable, one also concedes that sex is characterised by a good which is independent of and additional to its orientation to procreation' and so 'sex has other roles and is open to other meanings and purposes than procreation' (58). The peculiarity here is that even most of those opposed to contraception would not deny the conclusion that sex has other meanings and purposes than procreation. The key question is what is meant by sex having goods 'independent of . . . its orientation to procreation' and whether the separation of the various goods and total removal of the good of procreation from all sex within a relationship is morally relevant. Song has to defend a separation of sex from procreation at the level of a sexual *relationship* and not simply at the level of an individual sexual *act* and this cannot simply be done by appealing to acceptance of contraception.

Sex BC *and sex* AD

Song's argument also has to explain how the coming of Christ has brought about a change in the relationship between sex and procreation. His sole theological argument about the goodness of non-procreative sex is 'the connection between sexual intimacy and our knowledge of God' (59). He claims – with an appeal to Song of Songs and to Rowan Williams – that the delight experienced in erotic and sexual encounter and 'the intimacy of communion that one experiences with another' is in fact 'a foretaste of the intimacy of communion one will experience with God'. Sexual relationship 'may thus become a glimpse into the inner life of God and focus for us the very reason for our creation, that we might participate in this' (60).

No theological justification, no biblical basis, is offered for such incredibly strong claims about sex as effectively a means of God's self-revelation and grace. Indeed, a strong case can be made that, in contrast to surrounding cultures, the Old Testament is very careful to separate the sexual act from divine revelation. Davidson begins his monumental study of sexuality in the Old Testament by highlighting that 'there is a radical separation of sexuality and divinity in the Genesis account of origins'.[6] His first detailed study of the features of Old Testament sexuality (ch. 3) focuses on this and how 'any attempts to divinize or sacralize sexuality in Israel, as done in the pagan fertility myths and cult practice, is met with the strongest divine denunciation'.[7] There is nothing in the New Testament to challenge this Old Testament perspective, which is not surprising given that, as Davidson's chapter concludes, 'the various syncretistic religions of the NT milieu included the divinization of sex'.[8]

Even were one to grant Song's arguments relating sex to our knowledge of God, there is another paradox. This good of sex as a revelatory power or means of divine grace is presumably part of creation, a form of natural revelation. Central to the Christian confession is that God has made himself most fully known in the incarnation and that he makes himself known to us by his Spirit who now, post-Christ, fills his people in a manner unknown in the Old Testament such that our bodies are temples of the Holy Spirit. The significance of this breaking in of the age to come and the changes it effects are at the heart of Song's proposal. It would surely be expected that (as with the law) earlier forms of revelation are relatively *less* significant in the age of the Spirit after God has spoken to us through his Son. Song, however, argues that sexual intimacy is now even more significant as it offers 'a foretaste of the intimacy of communion one will experience with God' (60) and justifies patterns of sexual behaviour and relationship which, pre-Christ, were not acceptable within God's people.

This need to justify new forms of sexual intimacy post-Christ highlights a further problem: while the biblical evidence that good sex mediates God is weak, Scripture regularly warns that certain forms of sexual behaviour and relationship lead to separation from God. By proposing that post-Christ there is a new calling to covenant partnership as a form of *sexual* relationship, Song is effectively arguing that the change from BC to AD redefines sexual immorality. A form of sexual immorality pre-Christ has now not only ceased to be so, but

---

6. Richard M. Davidson, *Flame of Yahweh: Sexuality in the Old Testament* (Peabody: Hendrickson, 2007), p. 18.

7. Ibid., p. 85.

8. Ibid., p. 132.

has become a new divine calling and path of holiness. Scripture's acknowledged silence is therefore a serious challenge to Song's proposal. In both Testaments God's people are consistently and strongly warned about sexual immorality. Song notes that in passages such as 1 Corinthians 6 immoral sexual behaviour is related to eschatological exclusion (71). Given this, were the definition of sexual immorality to change significantly as a result of the incarnation one would expect this to be clearly stated in the New Testament. After all, other changes post-Christ, notably in relation to circumcision or food laws, are clearly stated even though these are not of eschatological significance. There is no such clarification.

Furthermore, if it is the separation of sexual behaviour from procreation at the level of a sexual relationship which is the distinctive feature of Song's third calling then it is unclear how the two key theological realities shaping his account – the coming of Jesus and the eschatological goal which he reveals – justify this. He can point to no place where Jesus teaches that there is now a new good of sex or that a recalibration of the goods of sex has occurred such that previously illicit conduct becomes good. Given his reticence about the place of sex in the new creation, Song also has no basis on which to argue that sex detached from procreation is a foretaste or witness to the world to come. Certainly, if in the new heavens and the new earth there is no temple because God is 'all in all' (Rev. 21:22), it is hard to believe that eschatologically there is still sex as a 'glimpse into the inner life of God' (60).

Finally, and relating only to same-sex covenant partnerships, a notable *lacuna* in Song's account is how sexual desire or orientation is to be understood: why is it only post-Christ that God provides a holy way of life for those who are same-sex attracted? The traditional debate in this area has tended to revolve around whether same-sex sexual desire is (like marriage) part of God's good created order or a consequence of human sin and the fall. The latter option is not compatible with Song's account but the former raises the question as to why, if part of the diversity of sexuality in creation, it is only with Christ's coming that same-sex sexual relationships become legitimate. It is hard to see how his theological reconfiguration based on eschatology is able to address this question and so it appears he faces an impasse when it comes to locating same-sex sexual desire theologically within salvation history.

Same-sex covenant partnerships?

If Song's case for covenant partnerships withstands these four areas of critique then two main issues need exploring before he also has a case for same-sex unions. These are his hermeneutic in relation to the negative biblical texts about homosexual behaviour (chapter 4 in Song) and his claim (set out in chapter 3) that procreation is the only theological rationale for sexual differentiation and requiring marriage to be sexually differentiated. In relation to both I believe his argument faces further significant hurdles.

Covenant partnerships: A third calling or marriage reconfigured?

In conclusion it is helpful to unpack some tensions in Song's own account as to how to situate covenant partnerships theologically and to consider whether it is better to see them, not as a third calling, but as a transformation of marriage.

Covenant partnerships – eschatologically founded like celibacy?
The clear theological distinction between marriage and covenant partnership within Song's argument is that the former is rooted in creation and has no eschatological form whereas the latter, like celibacy, is rooted in the eschaton (and its rooting in creation remains largely opaque). Covenant partnerships 'share certain features with marriage' but 'they are theologically speaking *not* in fact the same and have a different place within the divine economy' (27, italics original) as they 'are eschatologically grounded' (28).

One question here is what covenant partnerships bear witness to that is not already borne witness to in either marriage or celibacy. Or, more precisely, what eschatological witness is given by covenant partnerships that is not given by the eschatological witness of celibacy? Song does not clearly answer this although one answer appears to be that a sexual relationship can now be legitimately wholly divorced from procreation. This lack of an answer from Song does not mean that there cannot possibly be such a third calling. However, if it lacks any theological necessity and adds nothing significant to Christian witness beyond what is present in the tradition's account of two callings then, particularly given the acknowledged lack of any explicit biblical basis, the case for such a third calling is weakened.

In fact, covenant partnerships seem to be a hybrid of the two callings of marriage and celibacy in which each is stripped of certain features that are essential to it. From celibacy it takes the embracing of life beyond procreation but removes the requirement of singleness and sexual abstinence. From marriage it takes the goods of faithfulness and permanence but removes the good of procreation.

To be fair to Song, there appears to be a tension or unclarity in his use of the language of eschatology. He frequently refers to his third way as eschatologically founded but at other times the language is more focused on the here and now. For example, covenant partnerships are a 'witness to the time between the times, when God's purposes for creation have been fulfilled in Christ, but where we await their final manifestation' (50). This alternative account could mean speaking of three periods in God's work, rather than just two, mapping on to the three callings he sets out:

1. Marriage rooted in creation and including procreation;
2. celibacy rooted in the consummation of all things; and
3. covenant partnerships as a witness to both the life beyond procreation here and 'now' but also witnessing to the 'not yet' character by retaining many of the features of marriage as a created good and by being sexual.

Covenant partnerships – marriage as covenant partnership?

A more radical reconfiguration of Song's proposal is one he explores briefly at the end of his book. It raises fundamental theological questions about the exact nature of his argument and in particular the relationship between marriage and covenant partnership. From the start Song is clearly arguing for 'a new theological category' (81) distinct from marriage. The two callings are mutually exclusive. One has procreation as an essential defining feature and the other has non-procreation as an essential defining feature. However, he finally floats the idea of *marriage as covenant partnership*. This would address a number of the problems raised above.

If marriage is to be viewed as covenant partnership then covenant partnership must become an all-embracing category of both procreative and non-procreative unions. This does not require the creation of a third calling but rather the reshaping of one of the callings – marriage – in the light of the eschaton so that it is simply a form of covenant partnership. This would have a number of benefits compared to a separate, third calling.

The articulation of the goods of covenant partnership is now the eschatological reshaping of marriage and its goods. Fruitfulness is an over-arching good which may take the form of biological fruitfulness in procreation (as in traditional marriage) but may not. Furthermore, the problems of distinguishing procreative and non-procreative callings are no longer present as both are embraced within the now all-encompassing category of covenant partnership. Most of the various problems raised with Song's account of covenant partnership are no longer present or at least not as strongly or in the same form as when covenant partnership is a distinct third calling. This understanding of covenant partnership could also claim a basis in creation if one were to accept Brownson's argument that the Genesis language of 'one flesh' refers not to marriage as traditionally understood but rather to the creation of a kinship bond between two people, an acceptable description of covenant partnership.[9] This could also solve the problem of how to locate same-sex attraction theologically, which is raised if covenant partnerships are only a calling post-Christ, and the biblical language relating marriage to God's covenant with his people could now be read (as Song appears to do implicitly) as referring to covenant partnerships, one form of which is marriage. Despite these potential benefits, this alternative account of covenant partnerships and their relationship to marriage raises a number of questions and highlights a number of important issues. In conclusion, four of these can be briefly noted.

First, how does this calling of covenant partnership relate to marriage as traditionally understood by Christians? It could be argued that the account above of marriage as covenant partnership – as long as it is limited to a male–female union – is not so very different in practice from the traditional account of marriage. The latter has incorporated within its account of the calling of marriage instances of both procreative and non-procreative unions, just as would this account of marriage as covenant partnership. The way in which this alternative account does this, and particularly its desire to include same-sex unions within the category of covenant partnership, will however lead to radical changes.

Second, a crucial element in Song's argument for covenant partnership is the theological difference made to sex and marriage by the coming of Christ. How might this have a place in this reconfiguration of his proposal? He describes what it might mean in terms of 'marriage itself as changed theologically by the coming of Christ' so that 'after the birth of Christ covenant partnership is the deeper and more embracing category, with procreative marriage now being the special case' (89).

This could represent a radical change in the nature of the calling which becomes something new and significantly different from that which it was before. Some have argued for a similar sort of development in relation to the nature and calling of political authority pre-Christ and post-Christ in which certain features pre-Christ are shed post-Christ. So, although a major reshaping

---

9. James V. Brownson, *Bible, Gender, Sexuality: Reframing the Church's Debate on Same-Sex Relationships* (Grand Rapids: Eerdmans, 2013), ch. 5. For a critique of this and other aspects of Brownson's work see my 'James V. Brownson: *Bible, Gender, Sexuality*: A Critical Engagement' available at <http://klice.co.uk/uploads/Goddard%20 KLICE%20review%20of%20Brownson.pdf> or, more briefly, my review in *Studies in Christian Ethics* 28.1 (2015), pp. 103–10.

of traditional teaching on marriage, this would not be an unprecedented form of argument. There may also be interesting parallels to draw between the nature and role of the law, given that Christ is 'the end of the law'.

An alternative option would be to view the effect as primarily epistemological – the coming of Christ reveals covenant partnership as God's purpose and brings to light what was always the divine intention in creation but which was largely hidden prior to Christ. Here it may be that the key shift is not simply the revelation of a new creation beyond procreation (which Song stresses) but a theme particularly noteworthy in the tradition, especially in Augustine and also Barth, although not prominent in Song's work: the fulfilment in Christ of God's covenant purposes through Israel leading to a change in the place of procreation. On this understanding it is not simply that a life beyond procreation bears witness to the fact that God's purposes in creation are transcended in the non-procreative eschatological future. Procreation was also central to God's covenant promises to Abraham and the divinely chosen path for fulfilling his covenant promises. Now that those promises have been fulfilled and the path reached its *telos* in the birth of Christ, procreation no longer has the same place within God's purposes in history. So Augustine contrasts the requirements before and after Christ in relation to the fulfilment of the historic covenant with Abraham and Israel:

> In the early days of the human race it was the duty of the saints to exploit the good of marriage to multiply the people of God, so that through them the Prince and Saviour of all peoples would be predicted in prophecy and then born. It was not to be sought for its own sake, but was necessary for that other purpose. But now, since there is a teeming abundance of spiritual kindred from all nations on every side to enter upon our holy and pure fellowship, even those zealous to be joined in marriage solely to beget children should be urged to embrace the more honourable good of continence instead.[10]

Song's concern to emphasize the change brought about by Christ would thus still have a place. Prior to Christ, divine revelation focuses on (perhaps even restricts covenant partnerships to) procreative unions (what we have traditionally referred to as 'marriage'). But this is a limitation of the broader created good of covenant partnership, and post-Christ, that wider, more fundamental category

---

10. Augustine, *De Bono Conjugali*, ed. and tr. P. G. Walsh (Oxford: Oxford University Press, 2001), para 9, p. 23. Karl Barth, in his discussion in *Church Dogmatics* III/4, §54.2, writes similarly.

is able to be revealed fully and to take shape in human history with 'marriage' contained within it.

Third, what is lost in this alternative account of covenant partnerships that Song's proposal retains? There are two main consequences of viewing marriage as simply a sub-set within covenant partnerships. First, there is no longer any distinctive calling tied to the good of procreation. Second, there is no longer any distinctive calling tied to the union of male and female. Both of these represent major losses in relation to the traditional Christian doctrine of creation and marriage within creation, whereas Song's account retains these while adding a third calling which does not give them a place.

Fourth, this raises the question of whether this reconfiguration of the relationship between marriage and covenant partnerships can respond to a number of important theological challenges in the light of Scripture and traditional Christian teaching. Many of the issues raised earlier against Song's account of covenant partnership as a third calling distinct from marriage are no longer as pressing. It remains the case, however, that as sexual unions, including same-sex unions, issues surrounding the relationship between sexual activity and procreation persist as does the significance of being made male and female. In fact these are arguably even weightier challenges as there is no longer any distinctive calling that embodies the significance of being made male and female and the created good of procreation. The continuing problem of a lack of support for this alternative account of sexual but gender-blind covenant partnerships in either Scripture or Christian tradition also remains a major problem and indeed leads Song to caution that this view of marriage as covenant partnership, whatever its attractions compared to that of a third calling, 'would constitute a very significant theological change' (91).

© Andrew Goddard, 2017

14. 'MALE AND FEMALE HE CREATED THEM'? THEOLOGICAL REFLECTIONS ON GENDER, BIOLOGY AND IDENTITY

Andrew Sloane

Introduction[1]

'Gender bending', as it was once called, has gone from the titillating sideshows of cabaret to mainstream social phenomenon.[2] What are we to do with that? Some, clearly, want to stick to their guns (so to speak, all Freudian allusions intended). Sex and gender are binary categories, established by God in creation,

---

1. An earlier version of this chapter was published as Andrew Sloane, '"Male and Female He Created Them"? Theological Reflections on Gender, Biology, and Identity', in David Starling and Edwina Murphy (eds.), *The Gender Conversation: Evangelical Perspectives on Gender, Scripture, and the Christian Life* (Macquarie Park: Morling Press / Eugene: Wipf and Stock, 2016), pp. 347–58. I would like to express my thanks to Morling Press and Wipf & Stock for permission to revise and reprint it.
2. See, for instance, the prominence of related issues on the Australian Broadcasting Commission's news website: <www.abc.net.au/news/2015-08-23/gender-diverse-community-ostracised-from-playing-sports/6710778>, accessed 24 August 2015; <www.abc.net.au/news/2015-09-01/what-it-means-to-be-genderqueer/6727080>, accessed 1 September 2015; and, of course, the innumerable news stories, blogs, and so on, in response to Caitlyn Jenner's transition from male to female.

and only ever disrupted, questioned or complicated by sinful will.[3] Others want to redraw the boundaries of embodiment and gender, and follow Facebook in theologically justifying the proliferation of gender categories.[4] I'm not satisfied that either of these options is *theologically* satisfactory. But in order to figure out a more faithful way of engaging with these issues, we need to be clear about what questions need to be addressed, what resources we can mobilize in this engagement, and what strategies we might use in seeking to navigate our way through them.

We begin by briefly rehearsing the evidence that has been used to render problematic traditional notions of fixed, binary categories of male and female and masculinity and femininity, paying particular attention to gender dysphoria and indeterminate biological sex (intersex). Important methodological questions regarding how theology should deal with the 'data' generated by scientific and sociological research must be addressed before substantive issues relating to a theology of embodied human identity can be explored. Having made a case for the mutual interrogation of theology and other disciplines, I will suggest that, while our bodies are fundamental to our being in the world and crucially shape our understanding and engagement with it, both what we are (ontology) and who we are (identity) are primarily determined by the relationships we form and in which we find ourselves. And at the heart of these relationships is the one we enjoy with God in Christ which affirms our creation in God's image, redeems the brokenness of creation, calls us into new patterns of social relationship and promises our full restoration and glorification in a transformed physical order.

---

3. Chuck Colson, *Blurred Biology: How Many Sexes Are There?*, available from <www.breakpoint.org/commentaries/5213-blurred-biology>, 16 October 1996 [cited 2015]; 'A Church Statement on Human Sexuality: Homosexuality and Same-Sex "Marriage", A Resource for EFCA Churches' (EFCA, 2013), pp. 3–4.

4. Susannah Cornwall, '"State of Mind" versus "Concrete Set of Facts": The Contrasting of Transgender and Intersex in Church Documents on Sexuality', *Theology & Sexuality* 15 (2009), pp. 7–28; Tricia Sheffield, 'Performing Jesus: A Queer Counternarrative of Embodied Transgression', *Theology & Sexuality: The Journal of the Institute for the Study of Christianity and Sexuality* 14 (2008), pp. 233–58. For the Facebook categories, see <www.telegraph.co.uk/technology/facebook/10930654/Facebooks-71-gender-options-come-to-UK-users.html>, accessed 15 July 2015.

Orientation – data and questions

The complex pictures of sex and gender and their interrelationships that emerge from recent work in biology and social theory are helpfully discussed respectively by Patricia and Kamal Weerakoon and by Justine Toh.[5] I will briefly sketch these pictures, before I focus on two elements that generate painful questions both for those who have to deal with them and for those who seek to reflect on gender and sex theologically: namely, gender dysphoria and ambiguous physical sex (intersex).[6]

We turn first to the biology. As Patricia and Kamal Weerakoon have shown, neither sex nor gender is a simple phenomenon. While humanity's sexed nature is fundamentally dimorphic, it is not a simple binary, biologically determined phenomenon. At its most basic level, it is the product of genetics: XY male, XX female.[7] However, from that basis in *genotype* things can get complicated, as *phenotype* (bodily form) develops in response to specialized protein and hormone production and tissue receptivity to it *in utero*, as also during childhood and adolescence. Physical expressions of biological sex, such as the development of mature ovaries or testes and secondary sex characteristics such as the size of the clitoris or penis, formation of labia or scrotal sack, breast development and so on, result from complicated interactions of genetics, epigenetics (environmental factors that influence the expression of genes) and developing anatomy and physiology. This can result in clear disparities between genetic sex and bodily form, such as Androgen Insensitivity Syndrome in which people who are genetically male (including having testes that produce testosterone) develop as physical females due to tissue insensitivity to male hormones (androgens). This complicated biological picture also influences gender and sexual orientation. The brain seems also to be a hormonally responsive tissue and its natural

---

5. Patricia Weerakoon and Kamal Weerakoon, 'The Biology of Sex and Gender', in Starling and Murphy (eds.), *The Gender Conversation*, pp. 317–30; Justine Toh, 'Enculturated or Created? Gender & Sex in the Context of Caitlyn Jenner's "New Normal"', in Starling and Murphy, *The Gender Conversation*, pp. 335–44. The following paragraphs draw heavily on their treatments.

6. Heather Looy and Hessel Bouma III, 'The Nature of Gender: Gender Identity in Persons Who Are Intersexed or Transgendered', *Journal of Psychology & Theology* 33 (2005), pp. 166–78.

7. There are variations even at the chromosomal level, such as 47XXY (Klinefelter's Syndrome) and 45X (Turner's Syndrome).

plasticity is influenced by prenatal, childhood and adolescent changes in levels of testosterone, oestrogen and progesterone. The biology of sex and gender is complicated indeed.

The picture that emerges from work in social and cultural theory on gender and sex is equally complicated, as Justine Toh has shown. If gender is coming to be seen as having some biological basis (no matter how complicated), cultural theorists seem to be moving in the opposite direction. Both sex and gender are viewed as cultural constructs, neither biologically determined nor fixed.[8] These views generally depend on post-structuralist critical theory which argues that all the ways we see the world and navigate our way through it are *discursively generated*. That is to say, we have no access to the world or ourselves that is not shaped by language and the cultural systems that are codified by them. Not only do our categories 'masculine and feminine' and the behaviours associated with them reflect culturally relative norms and values, but so also do our categories 'male and female'. While our biology is not ignored, male and female are not value-neutral phenomena but are already interpreted in the language and cultural systems that form us into male/masculine and female/feminine actors. Sex and gender are malleable, and subject to our will: people are free to choose both their social and relational expressions of gender and sexuality, and their sexed bodily form, in resistance to cultural stereotypes and heteronormative gender essentialism.

Intersex takes a number of forms, ranging from those whose bodily form does not match their genetic sex (e.g. Androgen Insensitivity Syndrome), through those with ambiguous genitalia (as with Congenital Adrenal Hyper-plasia), to those who demonstrate 'true' hermaphroditism (in which they have more-or-less well-formed male and female genitalia and secondary sex characteristics).[9] How do such people relate to our binary categories of sex? How do we understand them in light of God creating humanity as male and female when they fall neatly into neither category? The history of 'assigning' such people a definitive sex (and gender) at birth, often accompanied with a

---

8. Judith Butler is a key figure in this discussion. See, for instance, Judith Butler, *Gender Trouble: Feminism and the Subversion of Identity* (New York: Routledge, 1990).

9. Claire Ainsworth, 'Sex Redefined', *Nature* 518 (2015), pp. 288–91; Megan K. DeFranza, *Sex Difference in Christian Theology: Male, Female and Intersex in the Image of God* (Grand Rapids: Eerdmans, 2015), ch. 1; Looy and Bouma, 'Nature of Gender', pp. 166–71.

regimen of complex and invasive surgery, is fraught with pain and tragedy.[10] It seems as though our binary categories serve such people poorly.[11]

Gender dysphoria, on the other hand, is a little simpler to understand. People with gender dysphoria generally have a fairly clear biological sex, but they do not identify with that sex or the gendered behaviours that go with it. Their experience is one in which they are alienated from their bodies; they are at home neither in their bodies nor in the social worlds in which they find themselves. And this causes them significant distress – hence gender *dysphoria*.[12] For some of them the distress is so great that they feel they must change their bodies to match their experienced gender identity if they are to have any hope of feeling at home in the world. How do such people relate to our binary categories of gender? How do we understand the connection (and disconnect) between bodily sex and cultural expressions of gender, and how fluid can they be?

In light of such phenomena, it is not surprising that the categories of sex (male and female) and gender (feminine and masculine) have been rendered problematic in recent discourse.[13] These are questions to which theology needs to give an answer – both in order to speak meaningfully in our cultural context, and also to encompass the complex realities of the world in which we live. How to do this is a vexed theological question. But in order to address it, we need to deal with an important question of theological method: what role should the perspectives of science and sociology play in theological reflection? To this we now turn.

Strategies of engagement

There are many approaches to the relationship between theology and both biological and social sciences, and a number of different taxonomies have been

10. See the accounts in DeFranza, *Sex Difference*, ch. 1 and Daisy Dumas, 'The In-betweeners', *Sidney Morning Herald*, 1 August 2015, available from <www.smh.com.au/good-weekend/the-inbetweeners-20150730-ginojq.html>, accessed 14 August 2015; Looy and Bouma, 'Nature of Gender', pp. 171–73.

11. DeFranza, *Sex Difference*, esp. chs. 4 and 6.

12. Mark A. Yarhouse, *Understanding Gender Dysphoria: Navigating Transgender Issues in a Changing Culture* (Downers Grove: IVP, 2015), ch. 1. The disturbingly high incidence of depression and suicide amongst people with gender dysphoria in itself warrants the term *dysphoria*.

13. Matt Huston, 'None of the Above', *Psychology Today* 48 (2015), pp. 28–30; Cornwall, 'Transgender and Intersex'; Sheffield, 'Performing Jesus'.

proposed. For our purposes three general categories will suffice: conflict, conformity and conversation.[14]

The first sees science and theology as being in *conflict*: while they lay claim to the same conceptual territory, they make fundamentally incompatible claims and as such one or the other must give way. This is the line adopted by many conservative Christian groups. 'In the beginning', they say, 'God created them male and female'. Any departure from that is a sinful expression of innate human rebellion against God and God's ordering of the world. Some in this group see the experiences of a person with gender dysphoria as the result of directly willed sinful choices; others do not.[15] But regardless of origin of their dysphoria, they cannot be allowed to determine the patterns of their gendered relationships in the world, let alone the form of their bodies. Their bodily form is a given of creation, and comes with prescribed patterns of gendered behaviour; non-conforming gender *behaviour* is therefore an expression of a sinful will. While such views may account for the sociology of gender (by way of rejection of its claims), it is hard to see how they give any account of intersex. If the only categories we have are the binary ones of 'male' and 'female', how do we categorize those with ambiguous genitalia or a mismatch between their 'genetic sex' and the form of their bodies? Are they male or female, and how do we

---

14. For alternative taxonomies and discussions of relevant issues, see Richard F. Carlson (ed.), *Science and Christianity: Four Views* (Downers Grove: IVP, 2000). See also Malcolm A. Jeeves and R. J. Berry, *Science, Life and Christian Belief: A Survey and Assessment* (Leicester: Apollos, 1998), esp. chs. 3 and 13.

15. These discussions generally relate to questions of sexual orientation, and gender dysphoria is often conflated with or discussed mainly in relation to them. See Robert A. J. Gagnon, *The Bible and Homosexual Practice: Texts and Hermeneutics* (Nashville: Abingdon, 2001). For a briefer account see Gagnon's chapter (and response) in Robert A. J. Gagnon and Dan O. Via, *Homosexuality and the Bible: Two Views* (Minneapolis: Fortress, 2003), pp. 40–92, 99–105. See also the public statements and policy documents of the (Australian) Christian Democratic Party: <www.christiandemocraticparty.com.au/media-releases/all-australian-schools-must-stop-teaching-queer-sex/>; <www.christiandemocraticparty.com.au/2015-nsw-election/2015-nsw-election-policy-snapshot/>; <www.christiandemocraticparty.com.au/about-the-cdp/cdp-national-charter/>, accessed 24 August 2015. Such views are also reflected (with more or less vitriol) on news sites and blogs, such as: <www.theblaze.com/contributions/bruce-jenner-is-not-a-woman-he-is-a-sick-and-delusional-man/>; <www.russellmoore.com/2015/04/24/what-should-the-church-say-to-bruce-jenner/>, accessed 24 August 2015.

decide? People who are intersex seem to be effectively excluded from theological anthropology, unless they are subjected to almost arbitrary surgical assignment of sex. Furthermore, this strategy assumes that the Bible addresses the kinds of questions we are asking in the ways we are now asking them, and that our interpretations of Scripture and theology cannot be modified in light of our developing knowledge of the world. Such an approach cannot provide adequate answers to questions such as these.[16]

This brings us naturally to our next strategy, *conformity*, in which science dictates the terms to which theology must now conform. Old understandings of humanity as created male and female, and the associated idea that human sexuality is ordered towards either heterosexual marriage or singleness, are obsolete. We need to allow for a plurality of genders and sexes, and corresponding expressions of sex and gender in social relationships, bodily form and sexual expression. Such views are seen in a number of 'queer' theologies.[17] There are numerous problems with such strategies, including their tendency to adopt theologies of Scripture and interpretive strategies antithetical to evangelical commitments.[18] While they may be able to address questions of intersex and gender dysphoria, they do not do so in fidelity to the Christian tradition or its Scriptures.

---

16. It is both ironic and suggestive that many LGBTQIA activists adopt a similar understanding of the conflict between theology and science; but in their case, theology must give way to science. See, for instance, an example of public statements and policy documents of the Australian Greens: <http://greens.org.au/node/11021>; <http://greens.org.au/LGBTI>; <http://greens.org.au/policies/vic/sexual-orientation-and-gender-identity>. Such views are also reflected (with more or less vitriol) on news sites and blogs, such as: <www.theatlantic.com/politics/archive/2015/06/the-christian-debate-on-transgender-identity/394796/>, accessed 24 August 2015.

17. Thomas Bohache, *Christology from the Margins* (London: SCM, 2008); Cornwall, 'Transgender and Intersex'; Sheffield, 'Performing Jesus'. See also Via's chapter (and response) in Gagnon and Via, *Homosexuality and the Bible*, pp. 1–39, 93–8; and numerous web pages and blog posts, such as: <http://religiondispatches.org/transitions-caitlyn-jenner-gender-identity-and-christians-behaving-badly-again/>; <www.believeoutloud.com/background/christianity-and-lgbt-equality>; <www.gaychristian.net/>, accessed 24 August 2015.

18. While the evangelical tradition is not immune from critique and development, neither can it be simply dismissed or ignored. Furthermore, as Weerakoon and Weerakoon, and Toh have shown, the scientific and sociological evidence is not as definitive as others might suggest.

Thankfully, we are not bound by the options of either conflict and rejection of science, or conformity and accommodation to secular reason. There is a third option of *conversation*, in which science and theology are allowed to mutually interrogate each other.[19] This strategy has been adopted by Mark Yarhouse and Megan DeFranza in their work on gender dysphoria and intersex respectively.[20] Yarhouse outlines a threefold framework for understanding and dealing with the phenomenon of gender dysphoria: the *integrity* framework (male–female bodily distinctions are sacred); the *disability* framework (gender dysphoria is a non-culpable reality deserving compassion); and the *diversity* framework (trans-gender experiences are to be celebrated as part of diverse humanity), and suggests that each should inform our theology and practice where appropriate.[21] DeFranza recognizes that the phenomenon of intersex renders problematic a simple binary opposition of male and female. Furthermore, the way that maleness and femaleness have been seen as essential to our being created in the image of God, she notes, generates problems for our theology of God as well as for our concepts of sex, sexuality and gender in creation and in the *eschaton*.[22] I am not convinced by the ways in which she ties together the image of God, social Trinitarian thought and human bodily existence in light of the incarnation of Christ. Nonetheless, she rightly notes that, given that people with intersex are created in the image of God, we must allow our theologies to include them

---

19. For science in general, see: Jeeves and Berry, *Science, Life and Christian Belief*, esp. ch. 13; Alister E. McGrath, *Science and Religion: A New Introduction*, 2nd edn (Malden: Wiley-Blackwell, 2010); John C. Polkinghorne, *One World: The Interaction of Science and Theology* (Philadelphia: Templeton Foundation Press, 2007); *Reason and Reality: The Relationship Between Science and Theology* (London: SPCK, 1991). And for medicine and health care in particular, see Neil G. Messer, *Flourishing: Health, Disease, and Bioethics in Theological Perspective* (Grand Rapids: Eerdmans, 2013), esp. pp. xiv, xv, 48–50, 103–7, 163, 210. For an outline of an undergirding epistemology, see Andrew Sloane, *On Being a Christian in the Academy: Nicholas Wolterstorff and the Practice of Christian Scholarship* (Carlisle: Paternoster, 2003); John G. Stackhouse, *Need to Know: Vocation as the Heart of Christian Epistemology* (Oxford: Oxford University Press, 2014).

20. Mark A. Yarhouse, 'Integration in the Study of Homosexuality, GLBT Issues, and Sexual Identity', *Journal of Psychology & Theology* 40 (2012), pp. 107–11, adopts an 'integrationist' approach to science–faith interaction.

21. *Understanding Gender Dysphoria*, ch. 2. See also his brief discussion in 'Understanding Gender Dysphoria', *Christianity Today* 59 (2015), pp. 44–50.

22. DeFranza, *Sex Difference*, chs. 4–6.

in our understandings of humanity and human community, and to embody communal practices that include them in our corporate lives. Such strategies can allow for fruitful theological reflection on questions of gender, biology and identity.

A theology of embodied persons in relationship

We need to steer a path between two poles: (a) conservative attempts to reify particular cultural constructions of gender as fixed ontological expressions of a determinative creational/biological order of binary sex, and (b) postmodern attempts to render sex and gender radically indeterminate or self-determined, denying the givenness of creation and the goodness of creaturely embodiment. The rejection of gender stereotypes and the acknowledgment of the complexities of human embodiment revealed in the phenomenon of intersex need not entail the 'queering' of gender and sex. A theological anthropology grounded in nuanced understandings of creation, Christology and eschatology provides us with a way forward.

The first thing to note is that the biblical texts suggest that we *are* bodies; bodies are not things we inhabit, but the way we inhabit the world as the kind of creatures God has made us.[23] These bodies normally are formed as male or female, and the shape of our bodies informs the character of our relationships with others. Sex and gender *inform* our identity, but we are not *defined* by our sexed bodies or gendered selves.

The creation accounts also indicate that both our nature and our identity are fundamentally relational. The 'not good' of Genesis 2:18 is the absence of relationships of a particular kind: not *sexual* relationships *per se*, but the otherness of fellow creatures who require our commitment and evoke our delight.[24] The primeval community was intended to embody relationships of love, justice, fidelity and delight, both between God and humanity, and within the human

---

23. Neil G. Messer, *Respecting Life: Theology and Bioethics* (London: SCM, 2011), esp. ch. 1; *Flourishing*, esp. ch. 4; Gilbert Meilaender, *Body, Soul, and Bioethics* (Notre Dame: UNDP, 1995), ch. 2.

24. Claus Westermann, *Genesis: A Practical Commentary* (Grand Rapids: Eerdmans, 1987), pp. 10–11, 20–1; Andrew Sloane, '"And he shall rule over you": Evangelicals, Feminists, and Genesis 2–3', in Andrew Sloane (ed.), *Tamar's Tears: Evangelical Engagements with Feminist Old Testament Hermeneutics* (Eugene: Pickwick, 2012), pp. 1–29.

community, as well as the expression of fidelity and joyful service in the world. It is those relationships that define us and shape our identity – the relationships and the complex gifts, tasks and responsibilities they entail. Now it is true that sexual dimorphism and the resultant sexual relationships and procreative capacity are key aspects of human bodily existence. We are mammals – biological entities of a particular kind that reproduce sexually and bear live young; and we are entrusted by God with the gift and task of filling the world and ruling it as God's vicegerents – a task that presupposes the fruitfulness (and blessing) of progeny and an unfolding history of human engagement in God's world (Gen. 1:26–31). But the creation accounts focus primarily on the creation of human community and its nature and task, and only secondarily on matters of gender and sexuality.[25]

The embodied and relational nature of human existence is affirmed, as well as transformed, in our new primary identity in Christ.[26] Our redemption and final transformation does not erase our embodied nature; nor does it mean that our gendered, sexed and sexual being is somehow jettisoned. After all, Paul affirms that 'the body is for the Lord, and the Lord for the body' (1 Cor. 6:13 NIV). Further, our bodily existence shapes our relationships, making some relationships possible rather than others, and so shapes what identifies and defines us. I am son and brother and husband and father and friend; and both my maleness and the particular forms of masculinity that I express necessarily shape those relationships and the self that they form and inform.

Gender is another matter. Gender, understood as particular patterns of thought, feelings, relationships and behaviour, including characteristic dress, gesture and patterns of physical comportment, is largely culturally constructed

---

25. See Sloane, 'Genesis 2–3', pp. 21–2; Looy and Bouma, 'Nature of Gender', pp. 174–6.

26. See Oliver O'Donovan, *Resurrection and Moral Order: An Outline for Evangelical Ethics*, 2nd edn (Grand Rapids: Eerdmans, 1994), esp. pp. 11–75; Tom Wright, *Surprised by Hope* (London: SPCK, 2007), esp. ch. 10. The vindication of creation renders problematic attempts to 'queer' anthropology in light of Christology and the resurrection of Jesus, such as in: Elizabeth Stuart, 'The Return of the Living Dead', in Lisa Isherwood and Kathleen McPhillips (eds.), *Post-Christian Feminisms: A Critical Approach* (Aldershot: Ashgate, 2008), pp. 211–22; Sheffield, 'Performing Jesus'; Bohache, *Christology from the Margins*. Rather, while they are not erased (1 Cor. 11:2–16; 1 Tim. 2:8–15), Gal. 3:28 suggests that sex and gender are not binary categories that determine our identity; our identity is primarily found in Christ.

or shaped.[27] Note that 'largely' does not mean 'entirely', because some of those patterns are given to us in the shape of our bodies and the ways our different hormonal environments shape thought, feelings, relationships and behaviour. Again, while there is a spectrum of patterns rather than a set of rigid types, there do seem to be characteristic patterns of male and female brains with differing ways of engaging with the world, valuing particular features of it, and so on.[28]

Nonetheless, we must not reify these particular patterns of thought and experience into rigid ontological categories and assign our constructed visions of 'feminine' and 'masculine' to female and male bodies.[29] Feminine and masculine traits are observed as statistical patterns across populations (even more than is true of male and female), and many behaviours and attitudes are gendered differently in different cultural contexts; they are not eternal, transcultural, binary categories. We need to allow for a degree of fluidity in expressions of gender – a 'permission' that would, most likely, alleviate the distress of at least some people with gender dysphoria.[30] It is not, however, simply a product of autonomous human will as if, no matter the bodily form of my created existence, I can determine that I am female or male or transgendered or anything else.

Implications and suggestions

Such a view, of course, complicates both simple binary categories *and* their repudiation in queered or fluid-sex views of sexuality and gender. We need to recognize that male and female phenotypes exist as polar rather than binary phenomena. At either end of a spectrum of physical types lie versions of paradigmatic male and female bodies; and in between these poles there is a variety of male and female bodies, and some that are neither-nor or both-and.[31] A theology that seeks to force the world of human bodies into rigid 'male' and 'female' types fails to do justice to the realities of the world as it is. Intersex

27. Toh, 'Enculturated or Created?'
28. Weerakoon and Weerakoon, 'Biology'; Looy and Bouma, 'Nature of Gender', pp. 166–71.
29. This often involves a degree of arbitrariness, historical and cultural naivety, and even arrogance.
30. Looy and Bouma, 'Nature of Gender', pp. 173–4.
31. Ibid., pp. 174–6.

should probably be seen as an inscription of a fallen world's brokenness on particular human bodies and therefore a *disability*, given the ways it complicates the biology of reproduction. One of the ends to which we are ordered as creatures is the procreation of the human species, and so our theology of the body needs to include our procreative capacities.[32] But other variations of maleness and femaleness are complex expressions of the rich variety of God's creation. We need to accommodate this full spectrum of bodily forms in our theology of the body as a sexed body. On the other hand, our bodily existence is a given. Our bodies are not mere instruments, infinitely malleable expressions of our untethered wills.[33]

This brings us to two related matters. First, how do we understand bodies and their relationship to ourselves,[34] and what role should biomedical technology play in the reshaping of bodies? The apparent body-obsession of contemporary Western culture hides an ironic hatred of the body and its resistance to our wills.[35] At the empty heart of our culture lies the absolutized 'good' of choice. Our wills, unconstrained by ends to which they should be directed and unfettered from any external moral norms, have become the sole arbiters of the right (and, for that matter, of *rights*).[36] The body has become the resistant matter

---

32. DeFranza suggests that seeing intersex as a consequence of the fall risks those with the condition being dismissed as persons (DeFranza, *Sex Difference*, ch. 4). Her concern can be more adequately addressed by seeing sex and gender as a *spectrum* of physical and behavioural and psychological and affective and relational traits rather than reified ontological categories, and human identity as primarily relationally determined. For a discussion of issues of disability, biology and culture, see Andrew Sloane, *Vulnerability and Care: Christian Reflections on the Philosophy of Medicine* (London: Bloomsbury T&T Clark, 2016), pp. 96–9.

33. Oliver O'Donovan, 'Transsexualism and Christian Marriage', *Journal of Religious Ethics* 11 (1983), pp. 135–62. While he seems to operate with a relatively unproblematic binary of male and female, he helpfully reflects on issues of psychology and embodiment in relation to gender reassignment.

34. Even speaking of our relationship between ourselves and our bodies is loaded with dualistic assumptions that are, in my view, misleading and unhelpful. But that's a larger matter.

35. Meilaender, *Body, Soul, and Bioethics*.

36. David Bentley Hart, 'God or Nothingness', in Carl E. Braaten and Christopher R. Seitz (eds.), *I Am the Lord Your God: Christian Reflections on the Ten Commandments* (Grand Rapids: Eerdmans, 2005), pp. 55–76. See also the reflections in O'Donovan, 'Transsexualism and Christian Marriage', esp. pp. 149–52.

that the volitional demiurge seeks to dominate and control, conforming it to the image of what we choose. (These choices are ironically constrained by the market and technology, which render even our embodied selves into commodities.) Such perspectives have come to control much of bioethics and medical technology.[37] Medicine is becoming a commodity to be purchased from medical technicians, subject only to the constraints of the market and the demands of the 'client'. This false, even idolatrous, vision of medicine must be replaced by a properly Christian account in which medicine exists as an expression of a community's solidarity with and care for frail, finite embodied beings whose vulnerability has been exposed by illness, infirmity or misfortune.[38]

In such a view, medicine has a clear if limited role to play in the care of people with gender dysphoria or intersex conditions. Crucial to the diagnosis of gender dysphoria is the sense that the alienation they experience from their bodies is *distressing*, and is not a matter of choice. Caring for them requires that we do what can rightly be done to alleviate that distress or help them cope with it, so as to enable them to function as well as they can as persons and in their relationships. As Yarhouse notes, the key is to do only that which is required to help a distressed person.[39] Radical surgical intervention should be seen as a treatment of last resort, an accommodation to an otherwise intractable disorder.[40] Similarly, if we allow for some kind of spectrum of sexed bodies, we need not engage in complex and risky gender assignment surgery on children with intersex conditions. Other strategies will generally allow them space to navigate the world as the bodies they find themselves to be, and to determine for themselves what, if any, medical intervention might be required later in life. In neither case, however, is medicine a tool for the expression of an autonomous human will. This is not a matter of 'choosing your own bodily adventure'. Furthermore, medicine is not going to be able to 'fix' all the problems that people with gender dysphoria or intersex conditions might face. Many of them are the result of

---

37. Gerald P. McKenny, *To Relieve the Human Condition: Bioethics, Technology, and the Body* (Albany: University of New York Press, 1997).
38. This argument is explored more fully in Andrew Sloane, 'Christianity and the Transformation of Medicine', in Oliver D. Crisp *et al.* (eds.), *Christianity and the Disciplines: The Transformation of the University* (London: T&T Clark, 2012), pp. 85–99.
39. As in all therapeutic interventions; Yarhouse, *Understanding Gender Dysphoria*, esp. chs. 1, 5–7.
40. Robert Song, 'Body Integrity, Identity Disorder and the Ethics of Mutilation', *Studies in Christian Ethics* 26 (2013), pp. 487–503, makes a similar point in relation to body integrity, identity disorder and surgical amputation.

particular cultural patterns that are not subject to biomedical control. Indeed, much (but not all) of the distress such people face might be alleviated by the recognition that a wider range of expressions of masculinity and femininity should be allowed – and even encouraged – within Christian communities.[41]

Conclusion

Intersex and gender dysphoria are aspects of biology and gender that theology needs to address. They rightly call into question rigid binary categories of male/female and feminine/masculine, without thereby undermining the notions *per se*. They require us to formulate a nuanced theology of the body and understanding of our interrelationships as embodied beings, and to develop social and technological practices that allow us to deal with our fractured and flawed nature. I have suggested some directions such inquiry should take, as well as what I see as clear limitations on the faithful engagement with these issues. There are many questions I have not addressed, and a number of my suggestions are at best partial and provisional. But such is the nature of theology in a world such as this.

© Andrew Sloane, 2017

---

41. Looy and Bouma, 'Nature of Gender', pp. 174–6.

15. SHADOWS ACROSS GENDER RELATIONS

Elaine Storkey

Any biblical or theological study of family, marriage and sexuality will eventually be faced with a darker aspect of human relationships, that of violence and abuse. Without some theological engagement with the cruelty and brutality in the dynamics of human behaviour, our study in human relationships will be incomplete. In particular, the aspect of gender-based violence cannot be ignored. In one of many reports on this disturbing phenomenon, the United Nations Population Fund sees violence against women as 'probably the most wide-spread and socially tolerated of human rights violations'. The authors go on to suggest that it 'both reflects and reinforces inequities between men and women and compromises the health, dignity, security and autonomy of its victims'.[1]

My own concern with this subject began many years ago when an editor of a women's magazine sent me a package of responses to questionnaires, filled in by women who self-disclosed as victims of domestic abuse. Working through a couple of hundred of these in order to write a report for the journal, I became deeply disturbed by the painful narratives of these women's lives and experiences. For many respondents, the words they were now pouring out on to the

---

1. United Nations Population Fund (UNFPA), *State of the World Population 2005: The Promise of Equality: Gender Equity, Reproductive Health and the Millennium Development Goals* (UNFPA, 2005), p. 65.

page broke many years of silence. They found they suddenly had permission to reflect on the assaults and attacks they had suffered and to identify their ordeals for what they really were: betrayal of trust and belittling of their value and worth.

This unexpected encounter with the reality of violence in the home began for me a long involvement with the issue of intimate-partner abuse (a more accurate term than 'domestic violence'), through both research work and counselling. By the time I travelled to remote societies as President of Tearfund, many years later, I felt I already knew a great deal about the damage that could be inflicted upon women. Yet the global manifestations of gender-based violence still took me by surprise. I found patterns of violation in cultures as far away from each other as Haiti, the Congo and India. Many different forms of abuse presented themselves, most of which were family-based but some of which were not. Institutionalized systems of damage to women cut across both public and private spheres, and were often deeply engrained in pervasive cultural attitudes. It became evident that patriarchal societies have multiple ways of reinforcing male power over women, whether through the indifference of lawmakers, collusion of the police and military or reinforcement by religious authorities. Sitting unobtrusively with all-female groups, and listening as they quietly shared their lives and stories with me, it was possible to witness levels of vulnerability which went beyond what I had ever seen before. Often lacking economic, educational and legal resources, women were left unprotected against those who would exploit and harm them. The damage was both physical and social, affecting young and old. There was little doubt that violence constituted, in the words of another UN report, 'a continuum across the lifespan of women', and that in places right across the globe, women were at risk of violation from before birth to old age.[2]

Today, gender discrimination operates in different practices in diverse cultures, much of it taking a sexual nature. Selective abortion, female genital mutilation, enforced marriage, honour killings, sex trafficking, prostitution, sexual assault and rape as a weapon of war are all aspects of the way women's bodies become targeted for abuse. And although intimate-partner violence victimizes men as well as women, the gender ratio of abuse and the homicide rate for women victims underlines their particular vulnerability. The case studies below draw heavily on examples from countries where there are fewer legal safeguards for

---

2. United Nations Secretary-General's study: *Ending Violence Against Women: From Words to Action*, 9 October 2006, <www.un.org/womenwatch/daw/vaw/launch/english/v.a.w-exeE-use.pdf>.

women. Yet this should not blind us to the reality that there are aspects of gender relations in every culture which leave women at risk, and that no society is exempt from gender-based violence.

Statistics themselves provide sobering reading. In the UK alone, the 2015–16 *Violence Against Women and Girls Report* shows the highest ever recorded volume of prosecutions and convictions for rape, yet these figures reflect only a small fraction of the women who call Women's Aid and other helplines to report sexual assault. When we turn to domestic violence, we know from Crime Survey figures that 1.4 million women in England and Wales suffer this annually, and that 1 in 4 will endure it during their lifetime.[3] We know also that 140,000 women are living with the consequences of female genital mutilation in the UK, and that around 10,000 girls under the age of fifteen are likely to undergo cutting.[4] In yet another example of abuse, the Home Office estimates that between 5,000 and 8,000 people annually are at risk of being forced into marriage in the UK (most of them girls), with forty-six prosecutions since 2014.[5]

Global manifestations of gender-based violence can be terrifyingly dramatic as I found during eight years' research for *Scars Across Humanity: Understanding and Overcoming Violence Against Women*.[6] The task of this book, however, was not simply to identify and document the ugly manifestations of human brutality, or even to allow the voices of victims to be heard – although these were clearly necessary. The aim was also to address the question underlying every issue – why? What makes human beings inflict pain on each other, and damage the female of the species at a level unknown in the animal kingdom? What is it about human societies, that healthy gender relationships can become so badly distorted and malefactors left free to violate women with impunity? In the exploration of these questions we need to probe underlying assumptions about the nature of human personhood and the construction of identity. To do that,

---

3. *Crime Survey England and Wales 2013–14* (London: Office for National Statistics, 2015).

4. A. J. Macfarlane and E. Dorkenoo, *Female Genital Mutilation in England and Wales* (London: City University, 2014), <www.city.ac.uk/__data/assets/pdf_file/0020/266033/FGM-statistics-report-21.07.14-no-embargo.pdf>.

5. <www.girlsnotbrides.org/child-marriage/united-kingdom>; <www.independent.co.uk/news/uk/home-news/six-year-old-girl-learning-difficulties-forced-child-marriage-pakistan-a6889071.html>.

6. Elaine Storkey, *Scars Across Humanity: Understanding and Overcoming Violence Against Women* (London: SPCK, 2015).

we are inevitably drawn into theological and philosophical reflection. It is the purpose of this chapter, then, to engage afresh in theological reflection both to address those questions directly and to consider critically some of the proposed explanations.

Explanations are not hard to come by. Many academic disciplines offer analyses of human behaviour which in turn form the bases for responses to these issues. Biologists, psychologists, systems theorists, sociologists, political scientists, historians, legal analysts and economists have all proposed theories which have been used, often by others, to provide reasons for gender-based violence and for their widely diverse cultural forms. Inevitably, the various explanations differ widely from each other, as they draw on different assumptions. Sometimes, as in the first case study below, these different approaches complement each other and together offer a comprehensive framework for understanding. More often, however, the result can be fragmented or contradictory, as in the second example. Some theorists even maintain that their discipline alone has the framework and rigour to furnish a reliable account, and that other theories lack this.[7] Yet, those same theorists often work from assumptions which themselves are dogmatic and not held up to critical scrutiny.

When we explore the problem of gender-based violence from different explanatory frameworks, we quickly encounter explanations couched in cultural, economic, social, ethical, functional, biological, genetic, psychological, historical or legal terms. They all provide insights, especially when they are supported by careful study and detailed research. Each discipline asks its own set of questions, and often cites carefully compiled evidence to verify the conclusions reached. At the same time, however, writers may be unaware that they are not carefully scrutinizing the assumptions incorporated into their theories. Yet these assumptions inevitably play a significant role in how people understand the reasons for gender-based violence. It falls to us as theologians, then, to uncover and examine these, and bring a more critical appraisal to bear on them.

Selective abortion

When we turn to the issue of female foeticide – the practice of sex-selective abortion – a variety of different explanations quickly present themselves. The

---

7. See, for example, George Gaylord Simpson, quoted in Storkey, *Scars Across Humanity*, p. 153.

statistics are not precise because of the very nature of the problem, but the issue is clear enough. In India (and previously in China), violence against women begins in the womb. India has lost around ten million girls over the last two decades through the abortion of female foetuses and female infanticide. One doctor who fought hard against her husband's family in order to keep her own twin daughters, points out that the number of girls killed by female foeticide 'is much greater than any genocide of this world'.[8] This has left that country with an acute gender imbalance in the population, seen very evidently in the child sex ratio in demographic statistics. The distorted ratio is apparently getting worse rather than better. In the census of 2011, many areas of India showed a rapid decrease of girls to boys from the previous decade. In Jammu and Kashmir, for example, the proportions of girls dropped from 964 to every 1000 boys down to only 870.

Explanations citing technological advance

A simple explanation for this decreasing ratio of girls in the population is that it is caused by the impact of sex-diagnostic technology. And that is obviously one answer. India has more than 35,000 registered ultrasound clinics. In addition, ultrasound machines can be operated outside medical centres and are available in every part of the country. The proliferation of unregistered clinics, the widespread sale of scanners and the collusion of doctors in expediting sex-selective abortions make it increasingly easy to eliminate extra girls from the family at embryo stage. The ease and speed of safer abortions have therefore all compounded the threat to girl babies and reduced their numbers.

Legal and political explanations

Technology can explain why the problem has increased, but we need to ask why it has become so marked and persistent. The legal and political context is important, and many explanations put the blame on irresponsible governance and non-implementation of law. For more than forty years, India's laws have officially offered protection for unborn girls. The Medical Termination of Pregnancy Act of 1971 allows abortion in India only under very strict conditions. It must take place within twelve weeks of conception, there must be evidence of grave risks of injury or ill health to the mother, or there must be substantial risks to the child of severe abnormality and impairment. When this law failed to prevent widespread abortion, further legislation entered the statute books.

---

8. Mitu Khurna, quoted in <www.abc.net.au/news/2016-10-04/india-obsession-with-sons-millions-of-lonely-men-after-dowry/7903134>.

Following the spread of new technology the aim was to prevent its misuse. The Pre-natal Diagnostic Techniques (Regulation and Prevention of Misuse) Act of 1994, tightened in 2002, regulated the operation of scanners and prohibited their use for sex-selective abortions. Yet experts such as Sabu George have pointed out that millions of crimes continue to be carried out every year in relation to female foeticide, and very few cases are ever brought to court or result in convictions.

Clearly there is a massive gap between legal expression and public implementation. It suggests an absence of political will to enforce laws which protect the female child, an absence which leaves room for others to exploit. George points to the strong links between companies which manufacture the diagnostic machines and sections of a powerful medical fraternity who make profits from the sex-selection technologies. He believes that collusion between them, the politicians and the bureaucrats 'has made a mockery of the legal provisions'.[9] For the law to have teeth, its enactment is essential, ensuring high penalties for those who ignore the legislative provisions.

These are all crucial points. Both law and its enforcement are vital. Yet as George acknowledges, explanations couched in political or legal terms can only explain why a practice persists. They do not uncover the reasons why it occurs in the first place.

Economic explanations

An economic explanation might yield a deeper analysis. Poverty is still very evident in much of India, and the cost of raising children is considerable. Boys are an economic asset as they remain rooted in their family of birth, contributing economically and supporting parents in their old age. But girls leave to join the family of marriage. So in poor families it is no surprise that, if there are too many mouths to feed, the girls are the ones seen as disposable. The economics of poverty and deprivation are strong motivating factors for sex-selective abortion.

The economic argument cannot, however, focus on poverty alone. Most of the research points to the high level of take-up amongst middle-class families.

---

9. Sabu George and Brinda Karat, 'Don't Trash This Law; the Fault Lies in Non-implementation', *The Hindu*, 4 February 2012, <newsite.thehindu.com/opinion/op-ed/dont-trash-this-law-the-fault-lies-in-nonimplementation/article2858004.ece>; see also Randeep Ramesh, 'Foetuses Aborted and Dumped Secretly as India Shuns Baby Girls', *The Guardian*, 28 July 2007, <www.theguardian.com/world/2007/jul/28/india.randeepramesh>.

They are the ones more likely to investigate the sex of their unborn child and pay the fee for the diagnostic test and abortion clinic. The very poor more commonly resort to infanticide, leaving their newborn girl babies exposed in isolated areas. In many areas not afflicted by poverty there are even steeper gaps in the sex ratio. In Punjab, for example, there are only 846 girls per 1,000 males. In Haryana there are only 830, dropping down as far as to 774 in the rapidly developing, cattle-wealthy district of Jhajjar.[10]

The economics of affluence therefore also contribute to sex-selective abortion. This is further conflated by the economic drive of those who profit from the sale of scanners, offer diagnostic tests, run abortion clinics and dispose of foetal remains. Middle-class families want to maintain their standard of living, rather than see it decline through constant increase in their family size. But, more importantly, they still want sons rather than daughters, and we are back to the same, unresolved issue – why? To understand that we need to dig deeper.

Cultural explanations

An explanation which explores cultural factors regarding the preference for sons is likely to open up a more comprehensive understanding of sex-selective abortion. For centuries, in India's patriarchal society, sons have had a higher status than their sisters. Not only do they continue the family line, and preserve the name through generations, but the bonds between parents and son are reinforced economically and socially. Traditional concepts such as *paraya dhan* dictate that a girl is not seen as a permanent member of her birth family. So if she is given a share in its assets or property, the family will lose out. In some Hindu families, sons are even given religious significance. 'Through a son, he conquers the worlds, through a grandson, he obtains immortality, but through his son's grandson, he ascends to the highest. All that has been declared in the Veda.'[11]

Marriages are arranged, and the bridegroom's family is at a clear material advantage, as the parents of any potential bride must furnish the dowry. The dowry affects all sections of Indian society. A middle-class girl's family who want to secure a well-educated and successful husband for their daughter will have been saving for this since she was born. 'Decades ago, a wealthy bride's

---

10. 'Census of India 2011: Child Sex Ratio Drops to Lowest since Independence', *Economic Times*, 31 March 2011, <economictimes.indiatimes.com/news/economy/indicators/census-of-india-2011-child-sex-ratio-drops-to-lowest-since-independence/articleshow/7836942.cms>.

11. Vasishtha XVII, 5.

father would have been expected to give gold bracelets. Today it is jewellery, fridges, cars and foreign holidays – and the bride's family may end up paying the bill for the rest of their lives.'[12]

The dowry has been illegal in India since 1961, but this is another piece of legislation which is largely ignored. Women are particularly vulnerable, especially when the dowry is paid in instalments and the money runs out. The patrilocal culture, which requires girls to become part of the family of their husband, also requires them to be subject to the rules and mores of their new family, without the protection of their own parents. Many of them become homicide victims. With the rise of dowry-related deaths (girls killed by disgruntled parents-in-law and husbands) a further law was passed in 1983, designed to protect women from dowry harassment. However, most of the public debate since then has been on the misuse of the law by women, and police in some regions have watered down the requirements of arrest following complaints. Meanwhile, the victimization of girls by their in-laws continues. The Indian National Crime Records Bureau recorded a total of 24,771 dowry deaths in 2012–15.

In 2014 the International Center for Research on Women (ICRW) conducted a study on gender roles in India comparing behaviour among men ranked on a 'masculinity index'. In a society already prone to ranking and hierarchy, they found that linguistic ethnicity, caste and class all had a profound effect on how Indian men develop their sense of masculinity. The more pronounced this was, the more it affected their preferences for sons, their attitudes towards women and their likelihood of controlling their partners. The study found that one in three men surveyed did not allow their wives to wear the clothes of their choice, two in three believed they had a 'greater say than their wife/partner in the important decisions' that affected the family, and three in four expected their partner to agree to sex. Men high on the 'masculinity index' also showed a stronger inclination for violence towards an intimate partner.[13]

Culture, traditional practices, gender-expectations, attitudes towards wealth, family mores and religion all therefore play into the practice of sex-selective abortion. They are the expression of a pervading world view which ranks people

---

12. Raekha Prasad and Randeep Ramesh, 'India's Missing Girls', *The Guardian*, 28 February 2007, <www.theguardian.com/world/2007/feb/28/india. raekhaprasad>; see also KumKum Dasgupta, 'India's Missing Girls: Fears Grow over Rising Levels of Foeticide', <www.theguardian.com/global-development/ 2014/apr/09/india-missing-girls-rising-levels-foeticide>.

13. Katrina Beedy, *Borgen Magazine*, 29 January 2015, <www.borgenmagazine.com/ gender-roles-india>.

according to specific criteria of caste or gender, and which in turn justifies practices which have enormous consequences for the future of the country. In this kind of context, those made vulnerable by the world view are very likely to suffer.

Theological explanations

It is time to move on to the deepest level of explanation – one which addresses the problem from both ethical and theological perspectives. For below the cultural practices, the gender disparity, the economic pressures, the legal indifference and the technological advances lies the question of human identity. There are deep assumptions at play, not simply about the construction of masculinity or the nature of the family, but about the very meaning of personhood. The underlying perspective here is one which ranks human beings according to human-controlled criteria. People do not have equal significance before God, but take their place in a hierarchal structure of values, where women come lower than men, and the girl baby is at the bottom of the pile. When this gender and caste ranking is reinforced by religion, upheld by cultural rituals and absorbed into normality, the challenges are pushed to the margins. It becomes even more difficult to hold the prevailing assumptions up to critical scrutiny.

The significance of childhood also lies beneath foeticide and infanticide. A biblical theology of childhood is one which entrusts adults with the guardianship and care of youngsters; their well-being and nurture is in our hands. In the New Testament, Jesus draws a child towards him and issues a dire warning to any who would harm children. The vulnerability and lack of maturation of a child is addressed in positive, even loving terms. St Paul refers back to the time when as a child he 'understood as a child, and thought as a child', recognizing that it is only in adulthood that we 'put away childish things' (1 Cor. 13:11, AV). Jesus points to a child's simple trust and dependence as a role model for our relationship with God. Childhood is therefore defined as the accepted period of immaturity and vulnerability, with children in need of adult protection. At the same time, the child is also fully human, fully spiritual, and of equal value to an adult.

By contrast with this biblical view, the tragic narrative of selective abortion, infanticide and wide-scale foetal death indicates something deeply sinister. It is that children are disposable. Their worth is extrinsic and situational, not intrinsic and given them by God. So both embryos and new-born infants must meet the criteria already decided by an adult society or they can be deprived of the right to live. And the women who bear children are required to fall into line with these deep-seated attitudes, or suffer the consequences.

It falls then to the Christian biblical theologian to provide a different framework for evaluation, and offer a view of personhood rooted in the truth that we are creatures of a God who loves us. Our identity before God and our intrinsic worth are tied up together; they apply to us all, for God gives equivalent value to every one of his human creation. The practice of sex-selective abortion rejects the equal meaning and significance of human persons – a rejection that is both cultural and personal – and replaces it with institutionalized patterns of greed, pride, status, deceit, conformity and violence which are allowed to dominate the societal mindset and set the agenda. The result is a free rein for profiteers who turn the elimination of girl foetuses into personal gain.

The tireless campaigners against sex-selective abortion in India, fighting for laws which protect the female foetus, know these truths only too well. When we support their work and commitment with our own theological insights, we can begin to share their hope for both the unborn girl and the growing woman. We also demonstrate the impact of the biblical teaching of women and men together made in the image of God. To see women and men as co-stewards of the earth, equally accountable before God, showing each other mutual respect, offering neighbour love, nurturing the young and protecting the vulnerable, enables us to recognize the widespread acceptance of sex-selective abortion for what it is: a denial of our fundamental calling to be human.

The different explanations which operate in the case of sex-selective abortion and infanticide come together as a comprehensive whole. They each pinpoint one way of seeing the issue without contradicting each other. If anything, each element of explanation urges further examination to build up a composite picture. However, in other areas of violence against women, we see a different spectrum. Particularly when we try to understand rape or intimate-partner abuse we are confronted with explanations which are fundamentally at variance with each other, even mutually exclusive. This leads us to recognize that truth about our humanness is highly contested.

Intimate-partner abuse and rape

Intimate-partner abuse affects women in every continent and every society. In the United States, according to the US National Center for Injury Prevention and Control, women experience about 4.8 million intimate-partner-related physical assaults and rapes annually, with an estimated 1,640 in one year ending in death.[14] Half a world away in Bangladesh, the World Health Organization

---

14. National Center for Injury Prevention and Control, 'Understanding Intimate Partner Violence', factsheet 2006.

suggests more than 50% of women experience some form of domestic violence, with around 3,000 acid attacks reported in one decade. In both countries, as in the UK and elsewhere across the globe, the reported level of sexual assault or physical battering is known to be much lower than the actual incidence. And even if women do seek help following a crime, they often have no guarantee of redress. In Bangladesh, for example, out of 121 attacks reported in 2010, there were only seven convictions.[15] In many cultures, women who report a sexual attack will find little sympathy from the police or authorities. There are many records of wives being returned to their abusive husbands who are not charged but left free to violate them further. Over 600 million women live in countries where domestic violence is not even a crime. And even in the UK where it is a crime, Her Majesty's Inspectorate of Constabulary (HMIC) in 2014 exposed 'alarming and unacceptable weaknesses' in the way that police forces dealt with domestic violence.[16]

Violence in the home may take many different forms. In some Asian countries it can take the form of acid attacks. For refusing to comply with a partner's demands women can be scarred, disfigured, blinded and left with wounds which never heal. In the UK it can be physical violence, sexual assault or emotional abuse. Whatever the form, the purpose is normally to control a partner, restrict her freedom, bring her into line or increase her dependency. Male victims of intimate-partner violation suffer equally, although in much smaller numbers and often with a different outcome. Partners of both sexes might die as a result of injuries, but Karen Ingala Smith makes a penetrating observation from British homicide figures: men are more likely to be killed by someone they were abusing; women are more likely to be killed by someone who was abusing them.[17]

Rape also exists everywhere and shows no sign of diminishing. Current figures from the United Nations Women's Desk indicate an increase in most countries, both of the reporting of rape and of convictions. The main differences between countries lie in the existence of protective legislation and the level of its implementation. Some countries, like the Democratic Republic of the Congo, or regions, like many areas in Egypt, are commonly referred to as

15. Bureau of Justice statistics selected findings: 'Female Victims of Violence', September 2009, <www.bjs.gov/content/pub/pdf/fvv.pdf>.

16. <www.theguardian.com/society/2014/jul/02/domestic-violence-convictions-record-high>.

17. Karen Ingala Smith, 'Sex-Differences and "Domestic Violence Murders"', <https://kareningalasmith.com/2015/03/14/sex-differences-and-domestic-violence-murders>.

'rape capitals of the world', but cities like Delhi and Jakarta are also known for
the prevalence of sexual violence. Few people have contested UN Secretary
Ban Ki-moon's insistence in 2015 that the world has made 'uneven progress' in
combating violence against women, and that this still persists at 'alarmingly high
levels'.[18]

The impact of rape on a victim has been well documented. Long after the
bruises or scars might have healed, the emotional and mental reverberations
remain. The after-effects of shock, the sense of violation, fear, anger at the
perpetrator, anger at oneself and deep sense of loss, can continue for decades.
Harvard psychiatrist and specialist in trauma study Judith Herman warns about
the deep-seatedness of the effects: 'Traumatized people suffer damage to the
basic structures of the self. They lose trust in themselves, in other people, in
God ... The identity they have formed prior to the trauma is irrevocably
destroyed.'[19]

It is therefore crucial that an understanding of domestic abuse and rape is
developed within our churches, and not simply left to welfare, medical and
counselling services. If the ministry of the gospel is to make any impact on the
lives of those who have undergone these traumas, we need to incorporate
the teaching of appropriate pastoral awareness and skills into the curricula of
theological colleges and training institutions. To do that most effectively, we
need also to develop our theological approach to these issues, so our thinking
and compassion go together.[20] Once again, we pursue our reflection against the
backcloth of the many other explanations of sexual violence against women.
Systems theorists, cultural anthropologists and functionalists have all developed
responses to the question 'why?' But given the limited space available here, I
will focus on two main clusters of answers which differ strongly from each
other: those that offer cultural explanations, and those that pinpoint biology
and evolution.

Cultural explanations

Since the 1980s the social sciences have been much more aware of the need for
gender disaggregation in statistics and research. In older approaches, issues
which affected women were hidden in research which looked at families,

---

18. CNN Library, <http://edition.cnn.com/2013/12/06/us/domestic-intimate-
    partner-violence-fast-facts>.
19. Judith Lewis Herman, *Trauma and Recovery* (New York: Basic Books, 1997), p. 56.
20. For a much fuller account of intimate-partner violence and rape, see Storkey, *Scars
    Across Humanity*, chs. 6 and 8.

institutions or work in a non-gendered way. By contrast, current students of psychology, sociology and social anthropology have more gender-aware research and more reliable data to draw on regarding gender-based violence.

Throughout the world, both social structures and social processes have been unevenly influenced by male perspectives. What happened within these structures and processes was formerly identified by such terms as 'institutional norms', 'deviance', 'patterns of nurture', etc., and was not seen as specifically gendered. So the fact that workplace patterns were often 'family-unfriendly' was regarded as a normal property of work, rather than derived from male definitions of it. Now, there is general agreement that the social constructions of gender are completely woven into the organization of human societies, and are fundamental to a person's life experiences. They are culturally varied: people learn how to be men and women in specific contexts, and gender values and ideologies become inculcated through habits and protocols. Furthermore, these habits will be formed against the backcloth of economic and social values with their built-in vulnerability for women. Explanations that refer back to culture therefore look at all the cultural predictors which frame our human expectations.

Social science research over the last few decades has provided a wealth of cross-cultural examples to show that the link between gender, culture and sexuality operates in the discourses of the family, economics, politics, social structures, jurisprudence, the military, history and religion. The presence or absence of laws, the understanding of human rights, the establishment of hierarchies and privileges, the restrictions on movement or dress, the attitudes of authorities and the interpretation of religious instruction, are all pivotal in the gendering of social reality. Taken together, they offer a persuasive reading of how gender-based violence can become shaped, framed and normalized.

We can illustrate this with reference to an article on gender-based violence in Nigeria. The author draws on a study which sees the connectedness of the factors above, and identifies a rigorous socialization process 'in which every member of the community is aware of what duties, responsibilities and roles are expected from them which is perceived as the correct order crucial for family and communal harmony'. She identifies the exercise of marital power as an aspect of this 'correct order'. The female partner anticipates what the other thinks, intends or requires, and defers to it, believing she has no power to resist, even fearing reprisals if she does resist. There is no negotiation on issues where she might feel differently, or any use of enabling strategies. Psychologically, the systems of inequality and the reinforcement of the *status quo* mean that this partner cannot even conceive the possibility of having input in decision-making.

The writer argues that this power imbalance significantly influences the woman's experience of conflict in marital relations.[21]

The experiences of victims of violence in other areas further affirm these cultural analyses. They point to processes that produce the sense of entitlement that men display in relation to women. The right to 'punish' their wives, the practice of polygamy, early, enforced marriage, the trafficking of girls for sex and rape as a weapon of war, all illustrate the negative undertones of the concept of 'patriarchy' – the system of male predominance which operates across the globe. 'Patriarchy' justifies male power and control, upholds it as normal and allows it to infiltrate into every structure of society. It creates gender stereotypes which excuse male violators, allowing them to abuse with impunity and, in many cases, blame the victim. In many cultures, a woman who is the victim of rape will be rejected by her husband; she may even be accused of infidelity and stoned to death.[22] And in some countries, even though rape might be a punishable offence, the penal code allows a rapist to marry his victim to escape custodial or financial punishment. It does not take much imagination to picture what kind of husband he will be! All this suggests that it is an uphill struggle to convince many cultures that all forms of violence against women are wrong. This would overturn deep-seated, gendered perceptions of worth, value and meaning. In the eyes of far too many, men who violate women are simply complying with patriarchal norms.

Patriarchy might reinforce entitlements of men, but many contemporary psychologists point to the fact that it also harms them. There is an increasing volume of research which looks at the way in which both sexes are its victims, although with different outcomes. One significant author argues: 'As long as men are brain-washed to equate violent domination and abuse of women with privilege, they will have no understanding of the damage done to themselves or to others, and no motivation to change.'[23] She agrees with many others who maintain that patriarchy brutalizes men and robs them of their full humanity.

Concepts of 'full humanity' are often assumed by social scientists. Although ethical evaluation is rarely made explicit, few sociologists or social psychologists

---

21. Nkiru Igbelina-Igbokwe, 'Contextualizing Gender-Based Violence within Patriarchy in Nigeria', *Pambazuka News*, 30 May 2013, <www.pambazuka.org/gender-minorities/contextualizing-gender-based-violence-within-patriarchy-nigeria>.

22. For a much fuller account of honour killings, see Storkey, *Scars Across Humanity*, pp. 59–74.

23. bell hooks, 'Understanding Patriarchy', in idem, *The Will to Change: Men, Masculinity and Love* (New York: Simon & Schuster, 2004), p. 27.

would demur from the understanding that gender-based violence is wrong, and that good reciprocal relationships, mutual respect and protection of the vulnerable are better mores for society. Yet, the question remains of how we know what is 'full humanity' and what it might rest upon, which is rarely examined by social scientists. To know how to respond to the problem more completely, we need to probe that question.

Explanations from sociobiology and evolutionary psychology

A strongly opposing set of explanations starts from a concept of our humanity. It is centred upon human biology. These explanations focus upon our 'evolutionary history', and argue that specific differences between male and female explain the paradoxes of human behaviour, including violence against women. The most prolific of the explanations argue that all the characteristics we can see currently in nature are most probably 'adaptations' – characteristics which have conferred some kind of survival advantage in the evolutionary history of the particular organism. They also identify the gene as central in the explanation, maintaining that individual organisms – animals, humans, plants, bacteria – are 'survival machines', whose purpose is to give temporary lodgings to our genes. Like all life on the planet, human life is driven towards pursuing genetic survival. Evolution has sculpted our brains with preferences that yield reproductive success.

These assumptions play heavily into analyses of gender. Because males produce far more sperm than females produce eggs, different strategies are needed for males and females to maximize their genetic potential. A man can have many children with little inconvenience to himself; a woman can have only a few, and with great effort. In many species, males direct most or all of their energy into producing strong offspring, and their success is entirely dependent on access to fertile females plus female parenting of their offspring. So, the theory goes, we can expect this to be reflected in human behaviour. For optimal gene reproduction a man needs access to many sexual partners, while a woman needs a safe environment to raise her children to adulthood. These needs predispose men's and women's choice of mates and of mating strategies.

Some evolutionary psychologists suggest that polygyny would have been the natural state in human evolutionary history because it enables men to impregnate many women in a secure setting without trespassing on the territory of other men and thus fuelling inter-male aggression. The males who out-produced other males in evolutionary history were precisely those who were willing and able to copulate with many females at the peak of fertility. And it is their genes which have continued down the generational line.

I have offered a very full critique of this biological reductionism in *Scars Across Humanity*, and there is space here for only a few comments. The question of the scientific value of sociobiology in particular has often been raised. Proponents have been criticized for their methodology, their lack of careful empirical research, their assumption of gender stereotypes, and the way they interpret all findings against the pervasive backcloth of biological determinism. On this theory, for example, rape is not an aberration, but, as Glenn Wilson proposes, an alternative 'gene-promotion strategy', most likely to be adopted when consenting sex is not available.[24] Apparently the human male, faced with 'the choice between force or genetic extinction', will obviously go for force. 'Non-receptive women can still get pregnant, so their protests are, genetically speaking, irrelevant.'[25] In another often-quoted text, *Why Men Rape*, the authors confidently assert that men use only enough violence in rape to accomplish the purpose of distributing their sperm to fertile females. The 'evidence' they submit consists of comments by volunteers at a rape centre that only 15% of the victims they spoke to reported excessive violence.[26] This spurious bit of research could be quickly contradicted by any conversation with Refuge in the UK or any visit to a hospital treating rape survivors in the Congo. Seeing a fuller picture of the brutal violence of rape raises huge questions about claims that it is a gene-promotion strategy. Even less gene-promotion happens when the victim dies!

More fundamental problems about the scope of the explanation also arise. The first is that the explanation lacks any ethical or moral understanding. No connection exists between what is naturally selected and what is morally right or wrong, and there is little space for those categories in the theory. In fact some positive biological or adaptive traits might well be considered by us as heinous in ethical terms. The second is that the explanation leaves us with a situation which cannot be redeemed or put right since, from the point of human reproductive history, there is nothing to be put right. In the 'ancestral environment' males who compelled women forcefully into sex may even have had 'greater reproductive success' than less aggressive males.[27] Evolutionary psychology does recognize that behaviour which was best suited for gene-promotion in the ancestral environment may not work today, but does not provide any solution

24. Glenn Wilson, *The Great Sex Divide* (London: Peter Owen, 1989), pp. 128–31 (reprinted Washington DC: Scott-Townsend, 1992).

25. Wilson, *Great Sex Divide*, pp. 128–31.

26. Randy Thornhill and Craig T. Palmer, 'Why Men Rape', *New York Academy of Sciences*, January/February 2000, p. 25; also at <www.csus.edu/indiv/m/merlinos/thornhill.html>.

27. Lee Ellis, *Theories of Rape: Inquiries into the Causes of Sexual Aggression* (Washington DC: Hemisphere Pub. Corp., 1989).

to the problems the theories leave us with. The third is that terms like 'justice', 'repentance', reparation' and 'remorse' have little meaning in this naturalistic framework. The violent abuser is simply, in Dawkins' terms, 'just a machine with a defective component'.[28] Our only hope, it seems, is that new adaptations might eventually make it easier for violence against women to be eradicated, but we really have very little idea as to how that might happen.

Not only does a materialist view of human life, which these theories rely upon, allow little space for proper analyses of power, it also shrivels our significance as human persons. It fails to connect us with our deepest experiences in life, or offer any guidance for the choices we might make in how we live. When a theory leaves no room for either human will or accountability, it justifies any behaviour in naturalistic terms, and exposes us to ultimate hopelessness.

Theological explanations

A theological explanation of violence against women also starts with a concept of humanity, but one rooted in our identity as persons before God, not in our biology. The understanding of human anthropology offered by biblical theology goes further than the social scientist appeal to patriarchy and directly counters the reductionist view of sociobiology. At its kernel it sees human beings as responsible agents – not simply a product of overarching systems or determined by their selfish genes. Human behaviour is certainly influenced by the contexts in which we live – by the requirements of our own bodies, by the way our sense of worth and self-esteem has been shaped through childhood and beyond, and by the prevailing attitudes and ideas which surround us. Yet human beings make choices; we have the capacity to reflect and decide on the morality of what we choose, we can marshal our will to certain forms of action. All this is part of our created humanness. We are not defective machines, but living beings who can respond both ethically and spiritually to the world we are placed in.

I have already noted how a theology of our creation as *imago dei* addresses foeticide, and it is relevant here also. Created as ethical, responsive creatures and called to uphold the moral structures of our created universe, we face the many challenges to our relationships. The biblical requirement of neighbour love would, on its own, rule out the dreadful practices of rape and violation we have been documenting. Even more would the theology of marriage, where wife and husband are called to show mutual love and respect for each other and live in troth and life-long commitment. A theology of justice, of right

---

28. Richard Dawkins, 'Let's All Stop Beating Basil's Car', Edge Foundation, 2008, <www.edge.org/q2006/q06_9.html>.

relationships and of protection of the vulnerable all require that we hold these patterns of violation to account.

However, it is with the Christian theology of sin that we gain a deeper understanding of human violence and abuse. Sin is a crucial concept in grasping the direction much of humanity has taken. In a nutshell it indicates that, though human beings are created with the capacity for good, we often do not live according to the life-giving norms God has structured into our creation, but instead choose a different way. The theological metaphors for that way are varied – embracing of evil, disobedience, rebellion against God, enthronement of self, venting of hatred – but whatever terms we choose, the evidence before us is pain and brokenness.

Sin is clearly manifested in the global oppression of vulnerable people, and in particular in violence against women. Its alienating and destructive nature means that people become cut off from God and from each other by the impact of sin on their lives; those sinned against are damaged by those who should be loving and supporting them. Sin's ability to distort and delude means that cultures, institutions and individuals become caught up in wrong ways of living, and begin to believe their own propaganda. Sin's addictive power makes it hard to break the bondage to violence or abuse that people are plunged into, and its structural implications mean that it becomes embedded in institutions and in families for generations. When sin fosters hatred, vindictiveness, hardness of heart and patterns of un-love, it is easy to see why so many people suffer. But without a theology of sin, it is very difficult to understand why some humans should treat other humans with such flagrant disregard for their well-being. Once we understand that patriarchy is not merely a cultural or economic edifice, but one built on the foundations of structural sin, we can see in a much fuller way the depth of its roots, and the difficulties in challenging its power.

Yet a proper understanding of sin actually brings hope to the discussion of gender-based violence, because in biblical theology sin never has the last word. It always points to the possibility of redemption and a new start. The theological answer to sin is Christology, where Christ's redemptive love, poured out on the cross, urges us to repentance and a bigger vision of our humanity. And those cultures who hear and respond to the message of redemption need also to hear how it speaks into the barbarity of all forms of violence against women. They need to recognize that it can bring change. It can spur on education programmes which challenge gender stereotypes and concepts of worth. It can undergird the drive towards more effective legislation, bringing robust protective measures and appropriate punishment for violation. It can institute greater healing and growth for those damaged by the brutality of others. It can take more effective steps towards economic justice and the empowerment of women. It can do all this because redemptive living is able to challenge sin, combat selfish gender attitudes and reject the distorted views of humanness which lie beneath. The challenge to theology itself is to recognize the urgency to make the implications of a theology of redemption evident in many more areas of life. The challenge to theologians is to serve with bold humility, alongside others, to address and overcome violence against women.

© Elaine Storkey, 2017

16. ON NOT HANDLING SNAKES: LATE-MODERN CULTURAL ASSUMPTIONS ABOUT SEXUALITY

Stephen R. Holmes

In the Appalachian mountains in West Virginia, snake handling as a part of Christian worship is still legal, and still practised by a small number of Pentecostal congregations. There is of course an exegetical basis for the practice of handling poisonous snakes in worship and, *prima facie*, it is strong,[1] but it is not one I have ever taken the trouble to investigate. The practice seems so self-evidently ridiculous, on account of the threat to health involved, that I see no reason to give time to exploring its supposed justifications; they simply must be wrong.

My suggestion in this chapter is that those of us who argue a traditional line on Christian sexual ethics are in danger of being heard by others exactly as I hear the snake-handlers: the conclusion pressed is so self-evidently wrong, again on account of the threat to health involved, that arguments for it are assumed to be inadequate before being heard. My argument is not merely that traditional sexual ethics are now culturally bizarre in the West, although that is true. Rather, I want to suggest that we have internalized into our church practices and teachings cultural assumptions which make traditional sexual ethics implausible even in our own terms. I fear that our conversation partners are right to hear us in the way I hear claims about snake handling.

If this is true, we need to learn to name and unpick these assumptions, and offer a different vision of Christian practice that is not based on them. This

---

1. Assuming we accept the longer ending of Mark as canonical.

paper is a modest attempt to begin that. Throughout, I pay attention to radical feminist critiques of contemporary cultural assumptions about sexuality. This may seem an eccentric decision, but this is the discourse which has most successfully exposed and critiqued the norms of our culture, and so it is a discourse to which we need to pay attention if we are to attempt the same work.

Introduction: what has changed?

The *secunda pars* of Thomas Aquinas' *Summa Theologica* treats moral theology, through nearly three hundred questions. What we now call sexual ethics is dealt with in just four of those questions, as a minor theme under the virtue of temperance.[2] One of those four questions, on the species of lust, is divided into twelve articles, of which one relates to same-sex sexual activity (or 'the vice against nature' as Thomas calls it). Most of Thomas's discussion concerns whether same-sex desire is properly considered lust or not. That it is wrong is evident already on the basis of the natural fittingness of male and female together, and the proper end of sexual activity in procreation.

Thomas may be right or wrong in this; what is interesting is the rapidity with which he can deal with the question. The issue was neither difficult nor controversial for him. The same could be said of any Christian moral theologian prior to about 1900 – indeed, writing in 1951, Barth could still describe the claim that 'the command of God' is opposed to same-sex relationships as 'almost too obvious to need stating'.[3]

Six decades later, we would struggle to be so sanguine.

Virtually every mainline Protestant ecclesial communion in the West is presently either riven by debates over the moral status of same-sex relationships, or recovering from a schism over the issue. Books promising new approaches to the question appear too regularly for most of us to read them all. It is virtually impossible to work as a theologian without being drawn into controversy on the topic (I have tried . . .) or to serve as a church leader without being regularly challenged by it.

What, we might ask, has changed?

Of course, it is possible to answer 'nothing'. There are those who claim, increasingly stridently, that Scripture (and, perhaps, the catholic tradition) is

---

2. Aquinas, *Summa Theologica*, IIa IIae, q. 154, art. 11.

3. Karl Bath, *Church Dogmatics* III.4 (Edinburgh: T&T Clark, 1961), p. 166.

clear about marriage, and that the widespread discussion is merely indicative of a more general failure of submission to proper authority in matters of faith and practice. This position is increasingly difficult to hold, however: a growing stream of revisionist proposals claim to be grounded on a commitment to biblical authority (and, perhaps, the catholic tradition), and it has become very difficult to dismiss all of them as just eccentric or mendacious.[4]

It is also possible to answer the question 'what has changed?' with 'everything'. Fifty years ago today, homosexual acts between two men were illegal in all parts of the United Kingdom; the legislation was suspended, but not repealed, in 1967 in England and Wales, but not until 1981 in Scotland and 1982 in Northern Ireland. It was only with the Sexual Offences Act of 2003 – not fifteen years ago – that parliament decided that the law should not concern itself with sexual acts between consenting adults in private. Yet now to query the morality of homosexual sex, to express an idea that was still enshrined in law in the last decade, is essentially unacceptable in public discourse. Whether we view this as a great triumph of human rights or as something more complicated, the astonishing rapidity of the change in cultural attitudes demands explanation, explanation that, when offered, will help us understand the nature of the debate within our churches.

Of course we cannot pretend our context here is merely historical, it is also geographical. There are significant parts of the world where the direction of travel is to steadily decrease the rights of LGBT+ people. I hope we can agree that such moves are reprehensible – whatever we may think of the moral issue, harsh legal penalties, possibly including death, are clearly disproportionate – but they are real. Many of the more painful international ecclesial disputes are reflections of this reality of differing directions of travel between, roughly, the global North/West and the global South.

The task of theology is always contextual. Each new generation of theologians in each particular human culture receives the biblical witness, mediated

---

4. See, for example, Michael Vasey, *Strangers and Friends: A New Exploration of Homosexuality and the Bible* (London: Hodder & Stoughton, 1995); Eugene F. Rogers, *Sexuality and the Christian Body: Their Way into the Triune God* (Oxford: Blackwell, 1999); James V. Brownson, *Bible, Gender, Sexuality: Reframing the Church's Debate on Same-Sex Relationships* (Grand Rapids: Eerdmans, 2013); Robert Song, *Covenant and Calling: Towards a Theology of Same-Sex Relationships* (London: SCM, 2014); and contributions, particularly Megan DeFranza's, to Preston Sprinkle (ed.), *Two Views on Human Sexuality* (Grand Rapids: Zondervan, 2016). My point is not that any of these books are right, but that each of them is a serious contribution to the debate that cannot be dismissed without engagement.

by the catholic tradition, and is called to repeat it in ways that are faithful to the tradition and comprehensible to the culture. Sometimes doing that will mean broadly accepting the context and reinterpreting the faith in the light of it. Thomas's great achievement was to renarrate his Augustinian inheritance meaningfully in the light of the Aristotelian renaissance. Sometimes the task will be to successfully resist the culture. In both the narrow cultural context of Nazism, and the broader one of Schleiermachian romanticism, Barth is celebrated for his ability to resist culturally-compromised forms of Christianity.

I propose that our present inability to settle our conversation about sexuality stems, at least in part, from the combined influence of a set of cultural assumptions that we have not adequately identified and evaluated. The urgent theological task in this area is not presently another re-examination of the biblical witness – although we will need to do that – but a naming of the assumptions which we, as late-modern Westerners, bring with us as we approach the Bible. I will argue that we have allowed, even within our church discourse, our accounts of heterosexual marriage to be determined by a number of cultural assumptions, and that this makes it extremely difficult for us to give a credible account of the biblical witness when it comes to same-sex relationships.

When I talk of 'assumptions' here I mean something deep – what Pierre Bourdieu described as 'doxa'. *Doxa*, he suggests, is that experience, common in ancient societies (or so he claims), where our categories for understanding the world so perfectly reflect the power structures in our culture that they serve to make those power structures appear natural or self-evident.[5] When a belief has become part of the *doxa* it has become too obvious to be questioned; indeed, it has become too obvious to be noticed.

We might look to the natural sciences for an example. As has been pointed out repeatedly, the scientific method relies on various philosophical assumptions, some easily stated (that observation of the world is not illusory, but conveys good information about the way things are), some more complicated (that the rationality behind natural events is internal to the physical world).[6] It is not hard, however, to find those who assume and assert that the validity of

---

5. Pierre Bourdieu, tr. R. Nice, *Outline of a Theory of Practice* (New York: Cambridge University Press, 1977), p. 164.

6. These points were classically argued by M. B. Foster in two seminal papers arguing that developments in Christian theology paved the way for the practice of natural science: 'The Christian Doctrine of Creation and the Rise of Natural Science', *Mind* 43 (1934), pp. 446–68, and 'Christian Theology and the Modern Science of Nature', *Mind* 44 (1935), pp. 439–66 and 45 (1936), pp. 1–27.

scientific method is self-evident; the underlying philosophical assumptions have become *doxa*.

Thomas and Barth both offered doxic readings of the question of same-sex marriage, which never occurred to them as a live question. We live in a different context, and we need to face this question with a seriousness that they never imagined. This is not to say their moral judgments were wrong; I have argued before, and will do again, that they were simply right. It is to say that the arguments they advance, such as they are, are inadequate in our contemporary context to defend their judgments as right.

This is a real and serious problem for us. The moral theology of marriage that we have inherited was forged in a context where same-sex marriage was unimagined, and so does not contain the developed resources to analyse same-sex marriage. I believe that a faithful development of the doctrines there assumed will lead us necessarily to oppose same-sex marriage, but it is an urgent task for our generation of theologians to offer the development that has heretofore been lacking.

The problem we face, however, is not just a collapse of a previously-secure *doxa*, but the rise of a new one. I propose that a set of assumptions about marriage and human sexuality have become part of the *doxa* in our culture, and so it takes great effort to even see them.[7] Historical and anthropological study can help. If we start to understand another culture that does not share our cultural presuppositions, we have a chance of seeing the assumptions, naming them, and being able to consider them. I will begin, then, with a review of patristic teaching on human sexuality, not because it is necessarily right, but because its alien assumptions help us to see that our cultural assumptions are at least contestable, even if they should turn out to be right.

A patristic account of marriage

If we ask the question, 'who should marry?', looking for guidance to the biblical texts, one plausible answer is, 'no one'. Paul says this straightforwardly and

---

7. It is common in the literature to note that our modern Western assumptions about sexuality all begin in the late nineteenth century, as does our modern language. Of course, we might argue that our Victorian forebears discovered and named something universal to all human experience, but virtually all theorists of sexuality resist that for reasons I shall explore later.

repeatedly in 1 Corinthians 7, and Jesus more than once hints in the same direction.[8] Whether this interpretation is right or wrong, it was certainly influential in the early church. Until Augustine, Christian interpreters of the Scriptures assumed the superiority of celibacy. For the orthodox, marriage was an acceptable way of life, but unquestionably second-best. The true Christian, they assumed and preached, should aspire to virginity.[9]

What of the Old Testament witness, which proposes a moral urgency about marriage? The patristic understanding, clearly expressed already just two centuries into the Christian era, was that the urgency of marriage stemmed from the reality of death, and so had been decisively reordered by the resurrection of Christ. Prior to knowledge of the resurrection, the only possible human response to death is the begetting of children. We marry to have children, and we must have children because we know we must die.

This idea is scattered all over the patristic literature. Writing against Marcion, Tertullian taught that sexual intercourse began after the fall, as a result of mortality. 'Where there is death, there is also marriage.'[10] He makes an explicit link with Jesus' teaching that marriage ends in the resurrection age: death ends in the kingdom and so marriage ends too.[11] The point became general in the fourth century. Chrysostom states it most pithily, almost echoing Tertullian, *Opou gar thanatos, ekei gamos*,[12] but Basil, Gregory of Nazianzus, Gregory of Nyssa, Athanasius, Jerome and Ambrose all make the same point.[13]

The temptation for the early church, then, was always to devalue marriage. Death is done to death – and so, of course, childrearing and marriage are decisively reordered. Now there is no need to marry, and so a dangerous error repeatedly arises amongst those who believe in Jesus, that real discipleship is celibate. The error is dangerous because it is so close to the truth that Jesus

---

8. In Matt. 19:10, Jesus' disciples suggest, seemingly incredulously, that he is proposing so strict an ethic of marriage that celibacy is preferable; Jesus' response hardly denies their judgment. In Matt. 22:30, Jesus asserts that eschatologically, at least, marriage will come to an end.

9. I have written more about this in my essay in Sprinkle (ed.), *Two Views*.

10. *C. Marcion* IV 38.5.43–45, p. 468 in *SC* 456; see also IV 17.5.30–33, p. 218.

11. *Res. Mort.* XXXVI.5.24–25.

12. *Virg.* XVI.6.70 (*SC* 125, p. 142).

13. So Josiah Trenham, *Marriage and Virginity according to St John Chrysostom* (Durham theses, Durham University. Available at Durham E-Theses Online, <http://etheses.dur.ac.uk/1259/>), p. 89 n. 102.

is risen, death is conquered, and so marriage is unnecessary. The logic is profoundly attractive to any community who actually believe the gospel. The Corinthians were merely amongst the first such, and so the first of their questions to Paul turns on the claim 'it is good for a man not to touch a woman' (1 Cor. 7:1).[14]

Paul does not disagree – not because he is misogynistic, not because he is horrified by sex, but because he believes in the resurrection. But he qualifies: although the kingdom is coming, it is not yet come, and so he warns of the continuing reality of sin. Since *porneia* happens, he counsels, be married, be faithful and be sexually available to each other. 'I say this as concession, not command' (1 Cor. 7:6) – our hearts are stony still. Better not to marry, of course, but, he remarks laconically, better to marry than to burn. So there is a mutuality of availability: wives own their husbands' bodies and husbands their wives'. In marriage spouses surrender themselves to each other so that both may fulfil their physical needs, but still it is concession, not command. This is not the best way – because Jesus is risen, marriage is unnecessary.

So the preoccupation of the early church with the ethical status of marriage was just right. This was not the result of some Platonic distrust of matter, as it is so often presented,[15] it was the result of the sure hope in the resurrection of the dead. The church of the martyrs believed in the resurrection, and so struggled with marriage, at least until Augustine. The genius of the Augustinian ethic is to see that marriage can be discipleship, not just concession, and it can be discipleship in just the way celibacy can. Celibacy is of course the Christian norm – to assert otherwise is to deny the resurrection – but both marriage and celibacy, well practised, are modes of asceticism, thick clusters of practices that serve to reorder our sinful and wayward desires and make us fit for the kingdom. Marriage, Christianly practised, is not a way of indulging our desires, but a way of redirecting them.[16] The only way we can make Christian sense of marriage as anything more than a pastoral accommodation to human weakness is to see it as a mode of practice for

---

14. Unless otherwise indicated all biblical translations in this chapter are the author's.

15. See for instance Adrian Thatcher's introductory text, and the works he references there: *God, Sex, and Gender: An Introduction* (Oxford: Wiley-Blackwell, 2011), pp. 194 and 201–2.

16. All of this is understood and rehearsed by the best arguments offering an affirming theology of same-sex relations. See, e.g., Rogers, *Sexuality and the Christian Body*, pp. 67–85 or Song, *Covenant*, pp. 1–22.

living in the kingdom, although in the kingdom we will neither marry nor be given in marriage.

As I said, I review this material not because it is necessarily right, although I happen to think that it is in all important respects, but because it is utterly different from our own cultural assumptions, even within the churches – which church today teaches unreflectively that celibacy is the normal mode of life for Christians? – and so it offers us a perspective from which we might perceive those things we assume without noticing.

Sexuality

The first set of assumptions we need to consider are in the area of human sexuality. Not about the nature of what is now called sexual orientation – that question will come in at the end of our reasoning, but only then. Rather, we need to think about the place of sexual activity in human flourishing in our contemporary culture.[17] The patristic assumption that celibacy was normal for Christians, the best route to holiness and maturity, is entirely alien to us; culturally, we have no space for celibacy whatsoever. Virginity is an embarrassing childish state to be escaped from as quickly as possible. As Bruckner puts it, 'Except for Christians, Jews, and fundamentalist Muslims, who still assign a symbolic value to the hymen and make its preservation a token of purity, waiting is no longer synonymous with maturation but with stupidity'.[18] Sexual activity is of transcendent human value. Foucault claims, famously, that, for us, '[s]ex is worth dying for'.[19] Our film industry presents a forty-year-old virgin as a self-evidently grotesque figure, tragic but full of comedic possibilities; our popular music has for five decades now equated first sexual experience with maturity and entrance into adulthood. The celibate is foolish, immature, childish and incomplete.

Further, to be celibate – even temporarily, after the break-up of a relationship – is considered unhealthy in our culture. A sub-Freudian narrative of sexual desire needing release or else being sublimated in pathological ways is

---

17. We must not forget in this argument that 'what we define as "sexuality" is an historical construction'; Jeffrey Weeks, *Sexuality* (London: Tavistock, 1986), p. 15.

18. Pascal Bruckner, tr. Steven Rendell and Lisa Neal, *Has Marriage for Love Failed?* (Cambridge: Polity, 2013), p. 8.

19. Michel Foucault, tr. Robert Hurley, *The History of Sexuality: Vol. 1: An Introduction* (Harmandsworth: Penguin), p. 156.

assumed.[20] Newspaper advice columns stress the importance of maintaining an active sex life into our twilight years, and counsel masturbation as an acceptable temporary solution, but assume without question that celibacy is dangerous. Eva Illouz argues that psychoanalysis, at least in the United States, 'quickly became more than a discipline, that is a specialized body of knowledge. It was a new set of cultural practices which . . . reorganized conceptions of self, emotional life, even social relations'.[21]

Lillian Rubin's study of American adolescence from the 1950s to the 1980s showed a reversal of desired reputation, particularly amongst teenage girls. At the beginning of the period, a girl who was sexually active would attempt to portray herself as a virgin. By the end, a teenage girl who was a virgin would typically pretend to her peers that she was sexually experienced.[22] Here, however, I raise for the first time a caution that will run through this analysis: while Rubin's data chimes culturally, the fact that it is specifically female teenagers who display this desire to fit in with shifting cultural norms invites feminist critique. bell hooks argues that a sexual liberation which has no space open for celibacy remains patriarchal: 'Men are socialized to act sexually, women to not act (or to simply react to male sexual advances).' Unless what she terms 'the stigma attached to sexual inactivity' is removed, there has been no sexual liberation.[23]

hooks offers a feminist argument that runs parallel, if counter, to the Freudian line; the two are brought into (violent) collision by Shulamith Firestone in her famous *Dialectic of Sex* (although without, at this point, the focus on celibacy). The book addresses the subsiding of feminism after attaining universal suffrage in the 1920s. In exploring reasons for this, she devotes a chapter to the relationship of feminism to psychoanalysis. Firestone first acknowledges the social significance of psychoanalysis: 'If we had to name one cultural current that

---

20. In describing this as 'sub-Freudian' I am deliberately evading the question of whether Freud thought sexual abstinence inevitably resulted in pathology or not. Certainly he regarded the attainment of healthy sexuality as an achievement (Peter Gay argues this well in *Freud: A Life for Our Time* (London: J. M. Dent, 2008)), and so (as Illouz puts it) 'problematized' normal sexuality (Eva Illouz, *Cold Intimacies: The Making of Emotional Capitalism* (Cambridge: Polity, 2007), pp. 8–9).

21. Illouz, *Cold Intimacies*, pp. 6–7.

22. Lillian Rubin, *Erotic Wars* (New York: Farrar, Straus, and Giroux, 1990).

23. bell hooks, *Feminist Theory: From Margin to Centre* (Boston: South End, 1984), p. 150. See further Carol Anne Douglas's exploration of celibacy as an expression of radical feminism in *Love and Politics: Radical Feminist and Lesbian Theories* (San Francisco: ISM Press, 1990), pp. 133–6.

most characterizes America in the twentieth century, it might be the work of Freud and the disciples that grew out of it. There is no-one who remains unexposed to his vision of human life . . .'[24] Her judgment on Freudian psychoanalysis is withering ('the emperor has no clothes on'[25]), raising the question as to why it not only persists in, but dominates, Western culture. Her answer is straightforward: 'sexuality' is the key problem of contemporary culture, and Freudianism not only names this, but offers a way of addressing sexuality which preserves patriarchy. It became, therefore, a way for a culture to pretend to address sexuality without confronting issues of gender justice.[26]

However compelling we find this feminist critique, its very existence affirms the reality of the cultural horror at celibacy for which I have been arguing. Within the churches, we have bought into this narrative to a surprising degree. If we speak of celibacy at all, it is as a rare and special charismatic gift. The underlying narrative supposes that our cultural assumptions about the unhealthiness of celibacy are simply correct, but that God miraculously protects some people from the otherwise-inevitable negative consequences when they are given 'the gift of singleness'. This stands in marked contrast to the patristic assumption that celibacy was the norm for redeemed humanity. One conception here begins in Freud and patriarchy, the other in reflection on the resurrection of Christ. It would be possible to argue that our churches have chosen badly.

Alongside this insistence on the necessity of sexual activity for human flourishing is the decoupling of sexuality from reproduction, and the rise of what Giddens calls 'plastic sexuality'.[27] Historically in the West, at least after the Christianization of the Roman empire, sexuality that was not directed towards procreation was frowned upon, even legislated against. In English law, the ancient (capital) crime of 'sodomy' referred not specifically to anal intercourse, or to male homosexual activity, but to any act terminating in ejaculation which was not directed towards procreation, including the use of contraception in marriage.[28] Procreation was, in law, the proper end of all sexual activity.

---

24. Shulamith Firestone, *The Dialectic of Sex: The Case for Feminist Revolution* (New York: Farrer, Straus, and Giroux, 2003 (1970)), p. 38.

25. Ibid., p. 39.

26. Firestone's entire chapter on this is explosive: *Dialectic of Sex*, pp. 38–64.

27. Anthony Giddens, *The Transformation of Intimacy: Sexuality, Love and Eroticism in Modern Societies* (Cambridge: Polity, 1992), p. 2.

28. Nikki Sullivan, *A Critical Introduction to Queer Theory* (New York: New York University Press, 2003), pp. 2–4.

Giddens traces the ending of this belief that the proper end of sexual activity was always procreation to a sociological shift beginning in the eighteenth century towards limiting family size. This is perhaps somewhat reductionistic. Birken argues a wider mesh of cultural moves, including the Enlightenment category of the individual, campaigns for women's suffrage, evolution and the new science of eugenics, and economic factors.[29] Whichever historical argument is more nearly right, there can be little doubt that the availability of safe and reliable contraception has accelerated the move to 'plastic sexuality', and the development of reproductive technologies has cemented the change. Not only is sexual activity not necessarily related to reproduction anymore, but reproduction need not be related to sexual activity either.

This change has been disproportionately transformative for women, as Giddens notes. He comments that '[f]or most women, in most cultures, and throughout most periods of history, sexual pleasure, where possible, was intrinsically bound up with fear [of death in childbirth]'.[30] This emancipation of female sexuality has of course been celebrated in cultural narratives of the sexual revolution, and surely rightly so – escape from the fear of death must be an aspect of human flourishing. Returning to the feminist critiques, this point is widely celebrated. Ti-Grace Atkinson, for instance, argues that freedom from reproductive function is necessary for women to be free. Discussing her position, Douglas raises several concerns about assumed universal desires, one being what if a woman chose to reproduce 'the old way'? Atkinson seems simply to assume that no woman will.[31]

If sexuality is not for reproduction, what is it for? Our cultural answer is clear: pleasure. We engage in sexual activity as a leisure choice, for enjoyment. Grant puts it well:

> As our sexuality has become increasingly detached from its essential purposes – relationships, marriage, and children – it has become simply a mode of consumption. As a result, human sexuality has become part of the entertainment industry – a choice to be catered to rather than a vocation that serves any greater goal. Our sexual choices are seen as just different modes of consumption within an infinite spectrum of choice, without any one choice having an intrinsic priority over the others.[32]

---

29. Lawrence Birken, *Consuming Desire: Sexual Science and the Emergence of a Culture of Abundance, 1871–1914* (Ithaca: Cornell University Press, 1988).

30. Anthony Giddens, *Transformation of Intimacy*, p. 28.

31. Douglas, *Love and Politics*, pp. 131–2.

32. Jonathan Grant, *Divine Sex: A Compelling Vision for Christian Relationships in a Hypersexualized Age* (Grand Rapids: Brazos, 2015), p. 80.

Unsurprisingly, this criticism of sexual liberation as consumeristic has been made repeatedly by feminist theorists. bell hooks criticizes Greer's *Female Eunuch* on precisely these grounds.[33] Luce Irigaray's ecstatic poetry questions the same point, without resolution: '*Jouissance* in the copula engenders form-body. Which is not limited to begetting a child. It has the power to do so. But that product is often a substitute for the profile of our bodies . . .'[34] Predictably, perhaps, given her Marxist orientation, Firestone is most direct, deconstructing the entire discourse of love and romance as at once oppressive and consumeristic.[35]

Once again, however, it is not difficult to see that our churches have followed this cultural shift towards a consumerist ethic of sexuality fairly uncritically. When Heather and I went through marriage preparation classes, the recommended book for sexually-inexperienced Christian newlyweds was entitled *Intended for Pleasure*.[36] Online critiques of American evangelical purity culture repeatedly characterize the message there as being about the maximization of sexual pleasure through postponing first sexual experience till marriage. Waiting will result in true sexual satisfaction, and true sexual satisfaction is what every Christian girl (evangelical purity culture is utterly disproportionately aimed at young women) wants.

It is worth noting finally here that there is a fundamental tension between these two cultural assumptions about sexuality. Grant again:

> In the realm of sexuality and relationships, the modern vision of freedom is expressed under two myths, the 'romanticist' and the 'realist', both of which have become pervasive in our culture. Romanticism describes the freedom of the *expressive* individual. It says we should freely express with our bodies what we feel in our hearts; how we feel about someone should determine how far we go with him or her sexually. This is encouraged by the recent creation of 'sexuality' as a type of distinct and core part of our identity that we must actively express to become a whole self. Sexual expression becomes an issue of personal integrity, of being true to the inner testimony of our desires, especially the sexual ones.

---

33. hooks, *Feminist Theory*, pp. 147–8.
34. Luce Irigaray, tr. Joanne Collie and Judith Still, *Elemental Passions* (London: Athlone, 1992), p. 79.
35. Firestone, *Dialectic of Sex*, pp. 113–39.
36. It appears to be still in print, despite one of the authors dying fifteen years ago: Ed Wheat and Gaye Wheat, *Intended for Pleasure: Sex Technique and Sexual Fulfilment in Christian Marriage*, 4th edn (Grand Rapids: Revell, 2010).

Realism, in contrast to romanticism, represents the freedom of the *utilitarian* individual. Realism tries to 'demystify' sex by reducing it to a sort of 'happiness technology' that offers fulfilment in the most immediate sense.[37]

Our sexual activity is apparently at once the most fundamental expression of our core identity and a bit of trivial fun. If we listen carefully to narrations of sexuality, we can hear both these attitudes being expressed. A young student speaking to the BBC in the summer of 2015 for example described herself as romantically lesbian but erotically bisexual. The emotionally fulfilling relationship she was seeking was with a woman, but in recreational sex she, as she put it, 'enjoys a penis every so often'. This cultural tension can also be seen in church life, if not phrased quite so crudely, particularly when we examine the variety of arguments offered in favour of revisionist sexual ethics. Sometimes the argument concerns a violation of the very being of LGBT+ Christians, other times it is an expressed impatience that anyone should be exercised over something so trivial as what consenting adults choose to do in private. In our culture – and in our churches – we have come to believe that sexuality is core to our identity, but that sex is an entirely trivial act.

Marriage

Our sociologists tell us of a transformation in Western understandings of marriage that has been accelerating since some time in the nineteenth century. The model now assumed to be normal is termed 'companionate marriage' in anthropological literature. Marriage on this understanding is a shared and private emotional project in which partners find true intimacy in their relationship, without reference to anything beyond. Clearly, this companionate marriage is egalitarian, not patriarchal. It is a coming together of two agents who each will expect to have their needs fulfilled and will act to fulfil the needs of the other.

The origins of this lie in the rise of marriage based on romantic love, rather than parental choice. We now expect to find our need for emotional intimacy fulfilled by our spouse. If that expectation is not realized, it is sufficient ground for ending the relationship. Sharon Thompson's study of American teenagers in the late 1980s found girls,[38] in particular, narrating their active sex lives as

---

37. Grant, *Divine Sex*, p. 60.
38. See Giddens, *Transformation of Intimacy*, pp. 49–52.

a quest for romance, for a 'pure relationship'[39] in which the relationship is sustained not by social mores or outside expectations, but by the satisfaction it delivers to the two people involved.

It is of course possible to argue that this pure relationship is an unobtainable ideal. Radical philosophical critiques exist – Pascal Bruckner asks, with considerable rhetorical verve, *Has Marriage for Love Failed?*

> Consider this current dream: everything in one, everything or nothing. A single person has to condense the totality of our aspirations, and if he fails to do so, we get rid of him. The madness lies in wanting to reconcile everything, the heart and eroticism, raising children and social success, effervescence and the long term. Our couples are not dying of selfishness and materialism, they're dying of a fatal heroism, an excessively great conception of themselves . . . Every woman has to be simultaneously a mother, a whore, a friend, and a fighter, every man has to be a father, a lover, a husband, and a provider . . .[40]

Whether it is an impossible dream or not, there is little doubt that this quest for the pure relationship has become the driving feature of contemporary Western relationships. Cinema, literature, and (perhaps particularly) popular music endlessly celebrate the ideal and the quest for its realization. There are three further features of it that I want to explore, which I will do through a reading of the successful romantic comedy *Four Weddings and a Funeral*.

The first point to draw out is what is *not* in the film: although it revolves around many sexual relationships, it is virtually devoid of children. The pure relationship is directed to the fulfilment the two partners find in each other. If it is heterosexual, they may choose to have children together, but that choice is almost incidental to the nature of their relationship. The pure relationship depends, that is, on the plastic sexuality I considered in the previous section.

The extent to which children are incidental to our present cultural accounts of the marriage relationship may be gauged, again, by reflection on advice given to married couples in newspapers and books. Children are a problem to be solved and a distraction to be survived. Still having an adequate relationship when the children leave home is one of the fundamental problems faced by couples, according to the culturally-dominant narration.[41]

---

39. The term is Giddens's: Anthony Giddens, *Modernity and Self-Identity* (Cambridge: Polity, 1991).

40. Bruckner, *Has Marriage for Love Failed?*, p. 30.

41. See, e.g., Anne Garvey, 'When the Children Leave Home . . .', *The Guardian*, 5 March 2003 or Elizabeth Bernstein, 'The Loneliness of the Empty Nest', *Wall Street Journal*, 1 July 2013.

Second, the single most successful relationship in the film is that between Gareth and Matthew. Although this comes as a surprise to the other characters when it becomes clear at Gareth's funeral, the film is careful to portray this gay relationship as in no way different from the various straight relationships. The pure relationship, because it is divorced from children, is an ideal available to lesbian/gay couples and straight couples indifferently. Illouz describes this dynamic in the academic literature: 'Sexual pleasure was . . . predicated on the achievement of fair and equal relations . . . [u]ltimately, such an idea of sexual pleasure blurred gender differences.'[42] The pure relationship is not intrinsically heterosexual, and its logic indeed leads in a different direction.

The very rapid embracing of same-sex marriage in the West is a demonstration of this reality. Historically, gay-rights activists (as they were once known) were ambivalent about marriage. In the theorized sexual revolution of the 1960s it was perceived as an inherently patriarchal and homophobic institution that needed to be overthrown rather than colonized.[43] Male homosexuality, in particular, generated subcultures that were extraordinarily promiscuous. One US study in the 1970s asked gay men how many sexual partners they had had, and 40% put the number at over 500.[44] The AIDS crisis of the 1980s led to rapid cultural change, and pursuit of the pure relationship became the public face of gay culture instead of celebrations of promiscuity.[45] If the ideal pursued by lesbians and gay men is identical to the ideal pursued by straight people – the pure relationship – then arguments against same-sex marriage are inevitably going to appear to be based merely on prejudice.

The final point to make about marriage in contemporary Western culture is that it is subject to extensive criticism and, perhaps as a result, is in decline as an institution. At the end of *Four Weddings*, Charles and Carrie cement their pure relationship with a vow to not marry each other. The film mocks marriage, or

---

42. Illouz, *Cold Intimacies*, p. 29.

43. For example, in the UK, the most significant pressure group, Stonewall, only began campaigning for equal marriage in late 2010, some time even after mainstream political figures had declared their support. Stonewall's campaign on the issue was careful to reaffirm the 'special and unique status' of civil partnerships for gay and lesbian people. (Quotation from a press release that has since been removed from the website.)

44. Giddens, *Transformation of Intimacy*, p. 15.

45. Obviously there were gay men and lesbians in the 1970s seeking a stable monogamous relationship, and there are still people (of all sexualities) who are very promiscuous; I am writing here about a change in the culturally dominant narrative.

more specifically the wedding, as a fairly ridiculous and inevitably insincere bourgeois institution. The pure relationship might flourish within this cultural form, but there is no sense in which it is necessary; indeed, it is very possibly detrimental.

The number of marriages each year in England and Wales has been declining steadily since 1972,[46] and there is little public perception that marriage has any particular value. Rather, it is a traditional institution that is subject to the suspicion and criticism that all traditional institutions are presently subject to. Quality of relationship, not legal status, is what matters. Of course, we need to add to this a feminist critique of the institution. In a patriarchal context, every heterosexual marriage will be distorting because it becomes a microcosm of the power imbalances that persist between women and men. Simone de Beauvoir's analysis of marriage as an institution in which a woman surrenders her possibilities of fulfilment in return for the protection and financial support that she needs but cannot obtain beyond marriage[47] begins a critique which only grows more trenchant.[48]

That said, all this analysis of the pure relationship takes us again, albeit by a different route, to the modern horror of celibacy. If we expect to find the emotional intimacy we crave in our relationship with our spouse/partner, then the single person is condemned to live without emotional intimacy, and so once again we find a cultural presumption that celibacy is necessarily unhealthy, a damaging, undesirable state. (And we find in feminist collectives practices of renewed sociality intended to provide emotional intimacy outside marriage.)

Just as with the cultural changes I outlined above concerning singleness, Western churches have generally followed these cultural changes concerning marriage uncritically and unconsciously. We have not even noticed that our accounts of what marriage is have changed radically. Christian couples are encouraged to have regular 'date nights' to maintain their relationship without the

---

46. See the ONS statistical bulletin available here: <https://www.ons.gov.uk/ peoplepopulationandcommunity/birthsdeathsandmarriages/ marriagecohabitationandcivilpartnerships/bulletins/ marriagesinenglandandwalesprovisional/2013#fewer-marriages-in-2013>, accessed 20 September 2016.

47. Simone de Beauvoir, *The Second Sex* (New York: Alfred Knopf, 1968), pp. 435–6.

48. Susan Moller Okin offers perhaps the most carefully worked-through reflection on this point that I know: *Justice, Gender, and the Family* (New York: Basic Books, 1989). See especially pp. 146–69.

'distraction' of children, and churches construct their programmes around the assumption that all adult members find their primary intimacy in their marriage relationships. This is particularly evident in the testimonies of celibate gay/lesbian Christians who present the challenge that they cannot flourish or find proper fellowship in (many of) our churches.[49]

Sexual orientation

Let me return to the question of sexual orientation. We now know that some people in the late-modern West are exclusively gay/lesbian. I am sufficiently convinced by recent queer theory to believe that this is a local reality. When we study the variety of human sexual mores across history and across cultures, we find that most people (who have freedom to choose their own sexual activities) have been sexually active with both women and men and have regarded this as normal for human beings. The late-modern Western assumption that the majority of people – lesbian, gay or straight – are sexually attracted only to men or only to women is very strange.[50] (According to Mitchell, even Freud saw this, claiming 'man and woman are *made* in culture'.[51])

It is possible of course that we in the contemporary West are right and the rest of the world is and has been wrong. We would require some very convincing evidence – which as far as I can see is presently entirely lacking –

---

49. See Wesley Hill, *Washed and Waiting: Reflections on Christian Faithfulness and Homosexuality* (Grand Rapids: Zondervan, 2010) and idem, *Spiritual Friendship: Finding Love in the Church as a Celibate Gay Christian* (Grand Rapids: Brazos, 2015); also Eve Tushnet, *Gay and Catholic: Accepting My Sexuality, Finding Community, Living My Faith* (Notre Dame: Ave Maria, 2014).

50. Jenell Williams Parris, *The End of Sexual Identity: Why Sex is Too Important to Define Who We Are* (Downers Grove: IVP, 2011) and Stephen O. Murray, *Homosexualities* (Chicago: University of Chicago Press, 2000) are good introductions to this material. Hanne Blank, *Straight: The Surprisingly Short History of Heterosexuality* (Boston: Beacon, 2012) covers the history of the Western invention of heterosexuality and homosexuality well. For a more radical account, programmatically using history and anthropology to deconstruct gender binaries, see Gilbert Herdt (ed.), *Third Sex, Third Gender: Beyond Sexual Dimorphism in Culture and History* (New York: Zone Books, 1993).

51. Juliet Mitchell, *Psychoanalysis and Feminism: Freud, Reich, Laing and Women* (London: Allen Lane, 1974), p. 131; emphasis original.

for such a claim not to appear merely imperialistic and racist. Note, indeed, that this argument is properly queer: it deconstructs heterosexuality/straight orientation just as effectively as it deconstructs lesbian or gay orientation/ homosexuality.

That said, if we follow through on queer theory, particularly the seminal work of Judith Butler,[52] we must follow this recognition with an acknowledgment that every society proposes – or imposes – certain narrated sexual norms to which members of the society are conformed by socialization.[53] Queer theorists uncover these norms in order to deconstruct them, but their reality is my point here. In the late-modern West, most of us are straight, gay, lesbian or bi. These socially constructed categories adequately define the reflexive internal narration of our experience of sexual desire.[54]

With this, I return to the various points argued for above. I have proposed that we believe that being sexually active is necessary to human mental health and to human flourishing, so much so that our functional definition of 'adulthood' or 'maturity' is being sexually active. Again, emotional intimacy is necessary to human flourishing, and I have argued that we believe that real emotional intimacy is only possible in the context of sexual intimacy – the pure relationship, which is necessarily sexual, is our defining paradigm for emotional intimacy.

I have also argued that these cultural assumptions about marriage have been accepted, and often supported and promoted, by the churches. If the churches were right to do this, then once we accept the fact of sexual orientation, which has become impossible to deny, there can be no plausible argument against same-sex marriage as a Christian option. Every argument we might offer will run up against the fact that to deny the possibility of sexual relationship to lesbian and gay disciples is to deny them any possibility of human flourishing or emotional intimacy, to condemn them to a permanently childlike, immature, unhealthy, dangerous way of life. That is not what God wants for any created human being; to propose it as a way of life is unspeakably cruel.

---

52. Judith Butler, *Gender Trouble: Feminism and the Subversion of Identity* (New York: Routledge, 1990).

53. See Nikki Sullivan, *A Critical Introduction to Queer Theory* (New York: New York University Press, 2003), *passim*.

54. J. R. Ackery's memoir has often been cited in this context. Asked 'Are you a homo or a hetero?' he comments that he had never heard either term before but 'there seemed only one answer' and so he found identity in naming. See *My Father and Myself* (London: Pimlico, 1992 (1968)), p. 117.

What then shall we do?

This recognition can help us to understand why conversations about sexuality are so often not dialogues, but simultaneous parallel monologues. Those of us who argue on the conservative side typically insist, out of faithfulness to Scripture and the catholic tradition, that marriage must be reserved for one man and one woman. We do not realize, however, that when we say 'marriage' we mean, or at least are heard as meaning, something very different from what either Scripture or the catholic tradition meant, something far more encompassing, something that is necessary for human flourishing and so that cannot be denied to all God's children.

We have, I am suggesting, unconsciously but thoroughly, allowed understandings of human sexuality and marriage that are simply pagan into our church life and into our teaching on marriage and sexuality. Because of that, we find ourselves unable to make sense. That which the Scriptures command is unliveable for at least some, and that which a proper pastoral concern seems to require is forbidden by Scripture. Should we be surprised that we are heard as talking like Appalachian Pentecostal snake-handlers? We are commending, with far more vigour – and often enough more hate – a practice that is just as bizarre culturally, and that is assumed to be even more inevitably injurious to health.

What, then, shall we do? We need to deconstruct with care modern notions of 'marriage', to find what in them is acceptable to the gospel and what in fact from the Father of Lies. Radical critiques such as Foucault's and Bruckner's will help us, showing us ways to think about sexuality that are not dependent on the sexologists or the psychoanalysts, and (in Bruckner's case) the tragic overinvestment in the marriage relationship in contemporary society, and how that leads to spiralling divorce rates and broken relationships. As I have tried to show, radical feminist theory offers many of the critiques that are missing from contemporary theology, and while its positions cannot simply be borrowed, they can be studied and learnt from.

We urgently need a renewal of the vocation of celibacy in our churches, particularly for straight people, so that we have visible lived testimony that the lies about sexual activity being necessary to human flourishing are just that. To make this possible, we need to reorder our church lives so that single adults can find fellowship and intimacy within them. We need to develop and teach an account of marriage that is much more modest, much more realistic, but also much more serious in its refusal to contemplate divorce. We need to explain credibly that marriage, Christianly understood, is an ascetic practice, just as much as – perhaps more so than – celibacy. We need to recover the centrality of procreation to the married vocation.

I should say that these prescriptions are not predicated on a conservative position on human sexuality. Rather, these tasks are urgent for the churches to be able to talk about marriage and sexuality in a way that makes any sense. Once we have become able to do that, we can debate positions. I have made no secret of my position on the question, but the argument above is about establishing the context for being able to reach a meaningful position, not about which position we should in fact reach.

INDEX OF AUTHORS

INDEX OF SUBJECTS

INDEX OF TEXTS AND ANCIENT SOURCES

Note: **Bold type** indicates that biblical texts are treated substantially in a chapter.